Therapy with a map

A Cognitive Analytic Approach to Helping Relationships

Steve Potter

Therapy with a map
A Cognitive Analytic Approach to Helping Relationships

© Steve Potter 2020

The author has asserted his rights in accordance with the Copyright, Designs and Patents Act (1988) to be identified as the author of this work.

Published by:
Pavilion Publishing and Media Ltd
Blue Sky Offices
25 Cecil Pashley Way
Shoreham by Sea
West Sussex
BN43 5FF

Tel: 01273 434 943
Email: info@pavpub.com
Web: www.pavpub.com

Published 2020

All rights reserved. No part of this publication may be reproduced, stored in a retrieval system, or transmitted in any form or by any means, electronic, mechanical, photocopying, recording or otherwise, without prior permission in writing of the publisher and the copyright owners.

A catalogue record for this book is available from the British Library.

ISBN: 978-1-912755-85-1

Pavilion Publishing and Media is a leading publisher of books, training materials and digital content in mental health, social care and allied fields. Pavilion and its imprints offer must-have knowledge and innovative learning solutions underpinned by sound research and professional values.

Author: Steve Potter
Production editor: Ruth Chalmers, Pavilion Publishing and Media Ltd
Cover design: Emma Dawe, Pavilion Publishing and Media Ltd
Page layout and typesetting: Emma Dawe, Pavilion Publishing and Media Ltd
Printing: Severn

This book is magnificent. It is at the cutting edge of theory and practice in Cognitive Analytic Therapy, introducing relational awareness and developing concepts and tools for working therapeutically – with a map. It stimulates thinking and deepens understanding of the relational impact of trauma and the mechanisms from which healing occurs. What I also love is that it can be used by a range of professionals, not just CAT practitioners, across many settings. This book represents a tipping point for a new approach to 'helping relationships.'

Dr Siobain Bonfield: Discipline Senior Clinical Psychologist, Peninsula Health Mental Health Service, Melbourne, Australia

Could there possibly be a more timely, prescient gift to the therapists, counsellors and help providers than "Therapy with a Map"? Completed in the time of lockdown and social distancing this is a passionate and intellectually erudite expression of a yearning for a more relationally aware world. Steve Potter has crafted an articulation and explanation of how and why we must learn the art of being unsure and tolerating uncertainty within our traumatised worlds, despite the pressures that work so forcibly to demand more simplistic and reductionistic outcomes. This book offers us an opportunity to embrace the paradigm shift towards a more dialogic and relationally aware approach to working alongside others, whilst also providing guidance on the essential tools that have emerged through the field of Cognitive Analytic Therapy. For if we are to work towards a meaningful offer that is more relational, from therapists, from services or within society, then this book demonstrates, "It is easier with a map".

Dr Nick Barnes: Honorary Senior Lecturer University College London

If you have ever curiously picked up a map, traced over the journey, scribbled one down or had an 'ah-ha' moment of recognising where you are, you'll want to pick up this book too! Steve Potter takes us on a rich journey in how you can map, understand, navigate and heal relational patterns; whether you are new to this area or a practicing CAT therapist, there is something in here for everyone – thought provoking, full of practical ideas and beautifully written – an utterly welcome 'how to' map and 'what if' book at a time when our world is reawakening and reaching out to the importance of human connection and relationships for our health and wellbeing.

Dr Lucy Cutler: Clinical Psychologist Jersey

Steve Potter has given us a gift: a "translation" of the (more) formal concept of diagrams in Cognitive Analytic Therapy into a more colloquial and collaborative shared creation. He invites us into a dance of exploration as he describes the simplicity and the profound depths which mapping can bring to light. He shows us that wherever two or more people are gathered in therapy, supervision teams, families and any organisations, mapping can enhance the understanding and the experience of what it means to be in relationship.

Annalee Curran: Founder member of ACAT

"Therapy with a map" is a fascinating journey into the depths of relation awareness and an excellent symphony of discoveries for both therapist and client. Steve's outstanding orchestration of therapeutic possibilities gives the reader a most insightful and innovative mapping tool, paving the way to a better society with a deeper understanding of ourselves and what surrounds us.

Alexandra Dariescu, concert pianist

An extraordinary tool for professionals to support clients retelling their stories and repairing relational signatures and journeys.

Dr Filipa Alves-Costa, Forensic Psychologist, PhD

Contents

Contents v

Foreword vii

Preface and acknowledgements ix

About the author xi

Introduction and overview 1

Part 1: How to map 17

    Chapter 1: Conversational mapping 19

    Chapter 2: Relationship mapping 37

    Chapter 3: Narrative mapping 65

    Chapter 4: Process mapping 83

    Chapter 5: Learning to map and talk 103

    Chapter 6: Writing and the therapeutic voice 115

Part 2: Relational awareness and relational trauma ... 131

    Chapter 7: Relational awareness 133

    Chapter 8: Relational healing 157

Part 3: CAT therapy with a map: beginning, middle and the end 171

    Chapter 9: Beginning therapy 173

    Chapter 10: What to do in the middle of therapy 199

    Chapter 11: Ending therapy 219

    References 237

Foreword

This impressive book by Steve Potter should become one of the practical and conceptual pillars of cognitive analytic therapy (CAT) and of relational approaches to human psychological distress and suffering. It is deeply thoughtful but also imbued with an evident warmth and reads effortlessly. The book represents, distils, and articulates the therapeutic wisdom and expertise of a lifetime of deep thinking and therapeutic experience by its author. Throughout it is also characteristically and relevantly, for good theoretical and clinical reasons, imbued with the humanistic and compassionate stance and style by which Steve has been known and valued by generations of trainee therapists, colleagues, and, I have no doubt, the clients with whom he has worked over many years. Indeed, this compassionate, curious and genuinely collaborative therapeutic stance is central and critical to the approach he describes and explores. The book conveys all this with a stylistically-understated but apparently effortless mastery – I was reminded of a 'master chef' type presentation! – of the therapeutic challenges and importance of relationality as the key defining factor and critical underpinning of human life, activity and well-being.

It should be noted, in an era of increasing commodification and 'technologisation' of most (Western) mental health services with their predominant, but unfounded, focus on endogenous individual and internal 'technical' dysfunction, whether cognitive or biomedical, that the evidence in fact unequivocally supports the view that mental health and well-being, and subsequently mental distress and disorder and their outcomes, are predominantly determined by relational and socio-political factors, both developmental and contextual. This assertion stands notwithstanding possible individual genetic and/or neurobiological variation and vulnerability. And the latter may frequently, as we increasingly understand, actually be caused by relational adversity. In this context this volume will therefore be an essential and supportive companion to those undertaking more relational forms of therapy, and will also act as a counterweight to the sometimes more mechanically-prescriptive ways in which even these are sometimes, in our day and age, taught and undertaken. This may seem paradoxical given that on the face of it the book concerns use of a 'technique'; but the key consideration is the manner and relational context this is engaged in and how it is undertaken.

In articulating his approach and in considering its theoretical basis Steve has developed fresh perspectives and advances key aspects of the CAT model developed by Anthony Ryle, around which the book devolves and develops. But he also acknowledges, discusses and makes creative use of a wide range of other writers and authorities. Ryle too incidentally always stressed that effective (relationally based) therapy could never simply be about assembling and administering a range of techniques nor 'manualising' them in strict order or detail. This does not mean of course that therapy should simply be an 'intuitive' venture or that outcomes should not be properly evaluated somehow – problematic as this is for obvious reasons – as Ryle also insisted. However, this is not the focus of this volume.

But although this is not a formal 'how to' or manualised technical book on therapy, it is full of practical wisdom and helpful tips for both trainees and experts, notably around its central focus on the importance and use of mapping, actually in a theoretically 'virtual' sense as well as literally, as a means of connecting, meaning-making, assisting people to move on fruitfully, and healing. Notably, as Steve and others describe, this can also apply more systemically and 'contextually', beyond individual therapy, to staff teams, care-givers, families, organisations, and to the broader socio-political context.

For those of us working in this field the book will be not only informative and thought-provoking but also reassuring and supportive, both clinically and personally, as I can testify from my own reading of it. It is a rich resource that will not easily be digested in one reading but will repay and reward repeated visits. As such it will be a resource for psychotherapy practitioners, teachers and supervisors, both in CAT and beyond, and also for non-specialists. It will also potentially be a helpful resource for those perhaps struggling themselves with many of the issues described, or with overt mental distress and disorder. Those who have been taught by or heard Steve lecture over the years will been aware of his broad repertoire of understanding and thoughtfulness, of his energy and commitment, and also of his innovative and uniquely personal linguistic and therapeutic insights. The book embodies all of these and also clearly benefits from his extensive experience in teaching and training in a variety of different cultural settings around the world. Addressing work in such diverse settings remains an important 'meta-challenge' to current models of therapy, although hopefully the more culturally sensitive CAT-based approaches described here and elsewhere should be able to make a helpful contribution. Few however may have been aware of the depth of background study, thinking, and vision underpinning his presentations and it is good to see all this brought together. It has clearly been a long while in the maturing and in the end rather quicker in the blending – as makers of fine whiskies would advocate. On a more personal note, and having spent quite a bit of time working together with Steve over the years in various contexts and in joint 'constructive dithering' as he might put it, it is a great pleasure and satisfaction to see this volume coming together and finally appearing. I commend it wholeheartedly.

Ian B. Kerr

Whangarei, NZ-Aotearoa, June 2020.

Preface and acknowledgements

Therapy is a shared experience. This book carries within it the voices of many clients and colleagues. Over the past four decades, I have had the privilege of working with people from all over the world and taught in a dozen different countries. I am writing to honour and celebrate the shared experience of client and therapist working side-by-side mapping out the patterns of interaction from the conversations which we are having and the life stories that are being remembered, retold and revised. All the stories of therapy in practice are entirely fictionalised but I hope have fidelity to the reality of therapy as I have learnt it from clients and colleagues.

This is not directly a book about a model of therapy. It is an offer to people in the helping professions to consider adding something to their work in the form of the skill of therapeutic mapping. In the process it shows the principles and practice of Cognitive Analytic Therapy (CAT) in the author's view. It presents CAT as a versatile therapy which can work with other approaches and is itself an integration of psychoanalytic, cognitive, narrative and systemic ways of working. Specifically, the book applies the conceptual tools of CAT diagrams and shows the activity of mapping as a therapeutic process.

The final editing of this book was done during the lock down and social distancing of the coronavirus pandemic. The talk then alongside so much uncertainty and loss, was of the 'new normal', globally and locally, which we would face once the spread of the virus was understood and managed. The 'new normal' pointed to many things, but one theme (hopefully explored in this book) was a greater relational awareness of each other and the social, economic and natural world within, between and around us.

My thanks for helping with this book go to a great many people. Foremost are those who have been clients and struggled with me to make sense of distress and find ways to talk about, map out and reshape lives. Also, warm thanks go to the very many groups of trainees, from all disciplines in the NHS and similar health settings internationally. The ideas described here have been crafted through running the 'Introduction to CAT' course with Annalee Curran in London over the past 19 years, and through three intakes of the Inter Regional Psychotherapy course with Hilary Beard, also many years of productive work as colleagues with CAT North/Catalyse and other practitioner trainings for CAT around the UK, and more recently the practitioner training in Jersey. They have been my conversational partners as trainers.

Thanks also to many groups and networks of practitioners: Iannis Vlachos and colleagues in Greece and the Hellenic CAT association, Marie Anne Bernardy in France, and colleagues in the CAT communities in Finland, Australia and New Zealand, Ireland, Italy, Holland and Spain. Thanks also to the network of Forensic CAT practitioners in the UK and especially to the multi-disciplinary group led by Nicola Kemp, Alison Bickerdike, Clare Bingham at the John Howard Centre. Thanks to working side-by-side over the years with the communities and groups of the Association for Cognitive Analytic Therapy in the UK. I have valued the open dialogue with ideas with Francis Creighton, Jenny Marshall, Jamie Kirkland, Rob Lam and Lucy Cutler.

This book would not have been completed without the sustained, motivational push from Anna Haigh to put my teaching and bits of writing together in a book. Anna helped greatly in the early stages and our shared interest in CAT as a co-creative therapy and helped me search for a writing style. Anna specifically helped in discussion of part three of the book. Many thanks also to coaching in the art of writing from N. Quentin Woolf and his skilful stewardship of the weekly meetings of the writing group at the Brick Lane Bookshop. Thank you to Ian Kerr as editing partner through three issues of the international Journal of Cognitive Analytic Therapy and Relational Mental Health. He has been a long-standing friend and wise voice.

Anthony Ryle developed the integrative and relational language, concepts and tools of CAT over 30 years. In the process he created something radically new, flexible and creative that is still ahead of its time. In the same spirit he brought people together as therapists from a wide mix of the mental health professions. His approach allowed the pieces of the psychotherapy jigsaw puzzle to be put together in a new way and left open borders for new pieces to be added. I hope he would have appreciated this book as one such small addition.

Thanks, above all, to my children and grandchildren for providing an endless source of love and relational awareness, and to Catherine, my inspiring partner for over 40 years.

Steve Potter, London

About the author

Steve Potter is a cognitive analytic psychotherapist based in London.
He has worked for many years as a trainer and supervisor in the practice of Cognitive Analytic Therapy. For six years he was chair of in the International Cognitive Analytic Therapy Association and previously chair of the Association for Cognitive Analytic Therapy in the UK. He has been closely involved in extending the application of therapy more widely. He has worked for the past fifteen years using CAT and relational mapping with teams and groups to develop relational awareness and reflective practice. He was Director of Counselling for the University of Manchester until 2006 and prior to that at Manchester Metropolitan University. He is interested in developing a relational approach to mental health that is versatile and responsive to our broad and varied mix of social and psychological needs in societies and cultures which are pluralistic and complex and in a profound global and local transition.

Introduction and overview

'There is a great deal of unmapped country within us which would have to be taken into account in an explanation of our gusts and storms.'
George Eliot, Daniel Deronda (Book 3, Chapter 24)

Introduction

Therapy with a map is a process of remembering and retelling the stories of our personal hopes and fears. It involves writing down the key words of our conversations on paper in front of us where we can see them and touch them. The process of mapping out patterns from stories about our lives helps develop self-understanding and solve problems. The client hopefully takes away a freer, more self-aware, storytelling relationship with themselves. It gives therapists an aid to keeping track and sharing their understanding.

Retelling our life stories in therapy is a search for a healing narrative. 'Story' has many connotations including ones relating to the sincerity, truth and reliability of the narrator. Therapists may wonder if the client is telling the whole story. Clients may wonder if the therapist can bear to hear the truth of their stories. Therapy with a map offers a framework strong enough to find the words that help.

Doing therapy with the aid of a map is a resource for any helping relationship. As in any use of mapping, it helps us find our way, notice when we are lost and survey the wider landscape. It also involves using the process of mapping to engage and track the therapeutic or helping relationship.

This book is about how and why the process of therapeutic mapping works. It uses mapping to introduce the tools, concepts and methods of Cognitive Analytic Therapy (CAT). It combines this with other relational, conversational and narrative approaches to our changing, collective needs for mental health, helpful relationships and personal growth. The process of mapping is not an end in-itself but a vehicle for a more open dialogue with each other about our lives. At the heart of this open, therapeutic dialogue is a process of learning to develop and use 'relational awareness' as part of a healing narrative which is co-created by therapist and client.

The words 'therapy', 'client' and 'therapist' are used throughout the book. They can be taken to apply generally to psychotherapeutic, counselling and helping relationships across the health, welfare and social work sectors. As much as possible the book speaks to the therapeutic partnership between client and therapist.

The book is divided into three parts

- Part 1 describes how client and therapist can use mapping as a shared activity.
- Part 2 seeks to describe the qualities of relational awareness and healing that are enabled by mapping.
- Part 3 goes through the stages of a relational therapy based upon CAT and built around mapping and writing from beginning, middle to end.

In the following pages there is an introduction to each of these three sections.

Introducing Part 1: How to Map

Four linked elements of mapping are described: conversational mapping, relationship mapping, narrative mapping and process mapping. The basics of learning to map and the interaction between mapping, writing and using our voices therapeutically are considered. The methods and the mechanisms of change and the dynamics of working together are explored. Generally, in Part 1, and specifically in Chapter 2, the conceptual tools of Cognitive Analytic Therapy (CAT) are detailed as the primary source of therapy with a map.

Mapping, writing and voicing as a therapeutic process

At the beginning of therapy, the client talks and the therapist writes down key words, spread out, here and there, on paper. It helps the therapist listen and keep track of the conversation. Words on paper amplify the spoken word and make it tangible. They can open access to the stories we tell of our lives and show the patterns of relating involved. The mapping makes a therapeutic discussion more equal, more transparent and open to negotiation. Talking about how the mapping is helping or hindering becomes a means of talking about how the therapy is helping or hindering.

Client and therapist will routinely stop and recap with the map. This helps see where they are in the conversation, in their relationship and in the process of mapping. Sharing the skill and activity of mapping is important. It helps build an alliance.

Mapping externalises feelings, memories and stories onto paper between client and therapist. It makes a parallel space alongside the interpersonal space of the conversation. It makes inky, tactile substances of our thoughts and feelings, and locates them, makes them visible and more real.

This multi-sensory experience aids a dialogue between mind, brain and body alongside the conversation. We see what we are saying. We touch the words that carry ideas and feelings. It is both containing and freeing of the conversation. We can look at the map and at each other, leaning in and leaning back. This movement of our bodies towards the paper or turning towards each other makes a more physical expression of the conversational relationship. The map frees us up to stop and ask questions or go back over things. We can use the map to see where there are gaps in our understanding. It invites shared 'finger pointing' choices to track the conversation and when to negotiate changes in direction and have moments of meeting around key patterns and connections.

Multi-sensory orchestration of different ways of relating

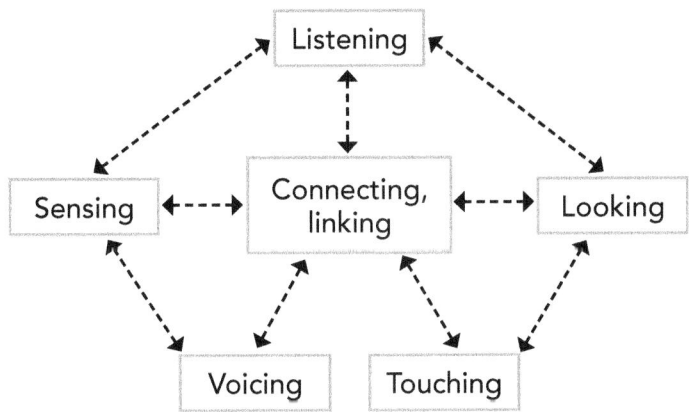

Maps are part of our lives. We have maps on our phones, maps that we sketch to help others find directions, mind maps to help us study. Maps may be one of the roots of our entry into spoken and written language (Wallace, 1989).

In the process of sharing the thoughts and feelings through the map, we touch the patterns of interaction in our memories and life stories. We do this literally and figuratively in a hands-on way. A triangle is created between what we hope to share, what is being said, and what is on paper. It is a space for the kind of transitional phenomena described by Winnicott (1953). The map becomes a transitional space and object. It is a shared object but one with which we each make our own relationship.

Jane's example

It is Jane's first session. With her permission, as she talks, I have been tracking her key words and phrases by marking them out on a big piece of paper. We are sitting side-by-side at a table. Like all of us, she talks and communicates not just with words but with her face, hands and eyes. Her ideas, feelings and problems are embodied. When I speak to clarify or connect with what she is saying, I turn and look to her and I point my pen at the paper. The link I make by speaking is paralleled by a link I make by pointing to the words on the paper. At this early stage, the pointing at words on the paper is not much more than a gesture towards another arena of communication. It is showing how meanings might be made between us.

As the conversation develops, there are a growing number of words written here and there on the paper between us. I am recapping with the map in a tentative fashion which I can only describe as hovering over the words on paper and shimmering between possible emotional responses. It is a form of 'constructive dithering'.

Jane says, as she points with her finger to the words on paper, 'I can see what I am saying'. One of the words on paper is sad. As she touches the word sad, a feeling of sadness seems to shimmer through her. In that second, Jane makes eye contact with me. We share a moment of feeling together which is unsteady but it is a move towards openness. It is partly a moment of remembering and reliving feelings for Jane but also partly a moment of meeting and tolerating mixed feelings, with the therapist, in the present, about embarrassment and anxiety around the sadness. The word 'sad' on paper makes it easier to negotiate with the feelings involved.

By going over the words and our thoughts and feelings, Jane and I begin to tease out a pattern of relating to herself and others. This capacity to make patterns out of a jumble of words may be something to do with the relational nature of our brains and our memory. We are biased to seek a coherent narrative and to put two and two together. The patterns of words which we are seeing on paper offer a scaffolding to explore this need and not be overly controlled by it.

The process of mapping is designed to keep the conversation open. To 'un-story' the stories which we are in the process of retelling. The activity of recapping is key. Jane gets involved and in sharing new links of thoughts and feelings, new stories work their way onto the map. It is now getting messy with words all over the paper, but it is 'our messy'. From it is coming small moments of clarification and shared ownership. We take time out to make a tidy map together. As we re-work our conversation from the messy map to the tidy map it deepens and extends our co-ownership of the activity and of the therapy.

As Jane continues talking, she rests her hand on one of the words as if to lift it off the page and get the measure of it. The word which her hand momentarily covers is angry. She says, 'I did feel that anger then but not now. Where has it gone?' Beneath the word angry, I put 'where has it gone?' in brackets and in small writing. We decide to come back to it later but the words on paper are there to remind us. We are marking out the emotional territory of the therapy.

Our focus of attention shifts to-and-fro between Jane talking and my sketching with words and arrows. We make links between thoughts, actions and feelings both from the past and in the present. The sketching is becoming part of the art of our conversation. If initially it got in the way of the conversation, or felt artificial, now it is more of a support. Like the piano accompanying the singer we are beginning to take it for granted but it is becoming essential.

We reach that point in our dialogue where sketches of incidents and moments in her recent life seem to be also mapping lines in the narratives of the whole of her life. There is more than one story coming from the words flowing through this conversation. The pattern of one story is discovered to be the scaffolding for many stories. Finding this out together through the activity of mapping helped us engage as working partners. Both of us are at the edge of discovering something new. There is an apprenticeship between us, like two people learning a foreign language together. The conversation is turning into an activity which we are authoring and creating together.

The art of constructive dithering
Throughout this book the shared, reflective, therapeutic process highlighted by the work with Jane is called:

- hovering between different points of view
- zooming in and out of the big picture and small detail
- shimmering with mixed feelings from the past and present with varying intensity, uncertainty, awareness, direction and meaning
- constructive dithering between problems and solutions, hopes and fears, open and closed stories, a focus on self and a focus on others.

This adds up to the therapeutic mechanisms of relational awareness. The process of feeling is assisted by an activity of mapping and talking, pointing to and touching the words on paper that touch us when we speak.

Maps offer a therapeutic space
Mapping helps find patterns from stories. The push and pull of words and phrases which accompany any conversation are put out there, externalised, projected and then taken back. 'Can I say that? I have said that. Should I say that?'

The mapping process can build a general confidence in navigating and negotiating our life stories and help us give shape to unformulated experience. Like geographical and street maps, this work of mapping helps us find our way until we know our way. By mapping and talking we have greater relational understanding of the personal and social landscape through which we move and live. Often, just two or three phrases written out on paper, apart from each other, can help hold and shape the joint, emotionally focused work of a session.

The therapist with the map as the assistant is hoping that it will bring new connections and help open the conversation in ways that are both safely paced and transparent enough to pause where it is good to pause and push where it works to push. It is as if somewhere in this shared activity with the map are mechanisms of mind, body and brain that help heal fragmented memories. The effects of early trauma or deficit can be reworked, 're-storied' and healed. The map is a therapeutic space, a micro-theatre for a variety of therapeutic mechanisms of change and healing. It is the midwife to a healing narrative that combines understanding of personal problems and symptoms of distress with new ways of relating to our self in the world.

In this approach the ideal of a free flowing, freely associative and exploratory conversation is supported. It is transference friendly, which is to say that it invites the replay and reliving of unresolved patterns of relating that make up the troubled parts of the client's sense of self.

Mapping is a three-way experience which takes the strain off the interpersonal encounter. It democratises the helping relationship. It offers a pathway to look at the dynamics of power and difference in the therapy room. Whilst the mapping process is unique and valuable as a mechanism of therapeutic change, it also yields a product. Maps can be used as a record. As described in Chapter 9, a principle product of mapping in CAT is a refined therapy map which holds and shapes the therapy through its middle and end phases and stands as a personal source of reference for the client after the therapy.

Whilst the focus of this book is therapy with a map, the active use of the processes of mapping and writing described here can serve other more general goals such as developing reflective practice and narrative competence or improving our ability to talk about ourselves and our world with each other. For examples and details of these wider applications see www.mapandtalk.com

Four layers to therapeutic mapping

In the next four chapters, different elements of the co-creative mapping relationship between client and therapist are separated into a chapter each, as follows.

1. **Conversational mapping** involves tracking a therapeutic discussion as it unfolds by noting down contrasting words and phrases on paper between us. This creates a mutual space for making links and choices about where we have been and where to go with the discussion. It helps connect with and own the feelings, memories and meanings suggested by the words mapped out. It refers to the work of Hobson (1985) and Meares (2016) and the conversational model of therapy (Barkham, 2016).

2. **Relationship mapping** works out on paper the roles and relationships with self and others in the conversations and stories that develop during the therapy. It helps pick out significant patterns of interaction that shape our personal problems, life history and self-understanding. It helps shape the therapy and describes the diagrammatic methods of cognitive analytic therapy developed by Ryle and colleagues (Ryle & Kerr, 2020).

3. **Narrative mapping** helps retell, relive, and rework the stories of our lives. It opens a capacity to share and 'hear' the untold stories behind our problems and ways of coping. It draws upon the ideas of narrative therapy (White & Epston 1990) and the developments in affective

neuroscience around memory reconsolidation (Le Doux, 1996; Solms, 2015; Knox, 2011; Lane, 2018). It seeks to draw out a healing narrative through the process of mapping.

4. **Process mapping** focuses on the here-and-now interactions between client and therapist. It looks at how the therapy is progressing by giving attention to patterns of relating between client and therapist and patterns from earlier relationships. It helps explore threats to the working partnership through enactments and transference. It draws upon relational psychoanalysis (Mitchell, 2000; Bromberg, 1998; Safran, 2000) and Ryle's view of transference (Ryle 2006). Process mapping work can be done at any time during the conversational, relationship or narrative mapping.

These four ways of mapping are layered. They play into and spring from each other. Narrative mapping depends upon the quality of the conversation we have created in the therapy relationship. It can show patterns that carry over from one story to another. Relationship mapping shows our part in the story. Finally, process mapping, with its focus on the here-and-now interactions in the room, draws its 'moments to map' from interactions in the other three types of mapping.

The contribution of Cognitive Analytic Therapy (CAT)

All three parts of the book are deeply informed by CAT, its founding father, Tony Ryle, and the extensive and diverse communities of CAT practitioners around the world. Ryle brought ideas together and he brought diverse people and professions together. CAT has a great debt to this creative interplay between therapy ideas and helping professions. Ryle's work drew on a rich mix of psychoanalytic, behavioural and cognitive ideas and the model has always had open borders and sought to integrate developments in the multiple disciplines that inform mental health. He was seeking a common language for psychotherapy (1978).

In the 1950s Tony Ryle was a GP in London with a wide social mix of patients. Through a pioneering epidemiological study with a social work colleague, his interest turned to their social and psychological problems as much as health problems (see his paper *The Whirligig of Time* (1998) for Ryle's own reflections on his career). He was Head of Student Health at the then new University of Sussex in the 1960s and 1970s where he saw the need for a collaborative and educational psychotherapy (Ryle, 1969). As consultant psychotherapist at Guy's and St Thomas's hospitals in the 1980s and early 1990s until his retirement, he developed a pragmatic, accessible model of therapy that could reach greater numbers of people than the then predominant models of long term psychoanalytic therapy. He sought an approach which took more account of the whole person in society than the prevailing behavioural therapies.

Ryle's research interest in linking therapy process to outcome led to a client-friendly list of short descriptions of typical problematic patterns of relating to self and others (Ryle, 1975). This was adapted and used with all clients in the form of 'the psychotherapy file'. The aim was a collaborative therapy focus around one or two problem patterns in the limited time of the therapy. These personal problem patterns (called Target Problem Procedures in CAT), offered a platform for thinking about the early learning that shaped our sense of self. In this way Ryle wove seemingly incompatible therapies of behaviourism and psychoanalysis into one by linking more insight-based self-understanding to more pragmatic, personal problem solving.

He was greatly helped from the late 1980's on by the ideas and clinical insight of Mikael Leiman who developed a second home for CAT in Finland and brought the work of Vygotsky and Bakhtin to the CAT model (Leiman 1992, 1997, 2004). There are full accounts of the CAT model and its development in (Ryle, 1990; Ryle, 1995; Ryle & Kerr, 2020). There is a practical, accessible and humanistic account of CAT therapy from the client's point of view in *Change for the Better* by Elizabeth McCormick Wilde (2017). There are books on CAT in forensic settings (Pollock, Stowell Smith, Gopfert 2006), CAT with older adults (Hepple and Sutton 2004) and CAT with intellectual disabilities (Lloyd, 2014). More recently a comprehensive book on Supervision and CAT (Pickvance, 2017) and a primer in CAT (Brummer, 2018) have been published. There is consideration of the social, dialogic and political dimensions of CAT in books by Pollard (2008) and Lloyd and Pollard (2018). There is access to a wide range of articles on CAT through membership as a friend of CAT on the ACAT website (www.acat.me.uk). Copies of the *International Journal of Cognitive Analytic Therapy and Relational Mental Health* are free to download from www.Internationalcat. org/journal/. For a wider reading list and supporting video and study materials relating to this book see www.mapandtalk.com.

This book draws upon CAT in two ways. On the one hand it is an open relational framework, with versatile tools, that can hold and shape a variety of therapeutic methods. CAT offers a framework for working with the common factors (Hubble, 1999) that reach across and animate all therapies. It has the tools and language for a relational approach to mental health work. It can be used to weave some of its techniques, concepts and tools into any contemporary therapy, counselling or helping relationship. On the other hand, as a distinctive clinical approach, it offers a uniquely psycho-social view of opportunities and challenges of a time-limited and collaborative therapy. On both counts, CAT has a following in several countries (www.internationalcat.org). It is not a manualised, diagnostic, or treatment-specific method. As an integrative and relational approach, it is not easy to isolate researchable variables. The research evidence is summarised elsewhere by Ryle and Kerr (2020) and Calvert and Kellet (2014) and in the *Journal of Cognitive Analytic Therapy and Relational Mental Health* (www.internationalcat.org/journal).

Some CAT therapists have combined its focus on reformulation, as the structure and shape of therapy, with therapies that explore how to be in a relationship such as the psychodynamic interpersonal model (Margison *et al*, 2016) or transference, interpersonal and relational approaches, (Mitchell, 2000). Others have focused on combining CAT with approaches from the third wave of therapies, Gilbert's compassion focused therapy (2013), acceptance and commitment therapy (Hayes, 2012), mindfulness (Kabat-Zinn, 1990; 2013), dialectic behaviour therapy (Linehan, 1993), or the variety of art, music and drama therapies. Any of these can fit within the CAT framework to create an integrative and relational experience of therapy. More recently, as practitioners have focused on clients with more complex needs, there has been interest in combining CAT with eye movement desensitisation and reprocessing (EMDR) (Shapiro, 2018) and related approaches, and with viewing CAT as a relational model of trauma (Howell, 2003).

CAT combines two therapies which are easily separated in the provision of treatment and care. First is a more pragmatic, cognitive and task focused therapy seeking to solve personal problems and reduce symptoms. Second, a more holistically focused and analytic therapy seeking to develop self-understanding in the process of solving personal problems. In combining these two Ryle brought the best of cognitive and behavioural therapies together with the more recent developments in psychoanalytic and relational therapies. In the process, a third therapy came into view which offered a more integrated, psycho-social view of the individual and of psychotherapy. This third therapy focus is summarised as 'relational awareness' in this book. Such awareness is built around the process of co-creative mapping. Mapping is the CAT gift that offers a framework for relational awareness in individual therapy, reflective capacity in teams, and working side-by-side in any social context whether family, couple or workplace and the wider organisation and social systems.

Mapping together has been a source of theoretical discovery. Tony Ryle, who pioneered the use of diagrams, was quick to spot that they helped clarify theories of what was then called personality disorder (Ryle, 1997b), and we might now, more generally, refer to as the consequences of relational trauma. The maps helped see the multiple interaction of several states of mind as part of the whole self-organisation. Ideas about dissociation, state shifts and narcissistic and emotionally unstable personality patterns would not have developed in Cognitive Analytic Therapy without the mapping tools and the wider relational awareness they enabled.

Introducing Part 2: Relational Awareness and a Healing Narrative

Relational awareness is the unintended fruit of therapy with a map. It is the ability to be simultaneously in dialogue with life, with self, with others and the world around us. Whilst the primary goals of therapy are solving personal problems, developing self-understanding and improving self-esteem, the process of mapping points to a further goal which in this book is introduced as relational awareness. Relational awareness is orchestral and integrative and battles with the fragmenting and disorganising impact of trauma, restriction and damage in our personal and social relationships. Relational awareness is the intervening variable between therapeutic activities such as mapping and writing, talking and listening and the goals of therapy. Kerr (Ryle & Kerr, 2002; 2020) describes CAT as a radically social model in that it understands individual and interpersonal psychology from a social perspective. It might equally be called a radically orchestral or integrative model since it offers tools and methods to be both socially and psychologically engaged without reducing one to the other. Developing and restoring relational awareness is an empowering, consciousness raising and healing process. It is easier to do with a map.

A yearning for relational awareness

This book is an expression of a yearning for a more relationally aware world. This is the author's yearning, but it is often the unexpected discovery of so many clients in therapy. Practically it shows up as joined up thinking, seeing patterns from the inside and outside. It is being able to handle empathy for self and others and the world around us in the same breath.

It is a deep concern that despite the evidence for relatedness being at the heart of human life we seem to a be a society caught by technological and political forces driving us out of a fully human dialogue.

Despite this there is creative work being done by practitioners and theorists in respect of trauma in the early years of life as described in chapter 8. There is interest in cultural studies and the social psychology of identity in relation to the struggle to form a coherent identity in a complex, transitional and unstable world. There are breakthroughs in the neurosciences and their applications to psychotherapy. There is a re-invigoration of psychoanalysis and the convergence between models. All these and other influences are part of a convergence of thinking. Some writers emphasise identity and agency, others attachment, yet others focus on meaning making but they are all dealing with joint activity in a complex web of relationships. Therapy with a map is a scaffolding for tracking the interplay of all these influences.

There are hundreds of different kinds of therapy. At times all are vulnerable to someone thinking their therapy is a complete model, entire and on its own. This is never true. All therapies are incomplete and can gain from the general pool of therapeutic wisdom. Good, flexible, integrative (I prefer the word orchestral), and relational therapy is the common direction of travel for the future of therapy and this book seeks to contribute to that. It draws on the rich variety of evidence for distinctive techniques and the general evidence for the common factors in therapy.

No single practitioner, or group of practitioners, can hold in mind all this richness. Part 2 of the book tries to get a taste of this theoretical richness. Chapter 7 proposes the qualities and dimensions of relational awareness as they have emerged from the practice of CAT with mapping as the central activity, whether in individual therapy or reflective practice and consultation with multi-disciplinary teams. Chapter 8 takes the idea of CAT as a relational theory of trauma and mapping as a mechanism of connecting with and reconsolidating trauma memories, and the patterns of coping arising from harmful early experience and its legacy of a limited sense of adult self.

Learning to be our own therapist

The common educational goal of all therapies is to help the client develop a therapeutic attitude towards themselves. All the way through therapy, in the minor and major moments, this new therapeutic relationship with self is being learnt regardless of whether the therapist realises or intends such an outcome. For many CAT therapists this fits well with Paul Gilbert's work on compassionate mind (Gilbert, 2013). For CAT and mapping, it might be called a compassionately relational mind in dialogue with self and others.

In becoming our own therapist, we are appropriating the therapeutic relationship as a relationship we can own and author with ourselves, with our problems and symptoms, with people that matter to us and the world around us. Therapy in this light is more like a course of learning and should end as soon as, but no sooner than, we have a good enough sense of, and practice in, being our own therapist. Tony Ryle puts therapy as education above any idea of therapy as persuasion (Ryle, 1994).

Looking outwards from the therapy room

Psychotherapists in the third decade of the twenty first century cannot just practice therapy as an individual emotional or cognitive practice. They must face outwards beyond the therapy room and the individual relationship. It involves a dialogue across differences of generation, gender, class, identity and culture. We are simultaneously psychological and social. Personal knowledge works within social ideology.

Looking outwards involves the therapist being a sociologist, historian, or anthropologist as much as a psychologist. Looking outwards from the words and language that have currency inside the therapy involves being interested in the arts and literature and the process of translating our personal language within and between cultures.

Psychotherapy has a mixed place in the popular imagination. It is dismissed, valued, and mocked in equal measure. The readers of this book will have their varied political and lifestyle allegiances, but there is something that the therapeutic imagination can bring to enhance all our dialogues regardless of differences. Our mental health and collective well-being will depend on an increase in relational awareness across all quarters and layers of society. Psychotherapy may have something to contribute to a much needed and broader programme of therapeutic education. This could not be truer at a time of global trauma and crisis both economically and with the current pandemic (at the time of writing). There is a need for a practical therapeutic language for reflecting upon the ordinary and collective trauma of not knowing the terms of interaction for normal life alongside the acute trauma and loss affecting so many people. It is as if global events whether epidemics, climate change, financial crises and inequalities are facing us with new global relationships, and we need a new quality of relational awareness to match up to them.

For Ryle, the development of cognitive analytic therapy always had an eye on this wider horizon. The tools and concepts arising from therapy with a map can help a more open dialogue between our localities, our tribal identities (old and new) and our world. We will need to find a thousand ways for group to speak to group, generation to generation, women to men, ethnicity to ethnicity, identity to identity, health to wealth, within us and between us.

With theory in mind

In the foreword to the ground-breaking collection of articles and research papers on what works in psychotherapy entitled 'The Heart and Soul of Change' John Norcross writes as follows:

> *'Let's confront the unpleasant reality and say it out loud: the rivalrous warfare among theoretical orientations in psychotherapy has impeded scientific advances and hindered the development of effective treatments, In the dogma-eat-dogma environment of "schoolism", clinicians traditionally operated from within their own particular theoretical frameworks, often to the point of being oblivious to alternative conceptualisations and potentially superior interventions. Although this ideological cold war may have been a necessary developmental stage, its day has come and passed. The era of rapprochement is upon us.'*
>
> (Norcross in Hubble et al, 2002, p xvii)

Nearly twenty years on from those comments, the rapprochement is slowly happening in the developing versatility of practitioners. The ideas of therapy with a map, as with CAT, is to be an active and willing part of this slow rapprochement. There are no ideas that are not part of a 'community' of ideas. Therapy with a map brings together the cognitive analytic approach with the relational psychoanalytic tradition from the USA (Mitchell, 2000; Bromberg, 1998). This book is also influenced by Hobson's (1985) conversational model and the work of Meares (2016) on the poetic development of mind and self through language and metaphor. Between them they have sustained a view, without being precious, that is poetic.

The other influences that flow from this mix include the relational view of infant development dating back to Bruner (1990) and Vygotsky (Daniels 2005) before him. These influenced Daniel Stern (2004) and Colwyn Trevarthen (2017) and many others to see the co-creative, developing and dynamic relationship between infants and their parents/carers as a central relational process to our human story. Their contemporary interest combined with CAT, has helped link back to Winnicott and the need for relatedness and the relational focus of the British object relations school (Mitchell, 2000; Josselson, 1995). All these writers in their own way, as practitioners and theorists, are grappling with our ambivalent (we want the wisdom but not the anxiety) quest for relational awareness.

The benefits of seeing therapy as multi-relational are more easily open to theoretical exposition with the accompanying activities of mapping, writing and voicing. It is working in this way in a co-creative partnership with clients, colleagues and systems that sustains an open dialogue across and within 'communities' of ideas.

The treatment story and the healing narrative

This book has grown from the stories of people of all professions providing healthcare. Its focus is on drawing out patterns of relating from life stories. Mapping with words helps the helper make a good formulation, find the right treatment and diagnosis. The treatment story is one side of the story of the therapy or the helping relationship. It involves formulating and mapping out links between the client's personal problems, life history and self-understanding. It is the story of what the therapy is about. It is the beginning story of the therapy as client and therapist gather a picture and find a focus. It is the answer to the question 'What's up?'. Alongside this 'What's up' story is another story of 'What will help?' This other story is one that is co-created between client and therapist. It is the story of the helping relationship and it needs, by the end of therapy, to have its own story. It is the sum of lots of little moments of partnership in understanding. It is the healing narrative. Therapy with a map, using the tools and methods of cognitive analytic therapy, works with both the treatment story and the healing narrative. Often, they will merge but they need holding separately in mind. Hopefully, this book will show how and why.

Introducing Part 1: Stages to therapy

Introduction
Having introduced in detail the tools and methods of mapping in Part 1, and the relational thinking around it in Part 2, the book goes on in Part 3 to examine the step-by-step sequence of beginning therapy, being in the middle and coming to the end. What do we do to get off to a good start? How do we keep on track and maintain momentum in the middle? How do we manage a temporary pause or permanent ending to therapy? What does it mean to say goodbye?

Beginning, middle and ending
The cognitive analytic approach offers a framework for shaping the therapy at the beginning, such that there is a distinctive experience of working flexibly in the middle of therapy and being honest and engaging about the end stage of therapy.

Chapter 9, the first of these three chapters, goes into the detail of preparing for therapy. How we begin sets the tone, the shape and pace of all that follows. It describes the activities and tasks at the beginning. It makes specific reference to the use of ideas and methods from cognitive analytic therapy and specifically the combination of moments of mapping, writing and voicing together. This leads to the most distinctive CAT idea of reformulation as a co-creative means of holding and shaping the time-limited therapy journey with the combined use of a therapy map and letter.

Chapter 10 is concerned with what to do in the middle of therapy. It is easily overlooked by the dramas of the beginning and the end. This is to be, as the bible puts it 'declaring the end from the beginning' or as poetically echoed by T.S. Eliot (1940) thinking that, 'In my beginning is my end'. It is tempting and understandable for client and therapist to think that once we have got to reformulate the client's problems that the hard work is done. We may think that all is revealed, the stage is set, and change will follow. In fact, it is only the 'setting of the stage upon which the therapy will do its therapeutic 'dances' (Ryle, 1990). There is a rich versatility to the techniques and directions that therapy can go in the middle of a time-limited or phased period of therapy. These are described in this chapter on the middle stage of therapy.

Chapter 11 is about the ending of therapy. Time itself becomes a self-conscious tool in the dynamics of the therapy relationship. Am I ready to finish? What will I be taking away? For the therapist, the question is 'Have I been helpful?', 'Is it the right time to end?' Ending will always bring feelings of frustration, relief, loss, and conflict. Mapping the unexpected dynamics of ending, saying goodbye, coping alone or finding other kinds of help can bring parallels with the ending of many other relationships.

Conclusion

The different elements of this book link to each other like the pieces of a jigsaw puzzle. The book is written from the point of view of the client as much as the therapist. The form of address is 'we'. As in, what are we doing here? Or, how are we helping or hindering? The form of address is not the patronising or finger-pointing 'you' of the accusative tense. The stance taken is one of working side-by-side. It is easy for the therapist and client to collude in a 'doing for you' or 'doing to you' rather than a 'doing together with' each other. It is not 'you' the client and 'I' the therapist but 'we' the therapy partnership. The book will no doubt repeatedly slip from this ideal and will be read as a book for therapists. Hopefully, client and therapist will both feel like subjects of the book. Therapists are also clients. Therapists who work well with clients always learn about themselves in every session they undertake.

Behind this book is a wish to share lessons learnt over many years. It is not meant to replace current ways of working, but to supplement and enhance them. The book can be read as a guide to one way of doing CAT. It contains most of the specifically CAT concepts. Or, it can be read as an introduction to mapping and writing as an aid to therapeutic processes in general.

Some readers will feel totally new to this approach and others will recognise it as their reason for working with the tools and methods of cognitive analytic therapy. Others may see it as an extension of a relational, psychoanalytic, or dialogic approach. Whichever way the reader comes to this book, there is an open invitation to take on the ideas and try them out as additions to current ways of working. The book hopes to encourage interest from practitioners across many professions and therapy traditions to see if there is a common ground to our involvement in helping relationships.

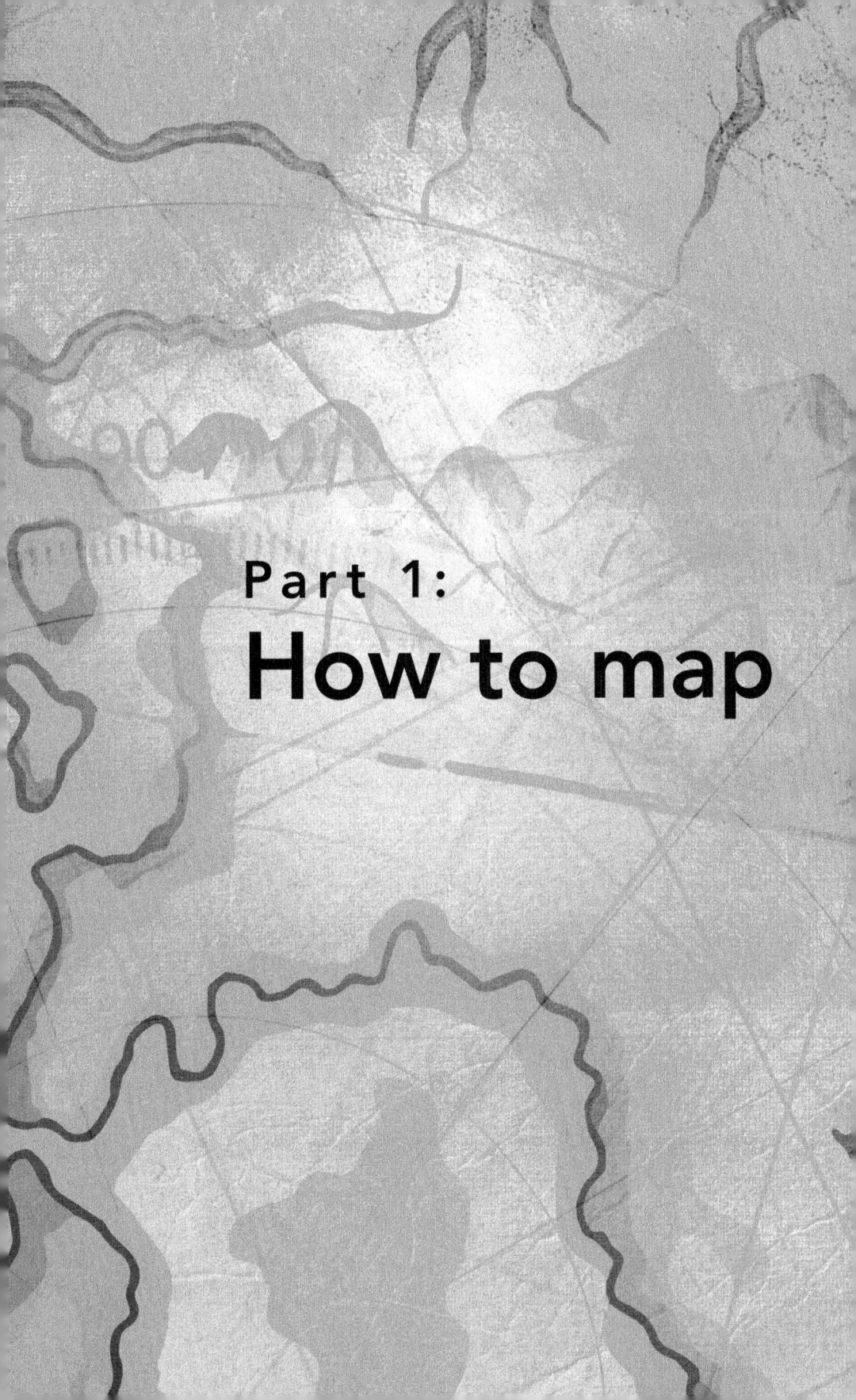

Part 1:
How to map

Chapter 1: Conversational mapping

Introduction

Mapping out our words on paper in front of us is a visual and tactile aid to a therapeutic conversation. Of the four variants of mapping described in this book, conversational mapping is the starting point and the first layer of mapping. It helps co-create an open and equal discussion in which client and therapist collaboratively negotiate control and direction.

This chapter describes how to do this and highlights the central role of recapping. It explores a heightened relationship with words and explores, with examples, the therapeutic mechanisms of 'hovering', 'shimmering' and 'constructive dithering' and their contribution to relational awareness. Some of the practicalities of mapping are explored and there are guidance notes for clients.

How to begin

The therapist says: 'It will help me listen and keep track if I can put the key words down on paper between us as they come up in the conversation'. Words that describe similar ideas and feelings are put on paper close together. Words are set apart that describe differences of action, feeling or view. The number of words used will vary. There may only be two or three distinct phrases. There may be a dozen or more. It can help to have a wide margin down the side of the paper for side notes – as memory joggers of background details to the conversation.

On a practical and visual point, make the words big enough to stand out visually but small enough to leave plenty of blank space between them. Put the upbeat or desired feelings (e.g. excited and happy) nearer the upper part of the page, and the down beat or feared feelings (e.g. ashamed, afraid) nearer the lower part of the page. The mixed feelings which could be good or bad go in the middle.

Putting words down on paper makes them external and visible in a way that helps negotiate with the thoughts and feelings they represent. They are within touching distance: literally, symbolically, metaphorically and emotionally. The presence of the mapping as an assistant to the conversation is a statement of intent. We are going to work transparently and co-creatively together.

Make mapping an ordinary part of the conversation

The offer of 'mapping as we talk' should not be made into something special or important at the start. It is an activity with the modest aims of helping the conversation develop, keep track of key points, and record memorable turns of phrase. It is not like making a map of the person or an assessment map of their character and its flaws. It is not a map of the client at all. It is a map to hold and shape the conversation.

The mapping is creating a scaffolding, an aide memoire to encourage free association or links and connections between what is on the client's mind, what is on paper and what is in the air between client and therapist. It makes a triangle between client and therapist, therapeutic conversation and map. Without a map to guide us, it is easy to get bogged down in detail, talk abstractly, or to be caught up in the interpersonal relationship. The shared process of mapping seeks to mitigate these risks. It can help us talk more freely, more sensitively, more collaboratively and more adventurously in support of a therapeutic conversation.

Just creating the conditions for a good conversation with the aid of a map is a healing process of recovering or discovering dialogue where it was blocked or never developed. This involves making sure the map is visible and within touching distance. Elbows can get in the way. If the therapist is right-handed then he or she should preferably sit to the right of the client. Or it is the reverse for someone left-handed. The ritual of a small negotiation of seating arrangements is not just visually practical, it sets the tone of working side-by-side at something together. The therapeutic relationship is nurtured through this shared activity. The taking of turns, speaking or not and the ebb and flow of the conversation is made more visible and control of its direction and intensity can be more easily shared.

Recapping with the map

After the conversation has developed a little, the therapist walks his or her fingers and pen around the map, showing their understanding of specific words and adding arrows to make links, checking for connection and agreement and reviewing progress. It involves pausing the flow of conversation and suggesting that it would help to just recap where we have got to so far using the map as our guide.

Recapping invites a different tone to conversation with more emphasis on reflection. It is modelling a higher level of discussion which is more deliberate and self-conscious. The activity is a tentative one of watching and waiting for the client's participation and with a readiness to pass the lead in recapping to the client. This is usually evidenced by the client getting a hands-on, 'pointing and linking' relationship with the map and thereby with the conversation.

Recapping can lead to moments of change in perspective. Tracking a sequence of words on paper may begin to highlight a pattern. A detailed interaction may suddenly open a view of the bigger picture. Or a moment that was in the past begins to show itself with all its emotion and memory in the present.

When we talk of past experiences, or any experiences that are not in the immediate present, then the qualities of interaction and feeling from 'back then' or 'out there' come alive in the room. Either in small and benign ways, or bigger and disturbing ways, memories become emotional actions and move us. The process of mapping can help hold, mediate and guide this reliving and re-enacting. Re-voicing what is on the map may trigger new emotional connections and responses as well as strengthen, or challenge, existing ones. It is an invitation to be rethinking, and rewording memories. It is revisiting of past links and previously forbidden, overly rigid, or muted responses.

The process of recapping is tactile. It involves circling, highlighting, under lining or crossing out words and arrowing lines of links or touching where two places co-act. It is a co-embodied experience as client and therapist lean in, turn away, look at each other and then the map. The body language of mapping is part of the body language of a relational therapy.

The act of recapping is a deceptive powerful therapeutic mechanism of change. Some words will be added, and others crossed out. Some words carry memories that were not noticed when the words were first said but come to full emotional attention in the act of recapping. The process of doing this needs noticing. The quality of recapping is key: it is open, curious, compassionate and in the zone of those taking part. It is descriptive and tentative, not interpretative. The use of the words on paper allows client and therapist to go at each other's pace, to check for understanding. Even so the client will fill the activity and have changing responses that are both characteristic of them and significant for the therapeutic process of developing relational awareness. How recapping develops can be indicative of how the client relates to themselves and the world around them.

As recapping the conversation with the map becomes an established routine, the role can be shared and turns taken. It integrates the activity of mapping into the conversation. Recapping also models work alone after the session with the map. It cultivates what Ryle called the 'observing eye' (Pickvance, 2017) and more generally a reflective, self-observing capacity (Ryle, 1997). The therapist, in her or his way of introducing recapping, is modelling a compassionate, open, and curious attitude to the conversation as it develops. It is inviting client and therapist to be participating observers.

Inevitably, recapping is likely to add mess to the map. A fresh and tidy version of a messy map can be made together surprisingly quickly. Making a tidy map may bring new connections, responses and clarifications. The therapist is curious about the process that comes into play with recapping. Is it a race for closure? Is it seeking to tidy up what is being said? What words and patterns are becoming familiar and accepted? Where do gaps seem to be emerging? For every important link that the process of conversational mapping makes, there is an equally important sense of gaps and disconnections to notice (see chapters 8 and 9)

Emma Smith (2020) in her acclaimed new book on reading Shakespeare, talks of gaps in the text, (in the story, in the characters) being the key to the opening of a relationship with his plays. She prefers the word gappiness to 'negative capability' as 'gappiness' is a more cheerful and open word. It points to the non-binary, 'in-between' experience that draws us into the drama on stage without offering an answer. According to Smith the trouble with our schooling in Shakespeare is that we feel we should know a 'correct' account of what is going on, whereas we are best entertained and provoked by experiencing Shakespeare as an active verb. Going to a play is 'Shakespearing' to being 'Shakespeared'. It is this quality of reading the story between the lines and behind the words that recapping offers and which is further elaborated below in the sections on hovering, shimmering and constructive dithering.

Sam's example of a map of two words

We began with one word on the map. Sam had described his father, who was usually a quiet man, getting very agitated at times with the family around him 'fratting' about. He would chastise them to stop 'fratting' about. On inspection the word seemed undefined, then and now, but opened feelings up of wasting time, going around in circles, being caught up in trivia and being at fault. Mulling over the word on the map helped him connect will feelings of anger at the limited life his dad had had to live and the job he had to do. It was a 'fratting job' as a travelling salesman. We looked for a word that stood in contrast to 'fratting'. The word chosen was 'dignified' in relation to longing to be doing something 'dignifying'. On paper we had two words that had appeared out of a short conversation: one at the top: **dignifying**, and one at the bottom: '**fratting**'. To our surprise, much of the therapy was concerned with moving up the ladder from 'fratting' to feeling and being more dignified. The two words and the piece of paper that first 'found' them became important to Sam. It opened a new relationship with his memory of his father and of his relationship with his own activities and values in life. He wrote a short letter to the words on the map.

Dear Fratting and Dignifying

I feel so sad about the loss and waste of life just fratting, fretting and worrying and not feeling anything was going anywhere. I realise for my dad it was the six years of national service, the boredom, the waiting. The life not lived. And then his job as a travelling salesman after the war. The Ford Anglia his company car. To my dad I want to say I understand how the family was a haven that sometimes felt like a hiding place and at times threatened to be contaminated by the 'fratting' feeling. I think I forgive him for that. I think I was raised in a climate of 'fratting' as if nothing more heroic or more dignified could be achieved. I make a promise to myself in this letter to stop 'fratting' and seek and look for dignity.

Thanks, from Sam

In writing the letter, Sam found another position to add to the map which he called 'treats and distractions'. He realised his mother would soothe his dad and the family by soothing and distracting from the distress of 'fratting' by offering treats. It was as if she was saying to the distress of 'fratting'. 'Let's leave the battles for another day.' It offered an escape from the distress but not a route to individual or family dignity. In initially putting the words on paper the process of therapy gave dignity, in the here and now, to Sam's recollections. It gave him a more relational, aware way of thinking about the word 'fratting' and made him less trapped by it emotionally.

Words on paper are dialogue buttons

Once out there on paper, words such as 'fratting' are like dialogue buttons. When we see them and touch them, we connect with them. Will the connection be curious or cautious? Will we enter dialogue or steer away from deeper thoughts and feelings? Will they help us negotiate with our own mixed feelings of approach and avoidance? These normal processes of conversational ambivalence can be transmitted and more easily negotiated with the relevant words on paper. As in Sam's 'fratting' example, the map may now be the site on paper of words for feelings that, when recapped, bring the inner feeling for the word more to life. A client points to the word 'sad' on the paper and says 'Seeing the word sad out there I can feel it touching me and it makes me feel sad. Somehow that is okay because it is as if the feeling is acknowledged and allowed'.

Words carry emotion, make meaning, and resonate with us. Or they jar and unsettle us. At their best they have a metaphorical quality. They offer an analogy. They carry the feeling through the words and meaning is transported. Hobson (1985, p56) gives an engaging description of language and metaphor in therapy: 'The colourful, vigorous, ambiguous language of metaphor generates *a sense of immediacy and life* which lures us on to explore what is dimly sensed'. He sees metaphor as breaking the rules of language games. We use metaphor to find our feelings and to fish for other people's feelings. Putting the words together is a co-creative and therapeutic experience at the heart of building reflective capacity.

Hobson refers to therapy as '…providing, and mutually elaborating, a feeling-language in a developing conversation' (p18, ibid). He describes a sensitivity to how passive listening become active listening, but also warns against the activity of talking and listening being a way of bypassing the therapeutic potential of the conversation. He seems to be saying that there is always an invisible threshold to the conversation, a moment of breakthrough that can be missed. The role of conversational mapping is to add a layer of fluidity to the conversation such that we can go back and forth and check for what was missed or not spoken. This fluidity is the lifeblood of relational awareness. Mapping can help navigate these movements.

Words spread out on paper as the markers of a developing conversation begin to point out the patterns to our relationships and stories. These key patterns are the stock in trade of Ryle and other cognitive relational approaches, but the latter tend to lose sight of the therapeutic importance of the developing conversation and its 'feeling language'. Hobson (ibid) talks of creating a conversation that can stand in 'mysteries, uncertainties and doubts' (p185, ibid) which echoes the core theme of the relational school of psychoanalysis in New York, as represented by Philip Bromberg's (1998) idea of 'standing in the spaces' between ego states, for example. Hobson views language as multi-relational; 'a broad conception of language which covers many different modes of being with other people'. Hobson talks of the key conversational dilemma being one of approach and avoidance. In a similar way Karen Horney's (1945) pioneering description of the parallel internal and interpersonal dynamics of emotional problems (she called them neuroses) distinguished between movement towards (dependently or openly), moving away (avoidantly or protectively), or against (aggressively or assertively) the other person in the therapy partnership. She also linked this to taking in (introjecting) or pushing out of difficult feelings as ways of managing the anxiety they produce. In writing dynamically in this way in the 1940s she offered a framework for the kind of relational awareness proposed in this book now.

Through a conversation with a map we are finding a new language, a new story, a new way of being intimately engaged with these lifelong problems of making sense of ourselves. Hobson says: 'it is important to own the metaphor as an action' (p59, ibid). The process of conversational mapping turns words into action and gives them an analogical role bordering on metaphor by just being out there on paper between and before us.

Wording and worded

In the ambiance of therapy, words take on a freshness and uniqueness of expression. Sometimes it's as if we are coining them for the first time when we speak. There is a gap between the making or the 'wording' of the word and the result of it being worded. This gap is the conversational and therapeutic gap in which there is space for what will later in the chapter be described as hovering and shimmering.

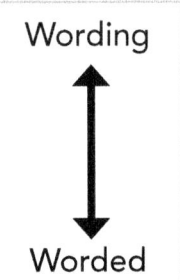

Watch a two-year old slowly pronounce words as they are simultaneously discovering and owning them on the tips of their tongues. We need this 'two-year-old' intimacy in the therapy room with words being worded. In this vein, it is not a surprise that therapy such as CAT turns to the latest generation of infant researchers with their common focus on the co creative, relational awareness and intelligence being nurtured through shared subjectivities in the first months and years of life. Whether it is through forms of vitality (Stern, 2010), play or musicality (Trevarthen, 2017), words are beginning to mediate the different emotional centres of the brain by the end of the child's second year. A feeling self with a capacity for self-consciousness and agency (Knox, 2011) grows through integration of different neuro-affective systems (Panksepp, 2012). Speaking feels like a form of action and movement for the two-year old. It is interpersonal and effortful. When we speak a word or phrase, we are wording. Or in the language of the Russian philologist Mikael Bakhtin (1981), we are 'uttering'. The uttering in our brains and the wording on the tip of our tongues and in our larynx is sensed and the voicing of what is worded feels like a deed, like an action. This process of creating space for the joint activity of considered speech is echoed and validated by the space for mapping words out on paper. We do not often know in advance which words will bring tears, or laughter, or shame. Or which words will pull us into feelings or push us to reflection or to shut off.

Part of therapy with a map is the process of reliving these early years in the discovery of language and repairing and healing damaged capacities or discovering new ones in wording and rewording. In **Chapter 8** on relational healing, memories of trauma that have never been worded and gaps in self-knowledge through the dynamics of association and dissociation are explored. Here in poetic form is a list of the qualities of words in the stop, start and flow of a therapeutic conversation with a map.

Uttering words is an action
- Which the map captures and illustrates.
- Words that speak out and show the way,
- Pointing to relationships in time and place.

- Carrying mixed feelings
- That make links and connections
- Which accuse, judge or blame,
- Or empower and validate.
- Words that are self-revealing
- As they hesitate and dither on the tips of tongues,
- Shouting or whispering true meaning,
- Or skip, bypass and deceptively cover up.

An illustration with Michael

Michael and I are sitting, side-by-side, at a table, with a big (A3) piece of paper in front of us. The paper is covered, here and there, with words in black ink, some circled, some in bold and in capitals, others in tiny scribble. All are linked by lines and arrows. We are just looking at it for some minutes in a contemplative silence. Michael seems pleased and smiles.

'No one will make head nor tail of this except me and you.'

'Do we make sense of it?' I ask.

'Yes.' He says, emphatically.

'It's ours. It is like our paths in the forest. Off the beaten track.'

I wonder if it will make sense in a week's time. I think we will need to tidy it up and, in the process, pick out the main patterns. Like many clients, Michael may want to hold onto 'our work'. Whatever happens to the map as a thing in-itself, the process of mapping, talking and reflecting together with it has done its therapeutic work. We have an alliance and a shared language. Out of nothing, in our first proper meeting since agreeing to do therapy, we have simultaneously talked and sketched our way into Michael's patterns of interaction with himself and the world. I have been an active participant, suggesting, pinpointing, clarifying, reacting. Have Michael and I done this work together? Admittedly I have been the one with the pen so far, but the map is his as much as mine. His hands are on it.

He seemed surprised at first that I was being so active with pen and paper and yet showing him what I was noting down. He said, as many clients do, 'Mapping together makes the therapist less scary. You can see them working things out, you can see a little of their vulnerability. It brings them nearer to your level. They are not claiming to know all about the mess in your head, but they are willing to go into it with you.'

Hovering

Hovering is a joint activity which becomes, through practice, part of the client's way of relating to themselves more generally. It is a capacity which allows reflection, relational mindfulness, mentalising, making meaning and testing a point of view. The hovering like a hawk, or helicopter, involves seeing here and there and taking in different points of view. Wittgenstein was all for seeing the bigger picture; 'Don't get involved in partial problems, but always take flight to where there is a free view over the whole single great problem, even if this view is still not a clear one' (Ludwig Wittgenstein, journal entry 1st November 1914). Hovering is both zooming in and out, a movement between picture and detail. It brings the multiple possibilities to life of seeing more than one perspective at the same time. The outward focus of hovering over the paper alongside another person enables an internal hovering and reflective capacity, which is doubly enhanced by knowing that the person beside you is equally giving attention in this way.

One exercise that has worked time and time again in training sessions and in therapy and supervision is to look mindfully over the map for a minute. This is neither looking at the whole map or any one detail but scanning over it and seeing what comes up. It invariably triggers a rush of activity to add to, amend or go around the map again. Hovering helps develop a focus and shared ownership over the conversation. It teaches also a shared reflective capacity. One client said it stops them dwelling too much or ruminating, because looking over the map took them out of themselves.

Hovering can help loosen fixed ideas to which we are overly attached through the pull of social identity and group allegiance. There is a push and pull to most conversations that nudge us into taking sides. The invitation from the map and the mapping process is to hover and to not take sides. It means seeing patterns without reacting immediately.

Shimmering

This ability to shimmer with mixed emotions is an ability also to tolerate the simultaneous experience of contrasting intensities, direction and colouring of feeling. These may be well or badly orchestrated. Shimmering helps us get alongside how our emotions are felt, triggered and put together. For example, we cannot understand anxiety if we don't see its link with unexpressed sadness or hard to manage anger, thwarted pride or feared shame. The root of this idea of shimmering (though not the word) can be traced to the pre-psychoanalytic idea of ambivalence as described by Bleuler, a mentor and colleague of Freud's in his early days. Ambivalent feeling links to ambivalent ideas and motivations. If I can tolerate the anxiety of ambivalence about feelings, about actions and about intentions, then I can develop a fuller relational awareness of the emotional context of the feelings which I am having. Hanna Segal who links the idea from Bleuler to Freud, Klein and Bion, views ambivalence as a useful quality and achievement rather than a difficulty as long we are in dialogue with it and not repressing the mixed feelings (Segal, 1992)

Shimmering outwardly might be between different actions and the emotions they involve. Shimmering inwardly is movement in and out of different states or between hot and cool feelings, or movements towards and away from the feelings aroused by others.

The concept of shimmering originates with the description by Mardi Horowitz (1998) of the emotional regulation of a state of mind. He saw that each state could be emotionally over-regulated or under-regulated. In conversational mapping the idea of shimmering is developed to include sensory awareness of all different feeling states and emotional coping responses within and between states and their orchestration. Our therapeutic goal is more harmonious orchestration. Or at least compassion for, and awareness of, discordant or shallow orchestration. Mapping helps us connect with the shimmering orchestration in our heads through a feeling for the emotion words on paper. It externalises feelings more safely by making them less intensely exposing. An increased capacity for shimmering holds feelings long enough to modify them by linking them, softening them, or refocusing and re-orchestrating them. Shimmering is not an end-in-itself. It can feel uncomfortable and a source of uncertainty and anxiety. It is a quality that if valued and tolerated can be a step towards a more open dialogue with self in the world and a greater sense of relational awareness.

Constructive dithering

The art of constructive dithering in for relational awareness

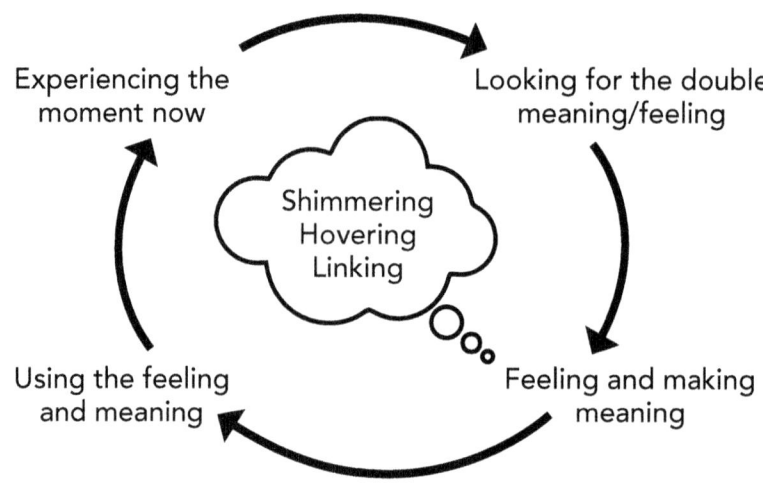

This idea is somewhat more unsettling to busy professionals with jobs to do and solutions to find and clients who want to stop suffering. It is the quality of constructive dithering. It is the combined work of hovering and shimmering. Much of the expectations of therapies and treatments for mental health are solution-focused and based on fixing and sorting things. There is an innate pressure to make our minds up and to get the story sorted (see page 73). Most of the key mental health professions put a stress on diagnosis, formulation, and clinical judgement. Clients largely expect their professionals to know what they are doing. They should, but part of knowing what you are doing as a therapist is to know how to dither. To know how to 'not know'.

Dithering is not proposed as a character trait, or a therapeutic mechanism in the manner of the timeless and popular detective TV series *Columbo*, whereby he would leave and then come back repeatedly with just one last unresolved thought or question. Dithering is proposed as a joint activity of being in-the-midst of important feelings, ideas and choices and just tolerating the messiness of the moment. It draws upon the research of Boston group on therapeutic moments. According to Daniel Stern's account, one conclusion of the research group after years of research was that a therapeutic moment is a moment of sloppiness (Stern, 2004). The idea of sloppiness links to Smith's idea of 'gappiness' and to the idea of tolerating the open and uncertain space of a world in transition with a yearning for relational awareness. It is the quality that is most forcibly not allowed in a traumatising world.

Therapists need to learn the art of being unsure and tolerating uncertainty at times when there might be pressure to be decisive, come to the rescue and pursue a course of action. Hovering, shimmering and constructive dithering builds resilience against uncertainty and anxiety. It is easier with a map.

John's example

Take the example of John, who is a young man, twenty four years old and in his first year at university. He says to me halfway through our first session that the main problem with him is that he is lazy, 'I am lazy, my mum says I am lazy, my girlfriend says I am lazy'. He says this, as if telling himself off, channelling their voices into the room. As he talks, he is relaxing in the chair; his body is a bit slumped back. We make eye contact and I think he felt judged because he sat up. I thought to myself, 'Perhaps you are lazy. What is it like being lazy? It would be lovely to be lazy'. My stream of thoughts does not develop into a conversation with him. I too, begin to feel a bit lazy. But there is, I sense, an accusing voice in him, or around him, which is part of the lazy dance in some way. If only we could turn this laziness into constructive dithering.

I put down the word lazy on paper. I speculate that it is his safe place or hiding place and the place he ends stuck in often. I have the word 'accusing' mixed with another feeling in my head to describe how his mum and girlfriend are addressing him and how he felt I was judging him just now for slumping in his chair. My reverie leads me to the question.

'How does your family view your behaviour?' I ask pointing to the map, as if somewhere they are hiding their feelings on the map.

'I don't know.' He says. 'They have given up on me.'

'Why?' I whisper, wary of sounding accusing.

'Oh, they were so frustrated.'

From the conversation a pattern is emerging. I put a circle around the word 'lazy' on paper and add the other words that have been part of the conversation. 'Frustrated', 'giving up'. He sits up a bit and looks mildly curious and concerned. 'Are the words on paper challenging?' I ask. He shrugs. I would like to think he is hovering, shimmering with me and I am encouraging him to constructively dither. He does dither between settling back down and getting engaged. He is in two minds but then seems to make up his mind.

'No, it feels cosy.' He says.

'You don't need anything from them. So, they ignore you.' I suggest. He thinks then says pointing at the blank space on the map, 'They get on without me. They get on with each other'. There is a pause. We are looking at the map without really connecting with it.

'My dad.' he says, as if making an unexpected link. 'My dad was unavailable. I think he was lazy with me and now they have all got the same response.' he says thoughtfully. He leans into the map and notes that, 'Wow, me and them? Everyone is being lazy with me.'

Part of the legacy of relational trauma, even in its mildest but chronically endured form, is gaps in self-knowledge (see pages 144 and 165). Becoming aware of a conflict within the self is upsetting and blocking the awareness is comforting. His cosy idea of himself in a bubble of laziness was a pattern born of self-protection.

In this process of active listening we now had a small array of words as in the figure above. These words are spread out on the paper between us. They are within our reach.

He says, 'I don't believe it'. We understand this to be his surprise at both the connections he is making and the absence of laziness right now in his work with me at making connections. It feels a little like he has woken from a long sleep. After more discussion I asked if he would write a letter to the Cosy with Lazy trap and bring it back the following week. In writing the letter and in reading it out at the following session and to his family he had created a new action tendency against the grain of his habitual lazy one. He is in a new dialogue with his pattern, with himself, me, his family and his partner. Step-by-step through mapping the conversation and making links that led to writing a short letter he climbed out of a restricted place in his life which had become his identity and his 'safe' hiding place.

> *Dear Cosy and Lazy*
>
> *I am twenty-four years old and you have become me. I am happy with lazy because it feels cosy. It is not that I don't want to do things or get on, but I never feel ready. Gaps have been created. I thought it was all about me. My character. But it is a dance I have fallen into with the rest of the family. We are all cosy and lazy when it comes to me. Partly it allows the others to be so busy and hard working. They are hyper whilst I am slumber. I doodle about. In fact, I am their constant. I do errands for them. Wait in for parcels. Listen to their heroics. If I stop being lazy, or if I show I am not cosy with being lazy, it will stop them in their tracks. They won't know me. It is like I have crawled out of my lazy seashell and they will tease me back in. I am not particularly scared. Just awake. You have become so much part of me that you risk becoming all of me. I am ready to move on.*
>
> *Yours, John*

Working together, side-by-side

One reason for mapping and talking together is to learn to work side-by-side through conversation and shared activity. Being side-by-side is like a parent and child learning to read, or an apprentice beside a carpenter learning to work with wood, or the midwife to the birthing couple. Many years ago, an Irish colleague Angela Mohan linked the sentiment of working side-by-side to a poem by Seamus Heaney, 'Side-by-side, about a love that's proved by steady gazing/Not at each other but in the same direction' (Seamus Heaney 2010, Human Chain).

A client says to their therapist in the third week of meeting and talking around maps and bits of writing, 'Well you don't like conflict do you'. The therapist is taken aback. It felt a challenging thing to say and an invitation to be in conflict. But it also felt personally familiar and true. The statement feels immediately like a dilemma to the therapist. If I take on the challenge, I may go head to head just to prove I can handle conflict and if I agree or do nothing it might seem like I am proving the client's point. Could mapping side-by-side help make something therapeutic of this conversational impasse? The therapist put the words 'conflict' at one end of a piece of paper and the words 'don't like' at the other end and asks if the client could help explore this and see what it means for each of them.

This is an open invitation to the idea of not liking conflict as a point of enquiry between them rather than a closed position that is avoided or fearfully fought over. In this example the therapist is neither revealing or concealing him or herself but getting alongside and doing work that might well be of therapeutic value for them both. Or to put it another way, it will not be likely to have therapeutic value for the client until it has therapeutic value for the therapist. The conversation gathered momentum around the words once they were on the map. The client explored his view that what he was familiar with was arguing and having it out. His parents were always 'at each other' (the phrase gets added to the map). He said people who were not willing to have a 'word fight' were overlooked. The therapist felt uncomfortable at the possible dismissing of him as weak because they are not able to argue. They talked more about the father being the main provoker of a head-to-head style of conversation. The therapist proposed drawing a dotted line between the words: 'conflict' and 'don't like'. Linked to 'don't like' he suggested adding 'being side-by-side' and linked to the word 'conflict' he proposed adding 'head-to-head'. With more discussion they decided that whilst the client was more at the head-to-head end of the continuum represented by the line, the therapist was more at the side-by-side end of the line. It was judged a useful therapeutic exercise, for each of them to notice moments and movements along the continuum when they arise in therapy. They now had an analogue or copy on paper, with which they might reflect upon the conversation between them. It created a safe scaffolding for the therapist to wonder what was on the client's mind and what he had noticed about the therapist that led him to the conclusion about conflict. It helped the client work with his perceptions of the strengths and weaknesses of the therapist and their echo in his own experience and memory.

In summary, the opposite of working side-by-side is going head-to-head. There are certain times in conversation when noticing the pull to go head-to-head is particularly important. We cannot help but go head-to-head at times. Otherwise some of the patterns of relating, judging, or idealising that make up the client's struggle, and the therapist's vulnerability will never see the interpersonal light of day. But creating a capacity to default to a side-by-side relationship is a hallmark of working therapeutically. Early and ongoing conversational mapping can help nurture this capacity.

Holding and pacing

In talking therapeutically, we want to feel safe, which means knowing the limits of the agenda and boundaries of roles. Holding implies looking after, taking care. However, talking therapeutically can be surprisingly absorbing and we can lose track of time and of each other. The role of mapping is to pull up every so often and see and say where our edges are. If our boundaries are too tight then nothing will happen in the conversation. If they are too loose then too much will happen in the hidden depths of the conversation. The process of conversational mapping can help hold the shape and direction of the discussion without it being narrowed or restricted.

Any therapy is a form of social and psychological development. As therapy develops, client and therapist alike will reach towards each other, reach beyond themselves and their current understanding, and reach within themselves to connect, repair and heal what is wounded or broken down. In order that therapy can be effective, this work must take place within the cognitive and emotional capacity of both client and therapist. Too far out of reach risks being overwhelming, and too easily within reach is unlikely to result in any meaningful change.

Vygotsky (Daniels, 2005) describes this cognitive and emotional 'reach' as the zone of proximal development. The therapist is leading the client into a zone of discovery and understanding, that is ahead of his or her current capability, but not so far ahead as to stop the client from engaging and internalising both what is learnt and how it is learnt. This idea is eloquently summarised by Vygotsky as 'What the child can do with help today they will do for themselves on their own tomorrow'.

Educationalists love Vygotsky's idea as it offers a developmental ladder to climb with a prospective student or child. Likewise, the therapeutic relationship can utilise the Vygotskian idea of working within the zone between what the client can do with help, and what they can do on their own. For Vygotsky's ideas to apply to therapy we need to stress the educational and tutorial aspect of a psychotherapeutic conversation. Through doing things together, noticing how they are done, naming what we feel and negotiating what to do next, the therapist and client move towards the shared goals of the therapy. Step-by-step the client learns to be their own therapist.

To sum up, there will be times when therapist and client overreach themselves. Or reach, and touch something that resists being held. At other times there will be the risk of under-reaching, of playing safe and erring on the side of caution. It is at these moments that mapping can help acknowledge the challenges and offer a framework for tracking a way forward.

Listening with a map: guidance notes for clients

Beginning mapping with the client can be helped by giving some notes as to what is intended. The following information sheet is one example that might be helpful both for conversational mapping and the mapping processes described in subsequent chapters.

> It may be useful to keep track of our discussion by making notes of key words, feelings and ideas that we can see and work with together. Think of them as listening maps. Initially it is likely that the therapist will be the one with the pen, but the paper should be accessible for both to add to the map. The benefits of mapping as we talk, or pausing at times during the conversation to make a mini map of a specific issue or moment are as follows:
> - They help us work together in an open and collaborative way.
> - The map allows us to see what we are saying which can be validating and a stepping-stone to being in a wider and deeper dialogue with ourselves.
> - We can keep track of the conversation and check if we share the same understanding.
> - We can recap some parts of what is being shared by using the map to go back to an earlier thought or feeling.
> - It can help us draw out patterns of relating to ourselves and others.
> - These patterns may help us see the influences on us, what happened to us, how we cope and choices we are making.
> - Though often the map will be ignored as the conversation flows the map notes are there as a point of reference.
> - There are various options for building on the maps across several sessions of therapy.
> - Rough sketches can be photographed and or taken away and tidied up.
> - Complex maps can be simplified for use in addressing a specific goal of therapy.
> - Working with the maps tends to help both of us feel safer and more involved.
> - The maps may also be annoying or confusing at times.
> - Discussing these feelings may help us talk about the process of working together.
> - The maps should not be given any status other than to help us listen and connect.
> - They should not be used independently as a record or assessment of the therapy.

Sitting or standing?

Mapping side-by-side is an act of trust. We are touching each other's thoughts and feelings and both clients and therapists have described it as a safe kind of intimacy through shared activity. The therapy room and its features and furnishing will mean different things to client and therapist. In many settings there is little control over the room or the choice of room. If it is soundproof that is a great relief. Ideally there is a table of suitable height.

Sitting side-by-side is the normal arrangement. It is what mostly will happen, but the conversational nature of therapeutic mapping involves movement. When mapping, the option of standing at a white board or flip chart stand should not be ruled out. For one therapist, the experience of standing up at a white board, with one client working and moving around beside them, was like they were dancing with the map moving back and forth, seeing the patterns develop from different angles.

As with the example of 'dancing around the white board', it is worth paying attention to the joint body language of mapping. It is not a 'heads bent over the paper' experience. Clients and therapists will, and should, shift attention between looking at the words on paper, and then looking eye-to-eye at each other or looking away. One client in the process of talking, switched between looking intently at the map as it developed bit by bit, looking at the therapist and looking at the ceiling as memories unfolded. She explained that looking at the ceiling helped her visualise the scenes she wanted to recall of events in her memory.

Conclusion

The combination of recapping, hovering, shimmering and constructive dithering, side-by-side as client and therapist, can help create a climate of relational awareness in the conversation. As clients we may not pay too much attention initially to the words being put on paper since we are caught up in our own flow of thoughts and feelings. But the feeling of 'words going down on paper' may stand for us as a sign that we are being taken seriously. They are an invitation to a different kind of dialogue.

The mapping helps the talking by tracking, holding, and guiding the developing conversation. The talk becomes dynamic and conversational. It goes places from present to past, from one person's view to another's from looking in to looking out. One topic leads to another one such that several themes are in play. This may happen in any form of therapeutic conversation, but it is easier to sustain and hold in mind with the aid of the conversational mapping process.

Chapter 2: Relationship mapping

'Estragon: We always find something, eh Didi, to give us the impression we exist?'

(Samuel Beckett, Waiting for Godot)

Introduction

This chapter describes the process of mapping relationships as part of therapy. Examples are given, and the therapeutic mechanisms of change that arise from working together in this way are described. We discuss the interplay of techniques with conversational, narrative and process mapping. The chapter is also an introduction to mapping templates from cognitive analytic therapy (CAT) based upon reciprocal roles and reciprocal role procedures. The origin of these ideas in the work of Tony Ryle is explored. (Their use in CAT is the focus of **Part 3** of the book.)

Reciprocal roles

Our patterns of response to each other are reciprocal. We push and pull interactions onto and from each other. What was clear to sociologists and picked up by Tony Ryle, was that in playing a role, we are in a reciprocation with one or more other people, as well as the inner parts of our selves. We are predicting, attuning to, or eliciting responses on the one hand. We are responding, reacting and coping on the other hand. We do this with varying degrees of intensity, intention and awareness. How well, how fairly or openly we orchestrate these roles and relationships is always at the back of our minds. Mapping helps us reflect upon roles and relationships in which we might be too involved otherwise.

The idea of role reciprocation offers an open framework for mapping patterns of human interaction without over-defining local and personal experience. For Ryle, it helped explain the repetitions of early patterns of relating and allowed the description of resemblances between roles enacted 'self-to-self' along with roles played out interpersonally and socially with others. He was interested in the life-shaping, emotional roles which are 'taken on' in our early years and later reproduced in the guise of personality and identity. What Ryle thereby added to the sociological idea of role was the psychoanalytic (object relations) idea of the internalisation and subsequent replay of patterns of relating as building blocks of the self.

Ryle introduces the idea of role in a very matter of fact way. He gives the example of the role at the railway ticket office. It is a reciprocation around buying of a ticket. Both parties know the roles. For Ryle, the more straightforward world of social role transactions can offer a scaffolding to get alongside the more intimate and implicit experience of emotional transactions. The social and emotional sides of the role live within each other. When queuing for a train ticket and under pressure of time, one person in the queue may react with brooding patience and the other person might be loudly complaining. Role, transaction, person and emotion are entangled in each other. Ryle was looking for a means of explaining this complexity without over-simplifying.

A key contribution from Ryle was to see, that in responding to a carer the infant gives back the elicited response of feeling cared for but also learns the other role of actively caring. For example, the infant who is in the role of being loved, also knows the role of doing the loving. The subtle internal and interpersonal dynamics of this exchange and the versatility of Ryle's idea becomes much clearer when mapped out on paper.

Doing and feeling – the two ends of a reciprocal role relationship

There are two ends, or poles, to the reciprocal role, one is the doing, or action end, and the other is the feeling or receiving end. The convention in CAT is to call each end a pole (like north and south poles). The line linking the two poles has arrows at either end to indicate there is a complex interaction condensed into two or more words. A circle or box is drawn around to denote that here is potentially a hub position on the map for several patterns of interaction.

The top end of the pole is usually the more powerful action end, which is often parentally, or adult derived. The bottom end of the pole is the more elicited, and less powerful child-derived emotional response. The doing end (top) has a 'feeling' part that can be teased out, but the dominant aspect is the action. In mapping, as in the adjoining depiction of a reciprocal role, we are looking for doing words at the top.

The bottom end of the reciprocal role arrangement will have a reactive, action element, but the dominant point is the subjective feeling of something being done to us.

If you care for me, then what you are doing in caring will leave me feeling looked after. I receive the care that you intend to give. If you keep looking after me in this way, and I keep feeling looked after, then this doing and feeling reciprocation between us becomes an enduring, central, role-bound, automatic relationship. I will expect it and I will help you care for and look after me. It may be mutual, and we take turns being in 'the-looking-after-role' and in the 'being looked-after-role'. Or we may inhabit either end of the role differently in an unequal allocation of power. I may take the 'looking after' for granted and be casual in its reception.

Putting the key words of the relationship down on paper before us opens a space up for discovery and exploration. The reciprocal role template is filled out a as personal, lived story using the words and phrases of the client. It is a springboard for reflection on feelings and memories and the aim in finding words for the reciprocal roles is to put on paper those that prompt us in the most open and connective way. As will be often repeated in this book such moments are opportunities for developing and healing relational awareness.

Our conversations about ourselves are peppered with stories of what we do to others or others do to us. In mapping out patterns of relating, we are listening out for whether it is a pattern local to a one-off story, or one that harks back to early roles and familiar ways of being. For example, if you repeatedly do something to me – and you are a powerful adult and carer in my life, and I am a child to you – then what you are doing is going to influence my relationship both with you and with myself. Imagine you are a parent bullying me in relation to me responding by fearfully submitting. This through repetition, will become an enduring role relationship and a part of my life story. It would be put on the map as bullying to fearfully submitting. It will be a relationship which I adopt automatically to myself. Since it is one of the relational patterns through which I know myself deep down, I will expect it, seek it out, read it into situations which I encounter, or elicit it from others. It becomes a pattern of interaction which is typical for me. Figuratively, perhaps literally, it is a map in my relational brain and my socio-emotional memory. Also, I may have seen this pattern become placed and rooted externally in the culture around me as what society does – 'parents bully-children submit'.

Asking questions which help map out reciprocal roles

As an exercise, the reader might find it an aid to the ideas in this book to take a blank sheet of paper and do the following. Look at the blank sheet of paper. Make it yours and welcome the opportunity to write on it. Think of a moment in the past day or two when you had a distinctive feeling or emotion. Write the words for that emotion or feeling down in the middle of the sheet of paper. Look at the word. Does it describe to some extent what you were feeling? Your thought about the feeling is now on your mind and out before you on paper. Draw a line, with arrows at either end above your words for feelings and ask yourself, 'Who was doing what?' or, 'What was going on that might have caused, provoked, invited the feeling that is there on paper in front of me?'. Put down the doing words without thinking too much about who it was coming from or whether you were doing it to yourself. Or it was a mixture of both? On the map now is a relationship between doing something as an action and feeling something as an impact. Look at the reciprocal relationship for a minute and wonder if now that the doing words are down on paper, do you want to change the feelings words? Is the reciprocation a familiar or unusual one? Is it linked to an emotional or social role that is part of how you are in life?

In summary these are typical guiding question to tease out the reciprocal role relationships.

- In that moment, or at that time what were you feeling?
- What was going on (who was doing what) that fed into, or elicited that feeling?
- What part did you play in bringing that feeling on or muting it?
- If other people were experiencing this being done to them or grew up with this being done to them, what would they normally feel in your view?
- How did (or do) you, or others and society around you make sense of this reciprocation then or now as you are recalling it?

Some reciprocal roles –good, bad, and mixed

To get the idea of reciprocal roles here is a list of common ones. Mostly the roles are those relating to care and neglect, love and abandonment, esteem and being helped or harmed in some way. In the box below the top four could be desired and valuable depending on how they are orchestrated and internalised. Think about how their meaning would change if adverbs were added as qualifiers. For example: 'terrifyingly' inspiring, 'lovingly' demanding, 'naively' trusting. Think of others you might add such as: validating-to-validated; loving-to-loved.

The middle four are mixed interactions in that they could help or hinder depending on context. Again, think of others such as 'being controlling-to-feeling controlled', 'supporting-to-feeling supported', 'advising-to-feeling guided'. Again, imagine adding adverbs that qualify the action of the verb such as 'cruelly' teasing, or 'over' protecting. Finally, the bottom four are most easily understood as harmful, though again the context and intensity may give them different meanings. Think of other harmful reciprocal roles such as abusing, denying and invalidating. Such reciprocal roles as these may be part of our deep sense of self and patterned into our memory. They may animate our life stories and shape our hopes and fears for the immediate tasks and times in front of us day-by-day. They are the nuts and bolts of developing relational awareness about aspects of our lives that were taken for granted, restricted, or greatly valued but are now overlooked.

Some reciprocal roles

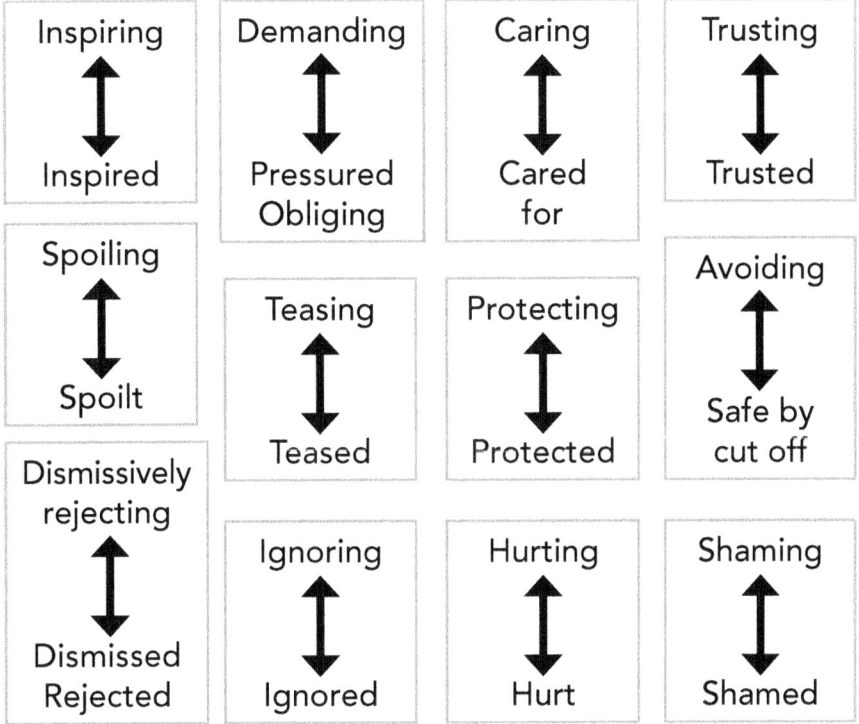

The list of reciprocal roles is not to be used in an off-the-peg way. Ryle (1975) viewed his idea of reciprocal roles as a necessary simplification. Indeed, to turn the 'off the peg' analogy around, the naming of a reciprocal role is a peg on which to hang a more bespoke noticing and negotiating of patterns of relating to self and others and the world around. The therapist should help the client with the process of mapping to discover the local language and colour of the reciprocal roles. The idea of colouring in the adverbs make them unique to the individual and avoids the risk of being clichés which are drained of personal meaning. Such moments of discovery are one mechanism of therapeutic change and an increase in relational awareness. The process is one of hovering, shimmering and constructive dithering described in the last chapter and explored further in **Chapter 7**.

A limited orchestration of reciprocal roles may be a key part of a specific culture, or institution in society. Restrictive or harmful patterns of reciprocal roles are at the heart of understanding the dynamics of racism and sexism and other dynamics of social power and abuse. For example, male roles at times of war, or the roles imposed on women in traditional societies or through mass media in a digital society. Or the structure of colonialism and positioning of groups and societies as inferior or exotic. The versatility of the reciprocal role idea is that it can help track simultaneously the internal and interpersonal psychology of relationships alongside their social and cultural organisation.

Reciprocal roles link inner and outer realities

In the development of CAT, the reciprocal role idea was the key to the process of making therapy maps. Or it could equally be put the other way around, that without the reciprocal role idea the distinctive method of relational mapping would never have developed.

> *'The development of diagrammatic reformulation over this period contributed to a more detailed and radical revision of object relations theory and to the development of a model of the dissociated personality structure of patients with borderline personality disorder.'*

(Ryle, 2003)

The more reciprocal roles were used to map key roles, states and positions in the person's life the more versatile they became as paper tools in the therapy. Here is a list of all that can be tracked and discussed with reciprocal roles through the mapping process.

Self to self and self with others
- Others do it to me
- I see others do it to each other
- I do it to myself
- Part of me does it to another part
- I do it to others
- I get others to do it to me
- I do it to things, ideas and activities
- It is now I see the world

- **Other to self-interaction:** what significant others were doing to me and the response they elicited or expected.
- **Powerful parent to vulnerable child:** as above but rooted explicitly in the memories and stories indirectly told of how we were treated in childhood and how we learn both ends of this early and formative interaction.
- **Self to self:** what others did or do to me is the only model I have for what I do to myself. I take it into my body and take it on as an identity and take it out into the world as a core psycho-social pattern of relating derived from others.
- **Part of me to part of me:** once a reciprocal role pattern is internalised it becomes part of an invisible orchestra within me of co-ordinated or conflicting actions and responses.
- **Self to others:** the pattern of relating which I have taken in as my own is one I can elicit from others. I project and push the pattern onto others or pull it from them.

- **Other to others:** this refers to intimately and indirectly observed interaction between significant others which is never aimed directly at me but even so is 'taken in through witnessing'.
- **Me to things, ideas and activities:** an interpersonal role response becomes, internally, a relationship with activities, objects, and beliefs.
- **How I see the world:** the reciprocal role on paper can track a central and enduring stance towards the world. It points to a basic orientation to the world. It is a 'deep-self' role and calls the shots on other role responses. It is the orchestrating, meta-cognitive part of myself.
- **The relational complexity of these different directions and intensities of interaction between brain, body, self and others, mind and society are explored further in Chapter 7 and from the point of view of relational trauma in Chapter 8.**

Reciprocal role procedures (patterns for short)

In the terminology of CAT, the patterns which animate and connect reciprocal roles are called reciprocal role procedures. These are specific patterns of action which come from either end of the reciprocal role relationship.

> 'The underlying assumption, based on CAT theory, is that every act or utterance can be understood as originating in one pole of a reciprocal role pattern and as being addressed, explicitly or implicitly, to the other pole (which may be represented by real or imagined others or by an aspect of the self).'

(Ryle, 1997, p.112)

To go back to the doing and the feeling ends of the reciprocal role in the preceding sections we might think of the doing end as made up of one or more actions. The reciprocal role of hurting to hurt might be animated at the hurting end by a procedure based around shouting abusively or by another procedure of hitting or threatening to hit. At the hurt end there might be procedures for stoically submitting, or fighting back or running away, or pretending it is for my own good. Teasing out the separate intentions, lived and felt responses to these different procedures may be a key part of recovering from the trauma of them.

The reciprocal role of **loving-to-loved** might be animated from the loving end by showing kindness or concern or by showering the loved one with gifts or by quietly and passively being there. In these helpful or harmful ways several procedures animate one reciprocal role. The aim of mapping is to pick up, and draw out into open view, these patterns of interaction. We want to see how they are driven and how much of us they control. We want to use the map to work out whether they are harmful or helpful or, most likely, how they are a mixture of the two. In the process deeper processes of guilt, undue responsibility (it was me that was bad) blame or shame can begin to be explored.

This section brings us inside the reciprocal role procedure by seeing it as an action (something done by somebody to someone or done to themselves) which has an impact. There is a resonance here with the ideas of Van den Hart (2006) and action tendencies based on his work with trauma drawn from the original ideas of Pierre Janet (Howell, 2003).

Action, impact, and response

As in the figure below, the top end of a reciprocal role is an action. The bottom end is experienced at first as a reaction. The purpose of relationship mapping is to open a dialogue with automatic, taken for granted, patterns of action and reaction. In this instance we want to see the action-reaction couplet opened into an action with an impact and then a response to the impact in the form of some way of coping.

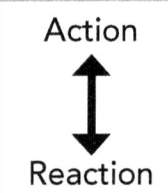

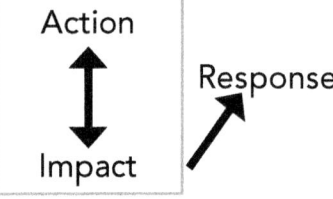

Daniel Kahneman in his book *Thinking Fast and Slow* (2011) makes very wide use of the way we process our immediate experience and calls to action. He argues that our brains are partly wired for fast responses. Fast brain responses are the everyday quick reactions. You are about to cross the road and you suddenly sense a car is approaching fast. You leap back out of the way onto the pavement. It's a quick **reaction to action** without second thoughts. If you stopped to figure it out with what Kahneman calls slow brain, the car would have hit you. Slow brain is our **second thoughts** brain designed to figure things out more reflectively. What makes humans smarter together is combining fast and slow brain. As in the many rich examples from Kahneman what makes us dumber is our use of fast brain reactions to respond to situations that warrant more consideration.

The reciprocal role depiction of fast brain is **action to reaction** as in the figure above. The more reflective and slower brain response would open the sequence up in terms of **'action-impact and response'**. Relationship mapping helps us learn to open our minds and feelings to the space between fast reactions and more considered responses.

For example, if you smile at me (your action), I may instantly smile back (my reaction). This reciprocation is a fast brain response. It is a rough and ready calculation so as to move more swiftly through life. It works well enough most of the time, but we need to have an ever-ready slower brain (or call it relational brain) response in case the smile is menacing rather than friendly. We don't want to be overthinking our reactions or unsure about our relationships with others but in part relational awareness is the hovering and shimmering presence of a choice between fast and slow brain responses.

If we were to map out the fast brain exchange as a reciprocal role it would look like the adjoining figure. Smiling is the action and smiling back is the reaction. But the process of mapping is one that seeks to see the roots to the interaction and the wider context. If we map it out a little more fully, I might see that when you smiled at me, it felt welcoming and safe. This put me at ease, I smiled back as detailed in the figure below.

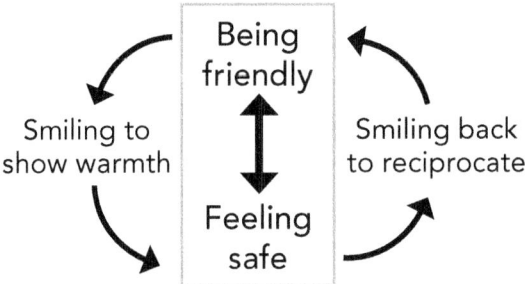

Drawing out the action, its impact and then my negotiated response of smiling back is at the heart of mapping our reciprocal responses to raise relational awareness and see the detail of feeling, thinking and behaviour. It is a process of opening the detail to dialogue and reflection. In the figure above there is a reciprocal role of being friendly to feeling safe. And the behaviour that is the expression of being friendly is marked by an arrow down the outside of the box. There could be many other behaviours that would serve as being friendly other than smiling. Or there could be plenty of other behaviours that indicate feeling safe and elicit a continuation of being friendly other than smiling back.

The dialogue between fast and slow brain is one basis of developing reflective capacity. The challenge we face in a complex, fast moving world is to know when to trust fast brain and when to use slow brain. Mapping helps develop the relational awareness to stop and think when we should have trusted our immediate responses or not. Mapping gives shared thinking time. The process of mapping slows down these fast responses and opens enquiry into the relational and the historical detail of their formation. With mindful relational mapping this can be done alone (see page 103 in **Chapter 5**) as a form of reflective self-care or in groups and teams. Mapping in this way is widely used for reflective practice in teams (Kemp *et al*, 2017) as well as in therapy.

The three-way relationship between **action, impact and response** is the first building block in the relationship mapping process. As in the example of Michael below, the relationships between action and response are not immediately conscious. There are links which we are not ready to make at first and are only made safe to explore through the mapping process.

Michael remembers the impact of being hit

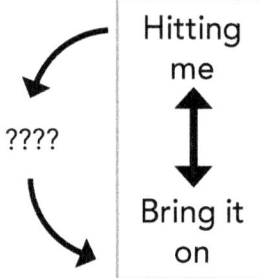

Here is an example of mapping a formative pattern of relating that shaped someone's identity as a man and his ways of relating to himself and others and to society at large. Michael talked of being hit as a young boy by his dad. Especially when his Dad came home drunk. 'It was as if my dad wanted to teach me a lesson which he found hard to live up to himself.'

I put the phrases 'teach me a lesson' and 'something to live up to' on one side on the paper, just as a note to the therapy conversation for later and not to be forgotten. I then tried to make a reciprocal link out of the distress of being hit as a child. Michael seemed very matter of fact about it. My first bit of mapping was as in the figure above, I put 'hitting me'. Michael agreed. I then wanted to put scared and hurt at the bottom end in response to the hitting (the feeling we would all feel in response to the impact of being hit), but Michael said 'No way, my response is to say, "bring it on". Michael added. 'I wanted to show my dad I could take it. That I could be the hard man and not the softy.'

I put 'hard man' as a desired place at the top of the sheet of paper (and added that is what Michael had to 'live up to') and I wrote 'Not the softy' at the bottom end of the paper as a defiantly avoided shameful place. We were both attentive to the mapping process, as if keeping tabs on each other. I showed him the action, impact response template and said that for me 'Bring it on' was a solution to, or a way of coping with a feeling. It was as if 'bring it on' was his 'action-reaction', fast track reaction. 'Hit me, bring it on, hit me, bring it on.' We understood that 'Bring it on' was a core belief or schema in cognitive terms, a defence in psychoanalytic terms, but also it had become an ideology and a key part of Michael's outwardly facing social identity and interior life as a man. It gave him control and esteem but made him dangerous to others and to himself.

What it hid was his core pain, his 'frightened child' feelings of fear and hurt which were still being hidden in the moments we were mapping. We talked about his dad's needs, or intentions, in hitting him. For Michael, his dad's intentions were not clear and so we left question marks as per the figure below).

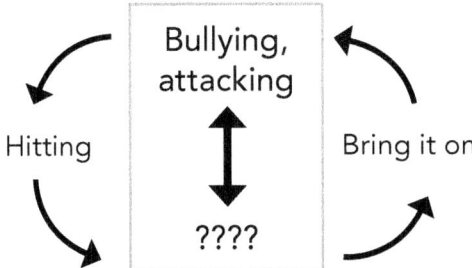

I wanted to create a space on the map that left a gap between the fast sequence of action and response. My aim was to find a way to open his relationship up with his ideas without challenging him so much that he shuts down. I didn't want the mapping process to be metaphorically another way of hitting him to remember his hidden feelings. We explored the context around his family life as a child and how his father was bullying and attacking in other ways besides hitting him. We touched upon an idea that he was going into the 'bring it on' mode to hide any vulnerability but also to take his dad's direction of violence away from his mother. He felt that if he was not soaking up all his father's rage, it would be aimed at his mother.

I checked with Michael as I added two more words and phrases to the figure above. At the top, where I had put 'bullying' and 'attacking', I showed that one procedure for doing this role was hitting. It is outside the box because it is one of the behaviours (or procedures) that maintain the bullying and attacking role. Someone else could bully with words or demands. Since Michael was not ready to look at the 'hurting to hurt', or 'frightening to frightened little boy' reciprocation that came wrapped up with the bullying, I pointed again to the question marks in the space at the bottom of the reciprocal role saying as gently as I could that we still don't know what this felt like. However, on the right-hand side, as in the figure above, I added 'bring it on' as his way of coping with and making sense of the hitting and bullying. 'Bring it on' was a coping and surviving response to a feeling that we had not yet named or allowed to be expressed. In this moment we were working with the CAT ideas of reciprocal role procedures to hold in mind simultaneously an emotional, interpersonal, and socially gendered memory by class, generation, and culture.

I wanted to begin a conversation about where the ideology of 'bring it on' took him. We mapped out that it took him to an identity as the 'hard man' where he felt that he was respected. As a young man it did win him respect from his dad before his death and, in a limited and damaging way, from the neighbourhood in which he lived. What brought Michael to therapy was a realisation that it no longer had any currency and cut him off from a relationship with his partner.

Michael insisted he did not know what he felt the impact was of the bullying and hitting. He said 'All I know is my response which is "Bring it on, I can take it"'. By leaving the impact blank and putting 'bring it on' as the response there was a space to come back to which we did in a roundabout way. Michael made a link to the idea of protecting his mother by being the one who could take his dad's violence. In one session Michael was describing a role which he liked of being a bodyguard and used the Hollywood imagery of 'being in the line of fire' and 'taking a bullet for the president'. As we talked about this role and some of his past roles in the security business, I explored what his mum would feel, if she was scared whilst he was protecting her. He said that he thought she was numb with fear. As he said this, he became emotional in a way that seemed to be a physical experience of loosening up. There was a softness in his eyes. He said of his mother 'I could see her giving in and it was as if she wanted me to give in as well'. We wondered if him taking on the fight left her safe but feeling guilty for being helpless to intervene. These were big steps to living with a more complex mix of feelings.

A week later Michael prodded his finger on the row of question marks on the map and said 'I know the words for those feelings. That little boy felt "effing terrified"'. We crossed out the question marks and carefully wrote 'effing terrified'. It was an important shift in emotional perspective and a recovery of disavowed empathy for the child he was (and has carried within him for years with hidden hurt and a 'survivalist, hard man' identity of 'bring it on'). He was stepping back, with the aid of the therapy map, from a lifelong fast brain response to feelings of being bullied. We later realised that 'bring it on' could be the tail that wagged the dog, in the sense that he was so primed and ready to be hurt that he became hyper vigilant and trapped in the hard man image and the social identity on the streets. He said that the map (below) helped him realise that he felt for his mum's suffering but not his own. He had always thought that showing feelings was being soft and giving in as weak.

Our work was like putting a jigsaw puzzle of memories and connections together. We were planning to complete it enough to connect with gaps in self-knowledge and feelings. The conversation with Michael weaved in and out of his memories and the story he was sharing.

The more complex map below shows all the work we had done and became our therapy map that guided the rest of our work.

The process of mapping is not simply a cognitive one but involves sketching out the known fragments and links and waiting for the emotional links to arrive. As the conversation develops the story unfolds and a more open and compassionate relational awareness develops. The above breakthrough towards empathy for himself and others became the driver of further change in his present interactions with his partner. In a later session our conversation hovered and shimmered around what to say and how to feel. The map came to the rescue. He borrowed the words from the top of the map 'I don't have to take it anymore or, make others take it, I can give in'.

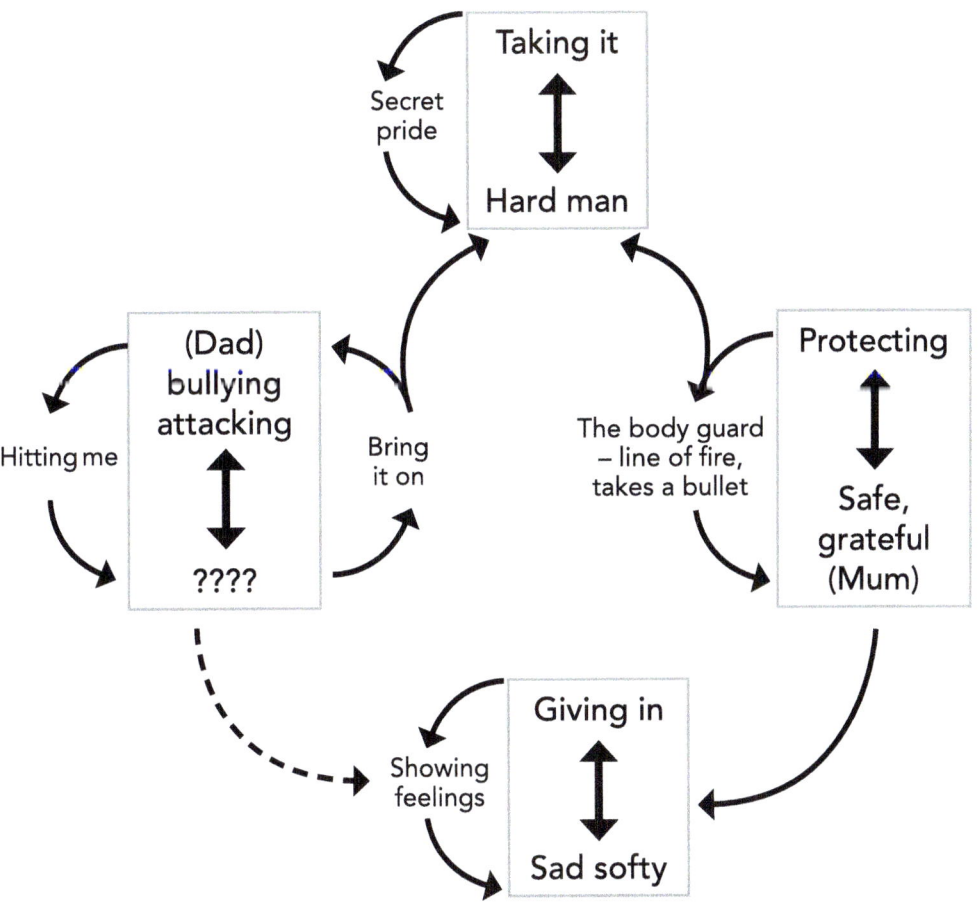

The shared process of mapping out relationships is a slow and patient re-orchestration of memories and feelings as we recover links and touch upon gaps in our self-knowledge. It is slowly building a shared understanding of the patterns of interaction and making a new, more open, and negotiable orchestration. I asked him some weeks later how his relationship was going, and he said with smile that things were better in that department. He could learn, he thought to be a 'happy, sad softy'.

As a way of consolidating our memory of the mapping moments I wrote a spontaneous letter to our therapy as it felt in that moment. Michael read it in a gentle way.

> *Dear Therapy,*
>
> *I think Michael had a moment of shifting just now. We have on his map that he did not do vulnerable or breaking down because that would be giving in, but he does now see that since his dad is long gone, he could explore if he can allow himself to be safe if vulnerable with his partner. I hope I can help him be a compassionate observer of this in the weeks ahead and that he might see that his style of 'bring it on' when he feels, or expects to be hurt, leads to him then, being trapped as the hard man. It seems that during his childhood his mum could not protect him but that he protected her and felt her vulnerability in a tender way. And his dad sold him a message that being hard was the only road to protection which cut him off from valuing any tender feelings. If now, Michael, within himself, can give in and allow care and tenderness from himself to his self, then others, such as his partner, are able to share in protecting him from hurt or danger. In the process they can value and accept him being a softy. I hope his relationship with these various ideas and feelings can be loosened up through moments of reflection with me and with the people around him over time.*

This letter consolidated his growing awareness and we added to the letter – *more than anyone it is me, Michael, that can give in to my vulnerable side and find softer ways of protecting myself.*

The letter is brief enough to be a ready source of personal reference and for him to keep and share. It is personal but not directly to him (it met him halfway at that point in therapy) and it works only with the map. There is more on the use of writing in relation to mapping and giving voice to therapy in **Chapter 6**. There is a further illustration of working with Michael in the Open Flowers Story on page 72. There is a related exploration working with trauma in **Chapter 8**.

Want or need

At the heart of the reciprocal role pattern of response there is an unconscious intention, need or desire. Developing relational awareness of it starts with the question, directed at the person and the map. 'If you are feeling this because of that (the doing words) what do you want or need?' It is often a healthy need, only partly fulfilled by the procedure through which it is expressed. By mapping it out and working with it over several meetings, its hidden, or taken for granted element, can be made more visible. It can be described using stronger or more touching words and connected with emotionally in the moment. The placing of the 'want or need' question is an invitation to think about motivation and awareness in that context and at that point or hub on the diagram.

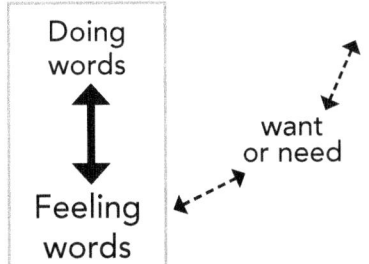

A key part of becoming aware is rethinking what we wanted in response to a powerful or difficult feeling at the time. What might we now say and feel we needed back then, looking at it on the map and from the safety and clarity of the therapy room? If the pattern is still in play now what would I want or need now? A small detail to note is the two-way arrow above the words want or need. This is to signify that what we recall wanting or needing is not just driven by the feelings at the bottom of the reciprocal role but by the range of coping procedures which we appraise as available to us.

As the mapping dialogue develops, what I want may seem positive (care, love, control or meaning) and the problem is in the limited options, then and now, for me to act on what I want. The limiting may come from the compulsion to respond in a fixed way.

The mapping process is one of consciousness raising at this point. In wondering what they wanted or needed, time past and present may slip in and out of the question, as in 'My needs now overlap with my needs then'. One of the mechanisms of change arising through the micro-process of mapping is bringing motivation and needs to the surface. We may realise looking at the map 'Oh, that was a silly way of going about getting that need met!', or conversely 'Everything else may be wrong but my awareness of what I want is good and healthy'. There are also feelings about our motives and needs that we would skip over in a conversation as too embarrassing, but with the map in front of us they seem more acceptable to share.

The client may answer that there was no space to think about what I wanted. 'I wanted what I was supposed to want but now you ask what I need.' Or they may say. 'What I wanted was good but my assumptions about what was possible, limited or stifled how I met those needs.' These are key points in recovering a capacity for agency. 'Authoring and owning' needs and desires is a potential moment of healing and increased relational awareness.

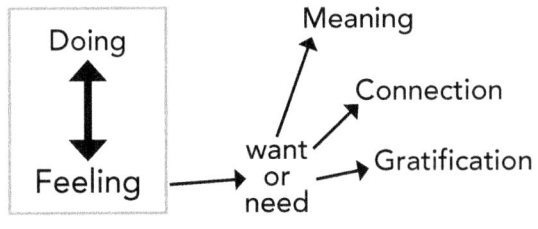

What we want or need can be theorised in several different ways as in the adjoining figure. Our first layer of needs can be framed biologically as a need for gratification. The frustration and sublimation of these needs are what Freud built his theory around. But these instinctual needs cannot be dealt with to any extent without meeting our other needs for connection, care and belonging. The turning point in the development of psychoanalytic thought has roots in Fairbairn and in Sullivan (though contemporaries they had no knowledge of each other), who put our needs for relationship centre-stage in human development and consciousness. Alongside these biological and relational needs may be a third need which is the search for meaning and understanding. Putting them alongside each other is an aid to thinking about the multiple tracks of need that simultaneously are in play when we respond to our feelings. One action (A hug from Mum or Dad) may meet all three needs. Mostly they are in play all at the same time with varying weight and direction.

In the same breath as mapping what I might want or need in response to a difficult feeling there may be the parallel question of what I do not want or need. I may not want to connect. Or, I fear gratification. Or I may find making meaning and understanding a far too unsettling experience. The activity of client and therapist exploring these options invites the client to construct options and reflect on past and present motives. The tension between what I want and don't want is mapped using the hopes and fears template on pages 76 and 104.

It was a major shift in psychoanalytic thought and practice to move from a *drive* or gratification model of human need to a relational one. This relational turn in psychoanalysis is well described by Stephen Mitchell (1988). It re-invigorated psychoanalysis in the United States. It offered a relational framework that could integrate all the threads of psychoanalytic thought. It makes sense that our primary need is to be connected, cared for and included because they are the main route to meeting our biological, cognitive, emotional and social needs for meaning.

Thoughts and ideas – the relational thinking involved in appraisal

Becoming more aware of our thoughts and ideas, and their relationship to feelings and roles and behaviour is common to all cognitive and psychoanalytic approaches. Some of our thoughts are automatic and out of consciousness as indicated when talking of the fast track response earlier. Others are locked up as opinions and fixed ideas of the groups and society with which we identify. Or they are dissociated from along the lines described by Sullivan in the phrase 'not me' Sullivan (1955). Or finally in some cases they may be repressed as forbidden and disturbing ideas along the lines depicted so richly by Freudian psychoanalysis.

Cognitive therapies look for the relationship between our more automatic thoughts and our deeper core beliefs. In this respect cognitive therapies offer a model of relational thinking. However, our thoughts, opinions and beliefs are born of two other more complex patterns of relating. One pattern is with the significant people in our lives with whom we find the ideas that make up our thinking. Changing our cognitive relationship with these ideas may be entangled with changing our relationship with the people with who we learnt these ideas. The other complication is our relationships with the ideologies and cultures of reflection and negotiation in the world around us. The assumption in mapping the psycho-social dynamics out is that we can move towards greater awareness of the appraisal system in operation in some of the patterns which we want to change in therapy.

The 'relational' mapping of our thinking is seeking to bring automatic thoughts and ideas to awareness. They are thoughts and ideas because they are both in our minds as thoughts and in our culture as ideas. Thoughts are circulating mentally, and ideas are circulating socially. The map is going to track them in both directions.

In cognitive terms we make an appraisal at this point in the sequence. It is a moment of self-observation. Supposing I am a boy who needs to cry as an expression of feeling upset because someone is hurting me. My appraisal (see map below) is a meeting between these feelings and an idea that for me

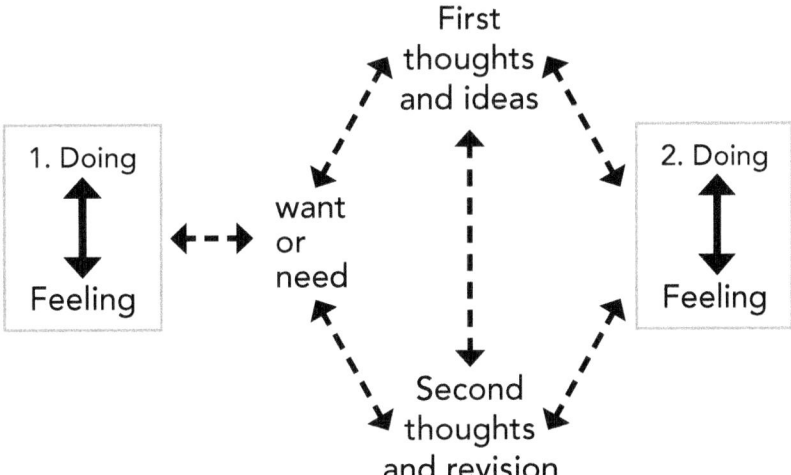

me and my culture, boys do not cry. My thought might be to hide my tears, cry later when no one can see. The cognitive appraisal of thoughts and ideas meets the emotional need in a procedural clash. In this clash does thought 'colonise' feeling or feeling hijack thought? The process of relational mapping helps us work out the answer. The diagram above shows how thoughts and ideas lead to a new reciprocal role (2) though it might equally find its new place by going into reverse into the initial reciprocal role (1) but at the other end of the role (i.e. I am now doing to myself what others were doing to me).

Powerful ideas will colonise feeling in childhood. We will submit to the ideology most forcefully on offer within the limits of our cognitive relational development and the intensity of our feelings and our limited power to negotiate. We do this by imitation and reciprocation and through the relational quality of how we use words. Our thoughts don't develop just in our minds but as ideas played out in the rough and tumble of significant relationships.

One client told of learning a key idea which soon became a core belief from their first day at school. They described themselves as a homely boy with several sisters and, naturally enough for him, on the first day at school he had gone in the playground to talk to the girls. An older boy soon beckoned him over to where the boys were and said emphatically, 'boys don't talk to girls.' The addition to this story was that exactly a year later, on the first day of school, he confirmed this social idea was now an automatic thought for him when he saw a boy talking to the girls in the playground and went over to give him the same gender-segregating advice.

These communally and interpersonally enforced cultural practices are the way in which ideas become our thoughts and beliefs. Mapping out the reciprocal role procedures helps us see how they work as relational thinking inside our heads and as ideas and ideologies in the network of interpersonal and community relations (both local and global, real, and virtual) around us.

To summarise, we may or may not be aware of, or give attention to, the appraisal we do with thoughts and ideas, but it leads us to consequences of further action. In turn these link to another reciprocal role that has its own triangle of action, impact, and response.

The sequences of response (through want or need to thoughts and ideas and a second reciprocal role) may take us back to our initial feeling which in turn reinforces the action of the reciprocal role. Ryle called these traps and they are a part of the psychotherapy file considered in **Part 3** of the book in **Chapter 9**. Or it may take us into a polarised split between two opposing pairs of reciprocal roles which Ryle described as 'dilemmas', of which examples are also in the psychotherapy file, and equally show up in the 'Hopes and Fears' map in the next chapter. Or it may lead to a snag in which a helpful new reciprocal role position is spoilt or forbidden in some way.

For Ryle, this drawing out of the pattern of thinking in relation to a recurring early relational pattern was the route to tracing the intimate and troublesome sources of our core beliefs. He saw the process of writing or mapping out of these procedures as the key to reformulation. They offer an overall understanding but also offer multiple points to change aspects of relating, thinking, feeling, or behaving.

Verbing the nouns

As an exercise in bringing the process of mapping alive nouns need turning into verbs or - as children say – doing words. Mapping with words involves bringing patterns into the active present tense. In this small step we bring history alive in the present or make the passive active which is a step to making them more relational and dynamic. Here are some examples of verbing the noun as a reciprocal relationship.

'**Lost: abandoning to abandoned**'

'**Told: storying to storied**'

'**Special: admiring to admired**'

'**Upset: hurting to hurt**'

This process of verbing the noun opens a space to look at the dynamics of feelings and the forces behind them and the forces around coping with them.

Words have a life of their own. Mapping out our patterns of interaction involves words becoming like actions. The proverb says sticks and stones may break my bones, but words will never harm me. Yet words carry memories, promises or threats of sticks and stones. As described when considering Wordsworth's poetry on page 129 they bring us back to the interaction and offer us an 'as if' experience of being again in the same role relationship. As discussed in **Chapter 8** on relational healing and working with the reciprocal roles of trauma some words evoke such memories as to take us into the memory - no longer as if we are in it again - but as if we are re-living it and have no outsider capacity to observe or mediate the experience. The map and the mapping process have the role of mediator to help bring a capacity to self-observe in such difficult moments.

Meta-cognition or reflective capacity and relational thinking

CAT and the process of mapping out patterns of relating is as cognitive as any other cognitive therapy. Where it differs is in its co-constructive, co-creative stance alongside the client with a focus on the relational origins and maintenance of the patterns of thinking. It offers a framework of ideas and methods that can reach more deeply into personal history and more widely into the social context. The process of mapping keeps looking for the patterns of feeling and relating around the troublesome thoughts and ideas. Key to this is a reciprocal role that depicts hovering above the mapping process. This reciprocal role is a meta-cognitive position or perhaps in Freudian terms it is a superego position. At its best it is a compassionate observer position, but often when mapping it emerges as a 'judging to judged' reciprocal role. It lurks or looms above our procedural thinking and mediates it in helpful or harmful ways. As in the figure below, the 'reflective capacity' reciprocal role, described in one way or another, needs putting on to the map. It plays the main part in shaping our appraisal of what coping or action procedure to follow in moving from one role to another. It may colonise or free up our attempts at thinking about the relationship we were in or are in now.

Reflective capacity and relational thinking

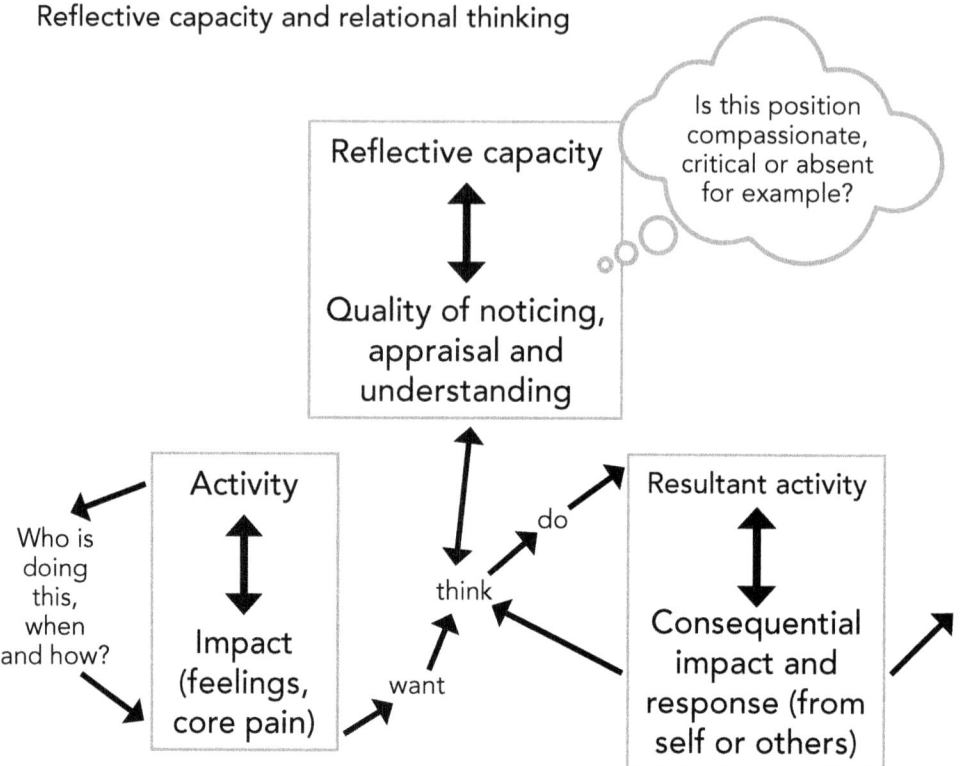

Roles on paper help with self-observation

Each of us has our own unique heritage of relationships and patterns of relating. A client writes on her map 'I did not learn these patterns from Martians, but from my mum and dad and they got them from the society in which they lived'. It was a way of reminding her that her current attitudes and beliefs with which she was struggling, were not some fixed part of her nature, but an outlook on the world which had stories of origin. How they had become part of her view was as important to the process of change as what the views were.

Mostly our patterns of interaction become so second nature to us that we find it hard to see or remember where we first learnt them. Mapping helps link our early learning stories of relating to our current patterns. Using the process of relationship mapping to bridge past and present interactions is a key mechanism of change. We learn our habitual patterns of interaction in our early years.

To say we learn them is an understatement of the dynamics involved. We were enrolled into them whether lovingly, 'smotheringly', forcedly or subtly, in ways which were so often repeated that they become the patterns that make us. The psychoanalysts call them 'egosyntonic' (Greenson, 1967) which is to say each of us can sense them, can feel their effects and act on them but we cannot see them from the outside. The social dimension of every role comes woven with our early emotional roles. We may see the social dynamic of it, but less clearly see our emotional investment. For example, we may say that we love the country of our birth but not feel the anxiety of what it would be like to not have such a secure attachment solution. Or we may love it and hate it for mixed reciprocation of including us and dismissing us through prejudice and exclusion at the same time. The reciprocal role map can help us explore these entangled dynamics.

The deeper more ego-syntonic roles have emotional roots in our family lives and early care in our cultures, such as in our responses through gender, class, ethnicity, or generation. We live with these 'deep self' roles as part of our make-up and way of being. Here are some examples. The carer, the clever one, the deviant, the bad apple, the outsider, the go between, the athlete, the chancer, the misery guts, the loser. These are all roles into which we are cast and take on as part of our way of coping and managing with the psycho-social environment in our early years. In mapping them out, writing to them and giving self-conscious therapeutic voice to them, we each discover our own phrases, memorable stories, and ways of freeing ourselves or living with them.

Us and them: across cultures, generations, and genders

A key moment of therapeutic breakthrough is when a client discovers from the map that what others did to them, they now, in some amended fashion, do to themselves. It can be useful to draw a small marker flag or two sticking up from the top end of a reciprocal role to indicate the name of the person in the family of who took that position. Similarly, it can be a road to compassion to see from the map and add markers to the map of how a reciprocal role was passed back and forward across the generations.

Looking at the reciprocal role 'egotistically demanding' and 'long-sufferingly obliging' as the key words at the centre of her map, a client pointed to the demanding top end of the role as her 'self-centred father' and their obliging and indulging mother at the bottom and then added, still pointing at the words on the map, 'It was the reverse gender with my mother's parents. My grandmother was "self-centred", "needy" and "demanding" and my grandfather was the peacekeeper and did the "looking after"'. Reciprocal roles can cut across gender differences when they pass from one generation to another.

Equally a pattern that seemed mostly about my inner life suddenly shows itself as an interaction with others. The mapping can step up to and handle the quite complex patterns of identity and state shift that are more common in global and fluid societies within which sit narrow local identities.

Sometimes the most simple and obvious connections between self and society are the hardest to see. We need to find ways with the process of mapping to set ourselves a little bit apart from them. A pattern which so far has been tracked on the map as personal pattern (this is me) can equally be tracked along the same lines as a familiar social pattern. One difficulty for Michael in the preceding case example was that his behaviour in his teenage years and twenties just seemed like what men do, but it was now beginning to feel odd and out of sync with the times. That men were not like him anymore was something his partner pointed out, and this prompted him to have the motivation to come for therapy.

Gender differences and differences between personal experience and cultural norms can be more easily reflected on with the map as guide. A map can be made of a specific group with inter-group dynamics mapped out from the 'push and pull' between 'us and them'. Such mapping can be used to mediate within a family or to help a client see the conflicting loyalties which she, or he, has between their grown-up status and their childhood allegiances. The map, with multiple places on it, tracks different self-states but also different identities and group allegiances. It makes it less shaming to explore prejudices through the medium of a map of the intergroup relations.

Casting of roles is a power relationship

The words 'doing' and 'feeling' could be replaced by role-casting and role-cast. Reciprocation starts with casting or initiating the role relationship. If I want you to be an obliging assistant in getting something done, I need to have a way to cast you in the obliging response such as by being demanding, cajoling, or encouraging. If our power and autonomy is relatively equal, then, either you are willing or not, to be cast in the role, and reciprocate. However, a large part of our role-casting and responding experience, is pre-verbal, and prior to our mental and linguistic capacity to map and negotiate a response in our minds. The power dynamic in every case is rarely equal. I may use intense pressure or threats to push you to reciprocate. You cast me in the role of rescuer, and you do things that invite me to rescue you. I cast you in the role as one who is self-reliant and find it as an excuse to neglect you. This role-casting is played out in our relationships on automatic pilot with only a background or vague awareness or capacity for self-conscious and mutual reflection. We are cast in roles that are part of our identity and culture. The mapping process is an attempt to trigger our curiosity and raise our awareness. As the patterns of reciprocal roles take shape on paper, we interact and develop a wider and deeper relational awareness of the balance of power and control.

Multiple roles and the patterns which orchestrate them

It is quite common to make a map with several separate reciprocal role positions on them. This is the case with the hopes and fears map in the chapter on narrative mapping and it is the case initially when working with our experience of several dissociated states of mind (see page 182). These separate positions may give us a general perspective as in the earlier example of Michael in this chapter.

The map allows us to move here and there, in out between detail and perspective from the overall picture to the detail of the patterns of coping and self-management (orchestration) that links one role to another or equally keeps them segregated. When mapping in this way it is helpful to keep in mind the idea of reciprocal roles as hubs or junctions on the map where traffic converges or gets tied up in knots. One client described them lyrically as the roundabouts in the traffic of his mental life. 'There is always more than one way out but also a risk of going around in circles.'

The distribution of several reciprocal role positions around a map can help track patterns of shift and disconnection between states which are potential social and psychological homes for the whole self. The mapping process can track and show the breaks in a divided sense of self whether driven by trauma and neglect or narcissistic entitlement. The mapping process of tracking links and gaps is hoping to build relational awareness and develop agency and ownership over the identified patterns of interaction.

Careless neglect and comfort eating: Maria 'maps' her pattern

Maria, a single, primary school teacher in her early thirties said at the end of the third session that there was something she needed to talk about but could easily skip. We wondered why she would skip it. 'It is boring' she said. 'I am fed-up with it and probably, yes, it is embarrassing.' Maria wanted to talk about being very overweight. It was not what she had come for therapy to explore. She had tried different diets and schemes, but they never lasted. In talking, as we had, about patterns of relating to self and others, Maria had started wondering if the over-eating was part of a wider relationship. 'I comfort eat' she said as she left the room. She said it in a way that implied the story didn't begin there.

The following week we decided to see how far we could get by making a map of the story and the relationship around comfort eating and seeing what the patterns were. There was an established sense of partnership and trust between us. We agreed to start with a big sheet of blank paper and put her first words at the centre of the sheet. **'Seek comfort through food because it won't let me down or expose me.'** We talked for a while about that single sentence on the paper in front of us. It implied that there were other sources of comfort that might or would let her down or shame her. We also wondered if it was instant gratification and worked because it did not involve demands on other people. 'It is always there, unlike people' she said.

Maria described going to the fridge door and routinely checking for what food is there and perhaps nibbling at something. Looking for the reciprocal role, I asked what she 'wanted or needed' that led to seeking comfort through food? She made the link that she wanted to be cared for and find someone there waiting for her (her key memory was of getting home from school and being home alone for the first two hours until one or other of her parents turned up) but expected that there would be no one there. We worked further back from that to the feeling of being overlooked and fearing being forgotten (a dreadful feeling that one day no one would come home).

Using our mapping activity, we were slowly opening a window on emotional connections to gather a fuller picture. Already we were seeing more than we could hold in mind without a map. We recapped the feelings in the air so far. 'I was pining for someone to be interested, to care, to notice me. I would secretly look through the letter box at other kids in the street and passers-by all of whom seemed so connected with the world.' Maria did not think her parents were unloving and at other times they could be very involved and demanding. She called their pattern of overlooking her a form of **careless neglect**. With that phrase we had a key reciprocal role of **careless neglect to feeling over-looked and pining**. We were not attacking her parents but getting alongside their spilt between being caring and being carelessly, neglectful because busy elsewhere.

Maria wanted to protect them. She said that she knew they had busy jobs. Putting these needs on paper reminded her of her awareness and assertiveness then and now. At the same time, it felt sad when we put down the words **'Forgetting-to-forgotten'**, to capture the reciprocal role that lurked beneath the idea that there was no one there. Her conflicting feelings were in the room between us and being acknowledged by the words on the paper.

In recapping our way around the map together our attention turned to how she never noticed the comfort in the actual eating. The emotion was all in the 'seeking' activity and the part that going to the fridge or the biscuits played in distracting her from a feeling of neglect. This helped explain the pattern of grazing becoming more like bingeing, since she sensed the comfort will not last because the action cannot continue forever and is not fulfilling it itself.

We then made an unexpected link which in hindsight seems obvious. Maria pointed her finger at the careless neglect phrase on the map and said 'Hey, when I am gorging on food I am also being carelessly neglectful of myself and my body'. This was a key moment of linking Maria's relationship with food to her relationship with herself. The **careless neglect to overlooked**

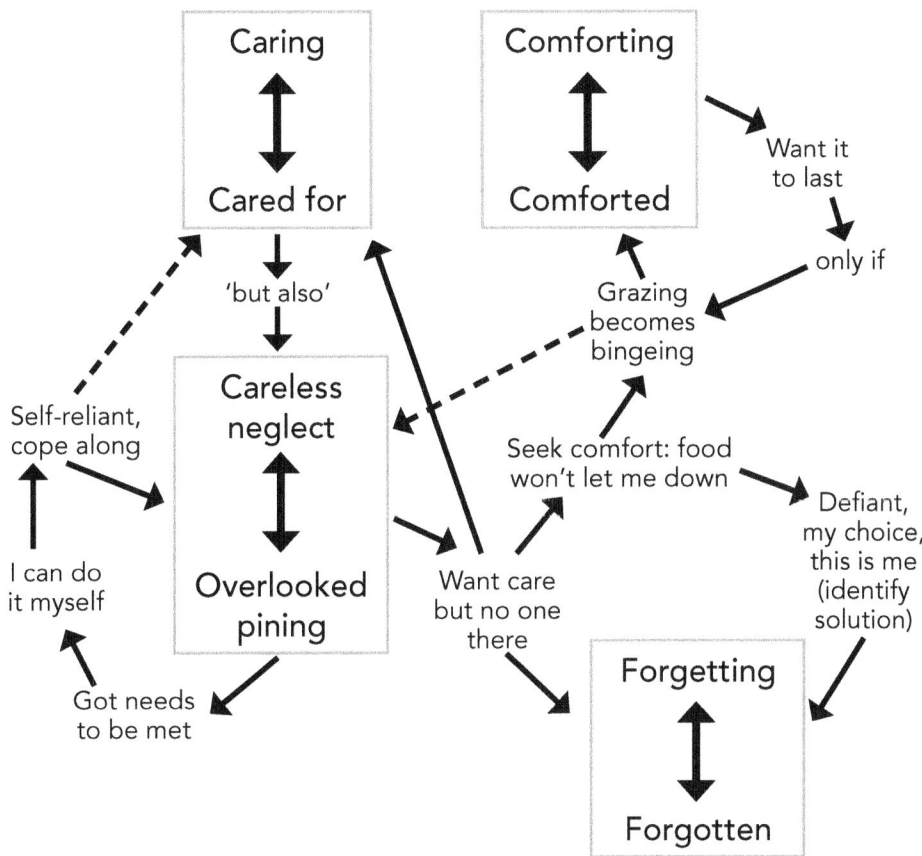

and pining reciprocal role was now acknowledged and owned as of her to within herself as well as of her parents to her. Led by Maria we drew out a pattern on the left of the map which acknowledged that she could care for herself and cope alone. As an aside, she said that coping alone was the model her parents had given her anyway. Her self-reliant coping was in doing her schoolwork and getting involved in after-school activities. This self-reliant coping had been a large part of her success and satisfaction in life so far. Even so Maria insisted speaking to the map, as if it was 'witnessing' her feelings: 'I really, really wanted someone to be there'.

The connection was upsetting and confusing. Maria said she felt that 'deep down I always felt about to be forgotten'. She protested 'They loved me. My parents loved me, but they didn't need me, or didn't seem to. Perhaps they did not need each other? They were just busy with their lives. They should have explained it to me'.

I said 'Well, that might be the greatest hurt of all, that it didn't make sense and was not explained. Now, perhaps, we are making some sense of it'.

Pointing to the **forgetting to forgotten** reciprocal role on the map, I said 'We are not doing this 'forgetting' now. We are remembering and understanding'.

Often there is a moment in mapping like this when a pattern emerges which locks the person's adult identity into a childhood way of coping. For Maria it came with adding an arrow from the phrases centre-right of the diagram. The phrase is **'defiant, my choice, this is me (identity solution)**. For her it meant the link between the 'comfort eating me' and the 'overweight me' was not up for negotiation. Maria felt it was just part of the landscape of being her. By adding the arrow linking this to the **forgetting to forgotten** reciprocal role, we understood that this a choice within a larger pattern. It was doing to her whole self was she was doing to her body. If she could see the defiant pattern within a larger picture of patterns there might be ways to change.

This shared experience of discovery with a map is delicate. Through the process of mapping, once links are made, elements of coping and feeling start flowing that have been kept locked apart. A 'feeling for feelings' is enabled. It may directly be the map and its details that are helping. But it may also be that the mapping process is gearing up the brain to make connections and not be so busy with the work of dissociation and segregation.

Maps like these can grow and grow. What stops them becoming too complex is that they reach a point of being good enough. In the illustration of work with Maria, awareness is the precursor to agency, ownership, and choice. Awareness is upsetting when it breaks through, but it is also exciting. The mapping together is an act of reformulation and restorying and in the process key memories are being reconsolidated and the relationships that make up personality and identity are out in the open. The map went on Maria's fridge door, so that she would spot when she was pining for care, and when she was carelessly neglecting or forgetting a part of herself.

Ryle's wish to make psychoanalytic ideas more accessible

For Ryle it is the primary task of therapy to 'carefully and accurately' describe central patterns of relating to self. Ryle explored the interaction between several contrasting emotional states in a brief paper which recast psychoanalytic thinking in terms of reciprocal roles. The paper was aptly called *'Self-to-Self, Self-to-Other: The World's Shortest Account of Object Relations Theory'* (Ryle, 1975). Ryle was seeking to make psychoanalytic processes more accessible and researchable. It had not occurred to him at that stage that these ideas would lend themselves very well as conceptual tools for therapeutic mapping.

In Ryle's paper the reciprocal relationship between being caring and feeling cared for was established as one pair of roles. He contrasted this with the counter position of being abusive and feeling abused. This opened the door to seeing the interplay between four locations for self or others: being cared for, doing the caring, abusing and being abused. The interplay between self and others, with their movements between these four different states of mind, point to a third, unspoken (by Ryle) couplet of positions of being neglecting and feeling neglected.

Ryle's aim was to offer an accessible account of the theories of internal patterns of relating called 'object relations theory', proposed by various British psychoanalysts. The reciprocal roles were easier to describe than object relations partly because they offered the subject and object end of the relationship. Understood in this way they might be judged to be more flexible in their application than the same ideas cast in psychoanalytic language. Mapping out reciprocal roles in this way needed therapists to be open, transparent in their thinking and collaborative with the client rather than interpret the client's underlying motivations from a superior intellectual position. Reciprocal roles offered a language that could bring the client alongside as an equal partner in the analytic thinking. In the process nothing of the richness of the psychoanalytic heritage of technique and theory needed to be lost. For Ryle this was in stark contrast to direct and powerful interpretations of the analysts who to his eye seemed to be tutoring their patients whilst keeping the processes involved in the dark.

Conclusions

Mostly we have set patterns of relating that make our personalities, and fix our social roles, status, and positions in the world. Our well-being depends in part on how varied or how limited these are, how much we know them and can negotiate and navigate them when they are unhelpful or distressing to ourselves or others. The security and apparent predictability of having set ways of relating comes at the price of them being so much a part of us that we find it hard to step back and see where they hurt or help us.

This chapter has described in detail the tools, concepts and methods of relationship mapping. In the process the methods and ideas of CAT have also been described in anticipation of talking through the steps to CAT therapy in part three of the book. The emphasis has been on the versatility of the ideas of reciprocal roles and associated procedures or patterns. Relationship or 'relational' mapping helps explore our interaction with ourselves and the world around us. Its focus might be summarised as the impact of significant people on the formation of personal and social identity. The versatility of the reciprocal idea, especially when mapped out, allows us to think about the dynamics of social difference and power as well. All that is described in this chapter applies to the use of mapping and relational awareness throughout the book.

Chapter 3: Narrative mapping

'But how could you live and have no story to tell?'
Fyodor Dostoevsky, White Nights

Introduction

The chapter begins with different forms of storytelling. This leads to a description of 'open stories' with some examples and the distinction between epic and novelistic stories. The pressure to be sorted and have a fixed and ready story is explored, leading to the central idea of drawing out patterns from stories using maps. The two templates for mapping, 'hopes-and-fears' and 'hide-and-seek' are introduced as a general framework for learning to map stories more openly and relationally.

To recap the earlier theme, the aim in narrative mapping, as in therapy generally, is to work between two therapy stories. One story is more focused on diagnosis and formulation. It is the story of what the therapy is about. The other story is how the process of change takes place, regardless of its focus or formulation. This is called the healing narrative in this book. It is the story of the co-creative and reparative nature of the therapy relationship. Between these two is another kind of split between stories of the present and stories of the past as explored more in chapter 7.

Dog stories

Sometimes when we seek help, we talk about the problems in our lives in the manner of dog stories. A dog story – no offence to dog lovers – is a story that tends to be told complete and contained, all-in-and-of itself. It is a story that has been told so many times it has become over-storied. There is no room for symbolism, metaphor, asides, innuendo, or transference. The 'telling' is all about the story. There are no openings. It makes great sense as a short form of exchange when dog owners meet in the park. The stories are stop gaps and in their sealed narrative there is no room for more open storytelling to break out. After all, the dogs will not sit around and wait for the conversation to develop. We can all talk in therapy in this way about our concerns and memories. Content and process are firmly segregated. What is therapeutic in the story is lost because of the way it is told. The mapping moment in such stories comes with the ending, and the space it creates for a different kind of storytelling. In time, it is an opportunity to consider the function of telling stories that are closed and sealed off.

Detective stories

The therapy conversation can sometimes take on the quality of a detective story led by client and therapist. It has the tone of getting to the bottom of something and solving a mystery. The therapist might be able spot themselves falling into this kind of narrative approach by the way they are asking questions and taking notes. The therapeutic habit of taking a history or doing an assessment over one or more sessions can become like a detective story. Perhaps there will be moments when a more investigative voice is required but the shift in tone in this way should be noticed and named. The therapist with a map should watch out for the therapy role reciprocation of being the investigator putting the client in the position of being under investigation. It smacks of doing the therapy to the client. It can take on the quality of digging deeper and deeper in search of some final discovery. 'Ah, it was your grandad's fault!' The past becomes the accused if not the client. The break from this tempting pattern may come in realising that it might help to stop digging for the hidden history. One client gained much relief and insight in realising with her therapist that they were not digging down into ever deeper discoveries but looking across the surface of different sides to self and different stories in her life.

Trumpeted stories

A variation on the dog story is the trumpeted story. In this mode, life stories can unfold in a collaborative way but every so often, and especially at moments of potential connection or emotion, the storyteller blows a trumpet about themselves, the key person, or event in the story. The story becomes trumpeted as if only one person can be the narrator and only one point of view matters. It is as if when connection and deeper meaning is being touched the shutters come down and the story becomes trumpeted as a solo account. Such a solo account can be forlorn, moving and a fine soliloquy but it distracts from the conversational quality of the narrative and therapeutic process.

It is quite possible for the trumpeted style of storytelling to come from the therapist. At important moments when the story telling is on the threshold of therapeutic connection the therapist harvests the feeling and the meaning with a trumpeting of their insight, theory and technique. The story telling process becomes all about them as the gatherer and re-teller of stories. Connection with, or perspective on, the other people in the story is lost.

Trumpeted stories can be entertaining and teasing, as if they are about to open-up and draw you in and then you find nothing to the orchestration but the sound of the trumpet. The mapping moments in trumpeted stories come wherever there is a chance to wonder about the part the trumpeting is playing in the story. Perhaps it can then find its place as a lament or call of people to come together or keep out.

Jigsaw puzzle stories

These are painful and important stories which require patience and compassion. They emerge piece-by-piece as unrelated details. Patterns are there but not easy to draw out. They may even seem to be parts of several different stories. A sense of narrative coherence comes slowly, if at all. It may be that the narrator does not know if all the pieces to the puzzle are available. Or whether there is space and time to leave them out in the open until the jigsaw is completed. Each piece in the jigsaw story may invite its own story and the very assumption that there is a larger story here may be challenged. The therapeutic mapping moments in a jigsaw story come with repeated sifting, sorting, and linking together. Completion may not be the goal. Important therapeutic moments may arise when realising that there are gaps in the picture and pieces in the jigsaw that are forever missing as unformulated experience and gaps in self-knowledge.

The 'sort me out' story

The sort-me-out story is a therapy story that goes to the heart of narrative mapping. The adjoining diagram is not a therapy map but shows how we struggle to hold stories open against the pressure to sort and close them. In mental health work, the pressure is to confirm a diagnosis, to carry out a treatment or select a medication. The pressure comes from the system but also can come from the client, or their family and friends.

The 'sort-me-out' diagram below starts on the lower left-hand side with (Box 1) **talking and listening**. As therapists and clients, if we establish a conversational quality to our discussion, then we are in a procedure of **sensing** and **noticing** and **engaging** and **sharing**. These lead in several directions simultaneously. Herein lies the challenge and the first point of the diagram. One the one hand we are finding the words that help us open or complete the story (Box 2). What influences us is that as we **hover and shimmer** (Box 3) over the words and the emerging story, we have mixed feelings and contrasting points of view. The therapeutic work of tolerating these also makes us go to the reciprocal role on the map (Box 4) of facing or risking **exposure and challenge** and feeling uncertain about the outcome and anxious for ourselves and our client (or therapist) as partners in the enterprise. On the one hand we need to tolerate the uncertainty and the tools of mapping and talking can help us do that. On the other hand, we want certainty, or at least coherence, sooner or later. Either we as client or therapist, or the system surrounding the therapist, will voice the call to fix this uncertainty with a story. The process of **storying and restorying** comes through the wording and negotiating at 1, 2 and 3 on the map. We are trying to slow the rush to sort the person with a closed story and instead, hold it open despite accompanying uncertainty and anxiety. When the story is

Chapter 3: Narrative mapping

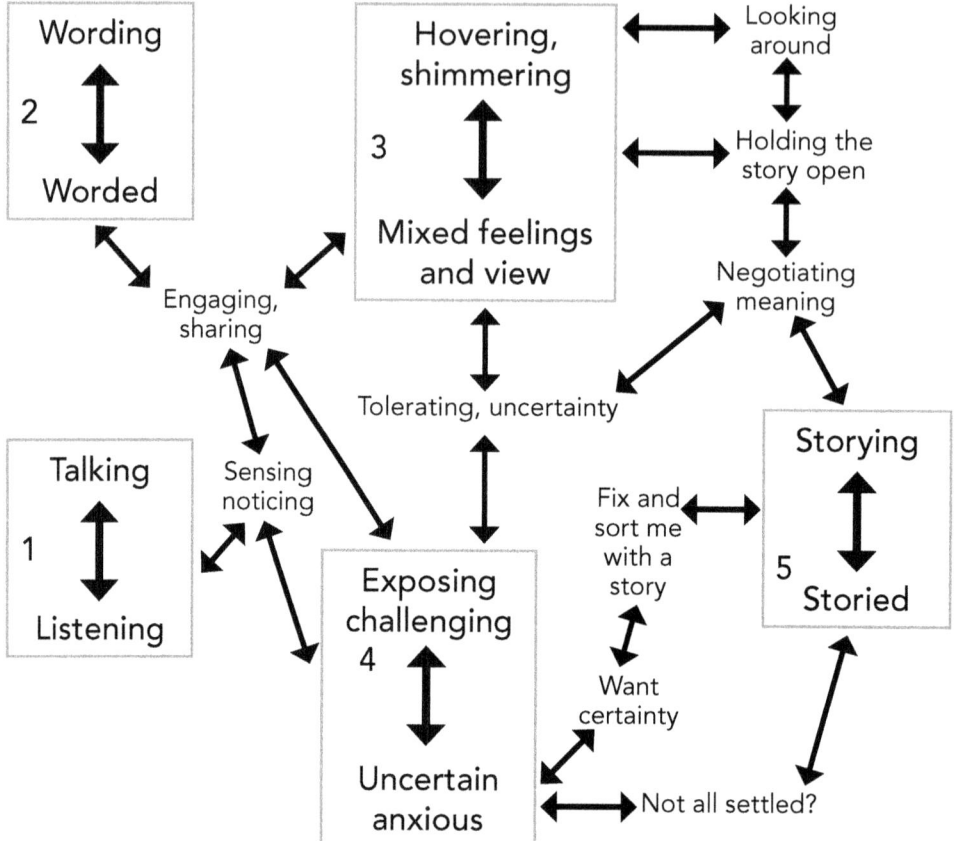

prematurely sorted, it often leaves an unsettled feeling. This is not the whole story, or it is not the one I wanted. We may go back to reopen it and stay longer with the mixed feelings and points of view.

Orchestral stories

There are times in therapy when several separate stories are being told, held open and retold and they begin to blend into each other and create a greater harmony. For example, stories of childhood and adolescence may be remembered as different events and experiences and the process of putting the stories together and finding patterns offers not so much a coherent whole but a sense of creating, orchestrating and managing something new and larger. These moments of creative awareness and insight are going to be called 'orchestral' throughout the book. The parts and patterns in the story are like instruments and music in an orchestra. There may be distinctive threads, but they weave together. This feeling of things having a shape is internalised as sense of agency and the ability to be self-possessed. To stay with the orchestral metaphor, the client, in telling their stories, feels that in the open space of the therapy, a life that had no good music to it was open to being orchestrated in a more composed way. This sense of an orchestral capacity can be the unexpected gift of therapy. Client and therapist should agree to look out for it and give it a thumbs up when it happens.

Life-story maps

At some point in the early sessions it can be useful to offer to work together on a life-story map as a way of tracking out the main patterns of relating through the whole of the client's life. This is an overview of the main family relationships set up as reciprocal roles, around which circulate life events, spread out on a large sheet of paper. Making the map may involve working at a desk or white board or with paper spread out on the floor depending on the person and setting. It may involve a big sheet of paper or stapling and taping several pieces of paper together. A life story map is likely to be quite full and more likely than the final therapy diagram to have short sentences and bits of biographical detail. Its purpose is quite different to the sketches of bits of stories or maps of moments.

Making a life-story map may need an extended session, over an hour and a half or two hours, or be split over two weeks. Agreeing to spend a session or two drawing out a life map can help the client step back from immediate difficulties and develop elements of a relational imagination which has both sociological and psychological dimensions to it. It is an orchestration of stories from the past. The client often sees the map as telling both 'local' stories about problems and incidents, and general stories about their wider sense of self. A life map can help tell the wider social stories of 'me' in the world by making links to gender, class, culture, and national identities. Such mapping helps to see common patterns across generations or across reconstituted families. It encourages an outsider's view (mixing a social and psychological perspective). Such detachment brings surprising flashes of emotional connection. One client could see the repetition of patterns of racism across generations. Another client could see a pattern of being a tough-minded woman in her mother and her gran. For all she knew, it was there in generations of women before them.

It is the first survey of life stories and some hot spots or important areas will be noted to come back to. Some therapists do a life map as a way of history taking, exploring the life story not just of the client but also of his or her family. The life-story map is not intended as a tool for a focused therapy but is more the big picture from which themes and target problems might emerge. A genogram (McGoldrick, 1985) in combination with a life-story map can also offer a rich historical, social and psychological perspective. The life-story map is a useful for personal development and coaching but can also be a powerful oral history research tool, equally useful for exploring social histories outside of a therapy context.

The life-story map will be crowded and messy, and a tidier version can be created which might ultimately comprise some of the focused sketches that make up the therapy map described in the next chapter. The life-story map needs a large sheet of paper and lots of notes. It is probably wise to bin the messy version and build on a tidier version which in turn will get messy and be replaced.

The process is an iterative one of exploration, connection and remembering. The process of tidying up and clarifying can be focused on alongside writing out prose descriptions or putting time aside to map out a specific emerging problematic pattern. The therapist may prefer to go away and write out a prose description of the feelings and connections arising from the work of life mapping. The client may also welcome the therapist offering to do this. Equally this can be done together in session and different technology will work in different contexts.

The life map is an extremely helpful resource from which to write a 'personal reformulation' in prose. For young people it helps them look back to preceding generations and the presence or absence of grandparents, the childhood experience of their parents and the major events in society or in the world. For older people it may be a wonderful way of looking at the whole run of life and connecting with preceding generations.

Sincere stories

An essential ingredient of therapy is a feeling for stories. The therapist's foremost job is to convey that they care about the client's life stories. The client's job is to be willing to discover more about becoming a sincerely imaginative, reliable and free narrator. Both are seeking to hear and see the key process of shaping and reliving a story in new ways. In the wake of World War II, many of the emerging therapies (which are still popular) had the idea of authenticity as their touchstone. In their view the therapist must be genuine. The search is for the true self. Winnicott, Kohut and Rogers all have this quality in their different ways. It is an understandable response to the dissociation and schizoid experience of two world wars in close succession. Richard Sennett in his work *The Fall of Public Man* (2002) and in his more recent work (2012) on tools and togetherness in working relationships choses to stress sincerity over authenticity. The focus is that being genuine in the relationship is a prior condition to feeling genuine in one's self.

From a narrative mapping perspective this makes sense. If the work together is sincere in drawing out patterns from stories, then we can live in the spaces between competing kinds of authenticity and uncertainty about how exactly we express ourselves. In one way it is a more modest and tangible goal to be sincere in the story-making relationship. We are not in pursuit of some ultimate truth, either out there or deep in the self. Some of the experiences and some of the events of history are too horrendous to comprehend or place within a narrative structure. Some stories are too hard to tell. Some stories have gaps in them that will forever be covered over. This theme is pursued later as 'gappiness' and gaps in self-understanding and relational trauma in chapter 8.

Epic and novelistic stories

The Russian philosopher Mikhail Bakhtin offers a rich perspective on genres and qualities of storytelling relationships. An account of his work is given by Michael Holquist in his book Dialogism (1990). One theme from Bakhtin is the contrast he drew between epic and heroic stories (like Superman or Homer's Iliad) and novelistic (for example the novels of Dostoevsky) stories. For example for an immediate and painful feel of the two narrative styles, a reading of Pat Barker's brilliant novelistic account of the experience of the girls and young women in the Trojan war (*The Silence of the Girls*, Barker, 2018) war historically described by Homer in epic terms only from the heroic male point of view. The epic account is more closed and not negotiable. It is handed down and given. The role of the listener is to listen in and be a spectator. There may be novelistic moments in the course of an epic narration but in the main it is one-dimensional and has no room for invention or dialogue. In contrast the novelistic account is open and uncertain. The listener is invited to participate and empathise alongside the narrator as author. The storying process is active and alive and unfinished. One story may slip into another. Events unfold simultaneously and with spontaneity. Dialogue replaces monologue. Put simply in a good novel there is an intertwining of several plots working in and off each other. Each plot has its own timeline and quality of space and location. Novelistic stories invite an orchestral experience of storytelling in the face of a multiplicity of narrative threads.

Contrasting story telling relationships

Epic	Novelistic
closed	open
certain	uncertain
storied	storying
one dimensional	multi-dimensional
and then, and then	here and there
declamatory	conversational
resisting dialogue	inviting dialogue

Looking at the contrasting list for epic and novelistic types of storytelling indicates that the direction of narrative mapping and therapy with a map is from epic accounts to novelistic accounts. Bakhtin defined this as the move from monologue to dialogue. We live our lives with epic accounts of our illnesses and turmoil in life and our own dreams and ambitions. It is for the therapy to help us move to a more open and uncertain accounts with multiple dimensions of relating and a capacity to tolerate an uncharted aspect to the future. In novelistic story telling we make links but live with gaps. In epic story telling there are no gaps but nor are there any links. The way of things is ordained and outside of time and dialogue.

The 'open flowers' story

By the middle of therapy, on Michael's map, there was a tiny drawing of a bunch of flowers tightly wrapped in paper. It was a symbol of his shyness or lack of skill in showing affection to his partner. It was both an unmet need and an untried skill as described in **Chapter 8** on relational healing. His partner Lisa had brought him flowers once when he was feeling low. He was very touched by it. As a child, tenderness towards him, or from his father to his mother was completely absent. His parent's roles were epic and fixed. He sometimes had the idea of going into a flower shop to reciprocate but didn't act on it. At my prompting he did go once and just imagined buying some flowers, looked at the selection and thought about his partner. It was a small behavioural experiment in facing new thoughts, feelings, and possible actions. He told Lisa of his experiment and she was amused but impressed: 'An imagined bunch of flowers is good enough for me. It's the thought that counts', she said.

On his 'flowers map', there were the words 'showing tenderness'. These were my words which he accepted as a goal for him to explore. And his words were on the map as 'sissy and weak'. There was also a judging phrase that came to him when he was doing the thought experiment at the flower stand with a voice in him saying. 'Who do you think you are? He pointed at the words 'bunch of flowers' and said. 'I think I cling to my familiar ways even though they limit me'. It hurts me inside when I think of changing, as if I am doing something forbidden.' As is mapped out and discussed elsewhere on page 49, Michael had been violently treated (in his dad's eyes for 'his own good' to make him a 'hard man') and had great difficulty in acknowledging compassion for the frightened child in him or the damage done to his oppressed and crushed mum. Together in the room, we wrote a short letter to the story of the flowers. The flower story was a path to change but it highlighted the double challenge. It is not just about changing behaviour and going through the motions of buying flowers. It is the self-conscious knowledge that he is both doing some caring for another person and healing something in himself. How to do this healing would only become clear through the flower buying experiment. By trying out the novelistic procedure of flower buying and seeing what he discovered about himself at each step he was in a small way acting as his own therapist. Having it mapped and now written out helped keep the whole sequence in mind as a small story. What was novel, began to feel less strange and he could challenge his pattern of shying away. With the aid of the map and a letter to the flowers he set off to be his own compassionate observer. For some weeks we forgot about the flower buying and then one week he remembered something he wanted to tell me, 'I took my partner a bunch of flowers'. By now this was something he had done several times. 'Usually I kind of hide them, hold them close to my chest, so that no one notices a man with a bunch of flowers. But this time, I held them out shamelessly and got smiles'. We were able to acknowledge that not only did he bring the flowers, but he had the insight for himself and for her of the meaning of not being ashamed.

Open stories and cover stories

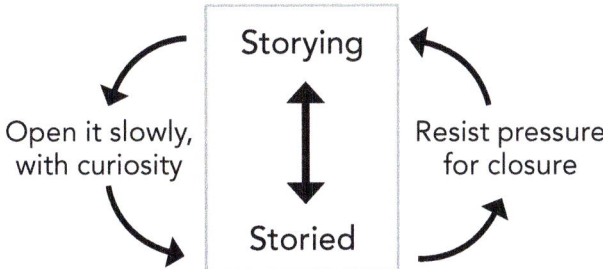

Therapy is seeking to find a way inside our major and minor life stories. To open them up to see different points of view and mixed feelings. This can be conceived on paper as a reciprocal relationship between doing the storying and being storied. The top end, the storying end, is enquiring, searching, opening the space up. The bottom end is receiving and experiencing the storying and the feelings of being storied. The challenge is to hover and shimmer and tolerate the uncertainty and anxiety that comes with resisting or delaying the pressure for closure and having the story sorted. Another way of thinking about this is to view therapy as a process of unstorying fixed and closed stories. We bring stories, our troublesome or hopeful stories, to therapy in the hope of compassionately and constructively unstorying them and then, slowly and constructively, restorying them. In the process we find that some experience has not been storied at all.

Some of our life stories are over-storied. They are cover stories, and like the dog stories and 'trumpeting' stories they work well. We feel safe telling them. They serve to protect us or give us familiarity when looking back. But they also serve as a cover for something less easy to relate to.

Therapy is partly about 'un-storying' the 'over-storied' story. It involves loosening the shape and line of it. We open it up to be inside it and among the characters and events. We want to see it from the other participants points of view whilst also being able to stand outside it with the 'anthropological' observer's, the painter's or the orchestral conductor's point of view. Re-storying is the healing, reparative and curative process. It is the reconsolidation of memories and, in the process of re-remembering, there is a process of working through.

The words on the map allow an opening between what is noticed and how it is named. How we name it will change what we notice. Other feelings or ideas may come to mind. This process of constructing alternative wordings and feelings for what is being remembered and described is more openly allowed and anchored with a map than without one.

The process of mapping, the externalisation of ideas and feelings onto paper leads to moments of sifting what is familiar from what is new. Sometimes the word on paper that was first said in a familiar way now feels new at the point of recapping it conversationally. A client looks at the words on paper and says 'its meaning has changed' whereas more importantly their relationship with its meaning has changed.

Maria and I had been mapping and talking for an hour. We had agreed an extended initial session of an hour and a half to help begin the therapy and considering the distance she travelled to get to the appointment. The map had markers of the conversations and links to key words in the accounts she had given. It started out as a sketch of one or two stories but had grown into a life-story map of lots of stories from her adult life, her childhood and elements of her parent's and grandparent's lives. It felt messy for us both but there was also a confidence that we were orchestrating something. We had been engrossed and, though nothing was sorted by the map, it was all out there. Maria said 'There is so much to see and so many connections that can be made. Perhaps things add up more than I realise'. They were jigsaw stories: initial enquiries to discover and recover new meanings and new connections – but gaps in self-knowledge and unfinished parts to stories. There were trumpet moments, though no dog stories.

In this disorder we had begun to have a another feeling all together. It could be called a feeling for stories. What we had before us on the table was not a therapy map (as described on page 186), but it was work in progress to take home add to or dwell on. We decided that for the next session we would pick out some key patterns from the stories. To finish the session and have some work to bring to the next session we wondered if there are one or two places that jump out as worthy of further exploration. She chose a moment from her childhood and a story about her grandmother. We photographed those two bits of the map with Maria's phone. We decided on the idea of writing short, spontaneous letters (no more than a couple of paragraphs) to those places on the map (Dear Childhood Moment, Dear Grandmother story) with which she made distinctive connections or felt troubled. There was no pressure to do this. If it did not feel right or there was no space or time, then we could pick up the conversation with the map anyway the following week. In fact, writing the letters gave Maria a sense of being an active author and participant in working therapeutically with the map. Her writing (which she read out) gave us a head start at the beginning of the next session. It was not so much what was written but the sense of being an active participant by writing that made the difference.

Patterns from stories

Perhaps the aim in working with stories in therapy is not to get them told but to be alongside them, in and out of them. We need to let the story breathe. We are listening and negotiating together as client and therapist to draw out a pattern from the story. It might be a pattern unique to the story, but we are expecting it to be a pattern that carries across several stories. If we can see the pattern, we can use it a template to gain perspective and think in general about the processes of restriction and change in our personalities and identities in the world.

The infant develops a feeling for stories before they develop a capacity with words. It is tempting to think we know words first and then begin to understand stories. However, we already know many stories by the time we begin to say words in our second year of life. We know these stories through our roles in them and through the maps our baby brains make of them. Stories of going to sleep, waking, pooing, eating, playing are enacted pre-verbally. Our feeling for stories is framed in these early months and years. It could be called relational awareness or as Colwyn Trevarthen calls it 'Affectionate, intersubjective intelligence' (Trevarthen, 2017).

Our entry into story making is the same as our entry into the world. Our first experiences of authorship are the beginnings of personal agency and individuality within a community. We feel part of a negotiating, map-making, story-making, co-authoring world with each extra orchestration of sensory, cognitive and motor development in the first year of life. We develop awareness through mapping and storying patterns of experience. The story gives meaning to the pattern of interaction and enables it to be transferred from one context to another.

The mapping process holds an 'open story' attitude to the reconsolidation of memories. This is a therapeutic mechanism of some importance as illustrated by Joseph Le Doux (1996) and, more latterly Richard Lane (2018). Le Doux sees that our systems of memory are dynamic and that a memory is not something like a photograph from an album that we take out and put back unchanged. The process of remembering involves some reshaping and relocating of the memory. It never goes back the same. To use mapping as an analogy for how the brain works: the memory is stored as a little map in a whole colony of maps organised in hierarchies and networks. In remembering the story in an emotionally engaged way with another person (and with the added dynamic of capturing something of the dynamics of the map on paper), it is relived and its place, in a web of memory maps, is redrawn (Le Doux, 1996). Lane describes how this process plays a part in remembering in therapy. From the point of view of mapping we are restorying, *and simultaneously* **restoring** our memories differently depending upon how, when, why, with whom and for whom we tell the story.

Jerome Bruner (1990) whose enormous contribution to cognitive and developmental theory lay at the roots of the cognitive revolution, drew an important distinction between paradigmatic and narrative ways of knowing. The paradigmatic way of thinking is one that sees patterns and is analytic. The narrative way of thinking is story making and more driven by feeling. Ryle adopted this idea seeing a creative and therapeutic interplay between the more 'paradigmatic' diagrams (mapping) and the more 'narrative' work of writing. However, mapping stories as a live co-creative process as they unfold has both paradigmatic and narrative elements.

'Hopes and fears' story map

The 'hopes and fears' template, is one of two (see the hide and seek template to follow) mapping templates that can hold open the process of telling a story and tracking and shaping its content. It is designed to facilitate mapping without intruding on the inherent dynamics and structure of the story. A more general version was introduced at the end of the preceding chapter under the title of what I really, really want.

The hopes and fears map starts at Box 1, with a reciprocal role of something being **challenging**. The question for the story then becomes one of when I am feeling challenged my hopes and fears are as follows. The **'hoping for'**

Hopes and fears map

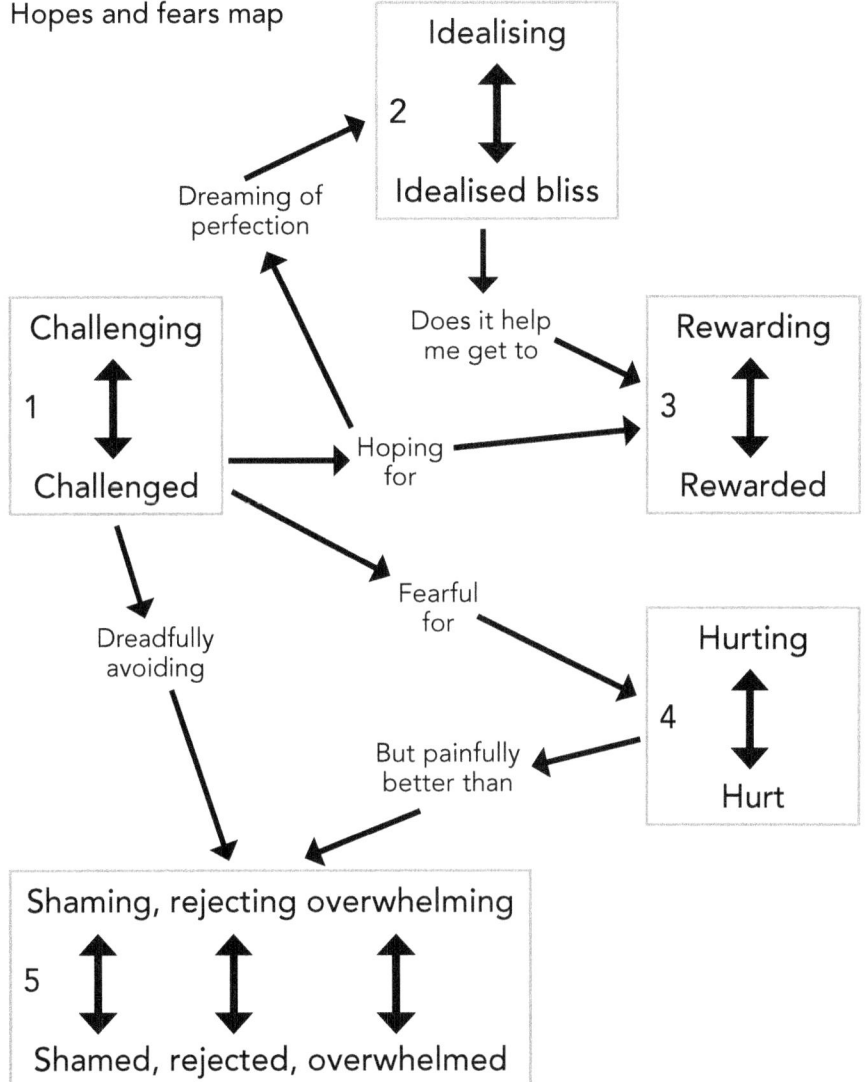

pattern of interaction might be a mix of finding a way to a **rewarding** place (Box 3) or dreaming of an **ideal** place of total fulfilment (Box 2). One question is how the ideal in Box 2 impacts on the more realistic journey to rewards in Box 3. Do our dreams hijack or enable our more realistic striving? Client and therapist can use the mapping process to work out the way the story can stay open to these two sought after positions.

Ambitions, ideals and dream places are part of all cultures and serve in part to give us motivation. The process of mapping out using this template is to open-up reflection of the function of our ideals and dreams on our behaviour. Is our ideal in this story an uplifting and inspiring motivator with which we can have a productive self-building or healing dialogue or an illusory dreamlike place where we hide and lose ourselves. Is the **'hoped-for'** place so desired that it works as a narcissistic solution (however fragile and costly) from which to look down upon others, or other parts of the self. The **rewarding place** in Box 3 could take many forms from being valued, appreciated, being in control, feeling fulfilled, being safe and so on. The **dreams** in Box 2 may be overvalued versions of Box 3 or sources of inspiration in pursuit of truth or triumph. One of the driving forces behind procrastination and avoiding exposure is to protect a bubble-wrapped dream place from ever being exposed. Our relationship with our thinking about our desires is considered again in **Chapter 7**-under the title of relational thinking and the narcissism invested in ideas.

In stark contrast there may be **feared places** (Box 5) that have such a long and now blurred history in the story of the self that they are so dreadfully avoided that still now the idea of coping with exposure to them feels unimaginable as it once did in formative years. What might in childhood have been unmanageable emotional experiences given the imbalance of power, might be more negotiable in adulthood, were it not for the pattern of avoidance and the way in which the feared place has been dreadfully avoided to the point of being dissociated in some way.

The feared places can be entangled in our emotional memory and as an effect of early restriction and trauma, it may be that we fear exposure to **rejection, shame and being overwhelmed** all in one as an intolerable and split off state of mind. We may find that in the yo-yo between our hopes and fears we find a painful but an understandable refuge in an intermediate state of hurt, 'stuckness' or neglect over which we have some control and for which we can offer a narrative.

There are possibilities for the naming of the feared and disavowed places. The one most likely to be near to awareness is Box 4 and the **hurt place**. Procedures developed to avoid hurt, or to accept and get stuck with hurt, may be more unconsciously driven by deeper fears of reciprocal roles of **shaming to shamed**, **rejecting to rejected**, **overwhelming to overwhelmed** as Box 5. These may be active possibilities in the current conversation being mapped. Or they may lie in the memory as deeply feared, partially dissociated and unformulated states of mind in the past. In co-creating maps with this template in mind the therapist, as lead mapper, needs to feel free to go off in different directions as part of keeping alongside the client. The template should never be followed like the instructions for the self-assembly of a flat pack. It works best as a template to hold in mind.

Hide and seek story map

Mapping activates our deeper emotions and puts them in dialogue with our capacity to feel and negotiate our feelings. Jaap Panksepp (2013) describes

Hide and seek

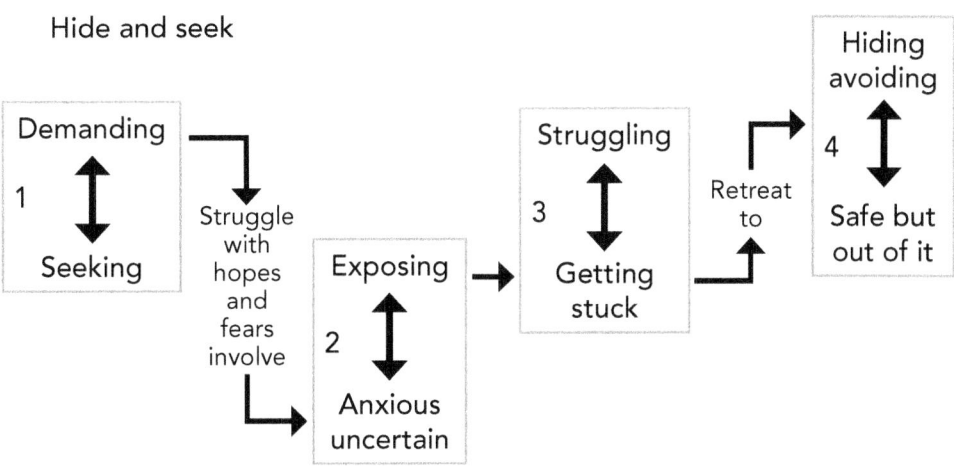

seven emotional subsystems in the substrata of the brain. These are defined by him as: seeking, playing, grieving, lusting, fearing, caring, raging. A working hypothesis for the mapping process is that our reworking and restorying of our memories of life experiences interact with these emotional sub-systems in helpful or harmful orchestral ways.

In the map of the hide and seek pattern shown in the figure above, the starting point is feeling pressured in response to a challenge from others or from within myself or both, as in Box 1. I respond to the challenge with hopes and fears battling for what I want and seeking to avoid falling into what I don't want (for examples see previous section and page 103). In the process, it can be personally exposing and, depending upon the kind of exposure, the client may be anxious or uncertain as in Box 2. They may resolve this in many ways, but some part of it involves times of struggling and getting stuck as in Box 3. Most of our problem patterns take us to a stuck place, which in the early days of CAT was called the **core pain**, in echo of James Mann's (1973) idea in brief psychodynamic therapy of chronically endured pain. Being stuck is one of our bad but tolerable places. It is preferable to the feared and unwanted places in the hopes and fears diagram on the preceding pages. The end of the sequence though is a familiar self-management procedure in which we retreat to a safe place or 'identity' solution (Box 4) where we are out of danger but at the price of being out of action. Such identify solutions are many but think for example 'the nice guy', 'the good girl', 'the loud mouth'. Much of therapy involves finding alternatives to hiding in the safe place or finding ways to notice when a place of escape and refuge has become something of a retreat and a prison. Most of the patterns of self-protection and hiding have a gain and cost.

It is most often the case that as we map our patterns of hide and seek with one story or one memory we are talking about and touching a general pattern of ours. The reflections in therapy with the map are around adding detail and colour to the specific memory but also looking out for familiar roles and patterns that have general application.

Here and there moments of zooming and linking

The capacity to see both here and there on the map can help us be in among the different elements and move around from one time and another, one state and another, or one identity and another, or one person and another. To understand one story, we need to move around within it but also see it in relation to other stories. Narrative mapping tries to create an analogical space that can be alongside this complexity. The mechanism of change in mapping along these lines happens when a client or therapist puts their left hand on one part of the map and their right hand on another and notes that they are both here and there at the same time. This part of the story depends on that part. As noted elsewhere mapping extends working memory in these moments of zooming and linking.

One of the mechanisms of change in therapy is a vantage point of seeing a bigger, or wider, picture and yet being able to zoom into small, or local detail. Perspective taking is a form of making links. We can use the map to say in detail that 'I feel this here because that is happening over there'. As we move in and out of detail and hover and zoom between picture and detail, we develop perspective taking skills. This develops both reflective and narrative capacity.

One way of communicating the value of these moments to clients and colleagues is to picture running up and down a perspective ladder. A therapy that is all big picture and perspective is of little help, nor is one that proceeds from detail to detail but fails to hold the larger context in mind. The more we take perspective from detail, or apply perspective to detail, the more we can observe ourselves and ultimately become our own therapists. It might be stating the obvious to suggest this process is easier with a map than without one, as the map provides a visual representation of both the larger picture and its component parts.

Conclusion – patterns from stories

The central idea of mapping to develop relational awareness within a therapy relationship is to listen to stories and draw out patterns from them. As the client searches for an account of what is going on in their lives, the therapist is listening out for patterns. Patterns of interaction, patterns of connection and gaps and breaks within and between patterns. Our memories swim between different stories. As we un-story and re-story our stories, side-by-side, we live temporarily inside them and re-organise and reconsolidate our memory of them. In therapy, the map of the pattern can work as a scaffolding or analogy for shaping and holding several stories.

We have a deep need for narrative coherence both in the developing stages of our early lives, in the little moments and in the grand narrative. Our basic human need for narrative coherence can equally be put as a need for a coherent pattern. Perhaps our social brains want stories to map out. Messy and unfinished stories make us anxious. We will manage our narrative needs by keeping up an appearance of tidied stories on the outside to which we ally ourselves and hide the unfinished, incoherent, messy stories inside ourselves.

There are three qualities to narrative coherence: first it is 'located' in time and place, second there is a known and understandable sequence and consequence to the story as events unfold and people respond. Finally, there is some message or perspective from the story in the form of a theme or pattern (Reese, 2011). From the point of view of therapy, it would be vital to add a sense of authorship through participation in or observation of the story. In the memory and repetition of the story, there must be a reliable narrator. Mapping the patterns to our stories helps us step back from trumpeting or dog storying and allows to be in open dialogue with our relationships with and needs for narrative coherence. There will always be gaps and pieces of the jigsaw of the story that belong in another story.

As we struggle to tell and renegotiate our life stories in therapy, the process of mapping out patterns and connecting with key words and phrases on paper may bring a kind of narrative tolerance. This is the ability to sit with a story until it opens up and live with stories different to our own. Narrative tolerance is a capacity to be outside our comfort zone of familiar tales and story lines.

Chapter 4: Process mapping

Introduction

This chapter is about mapping the immediate relationship in the therapy room. It requires skill, courage, and sincerity. For the therapist it involves seeing their part in the relationship and disclosing some of their own feelings and responses. For the client it may involve speaking truth to power and trusting that the therapist can openly work alongside differences of perception about how the relationship is being established and maintained. Mapping the therapeutic process brings safer ways of talking about transference dynamics and the wider relationship between client and therapist.

The following pages first explore how to move from hindsight to immediate insight about the dynamics in the room. It describes mapping the moment and gives examples. It draws upon the work of Karen Horney (1945) to explore the mapping of our processes of entanglement in therapy and naming the dance without blaming the dancer. There are checklists and exercises to increase capacity to work more confidently with the here and now. The qualities of working together by negotiating a shared understanding, and building a transference friendly atmosphere, are helped by a checklist of relational skills and of typical patterns of interaction. The chapter concludes with some reflections on the relational ethics of working together.

Hindsight really is a wonderful thing

Mapping and talking about the processes in the therapy room takes us to the heart of psychoanalytic thinking. We create a transference friendly space that is open to enactments and the repetition of patterns (carrying over and pushing into and onto us) of relating from one time, story and context to another. The more we can discover and hold in mind the transferred pattern of relating, the more we can see the interplay between past and present problems of living.

It is not easy to achieve awareness of the therapy relationship as it is happening. There are going to be times in any therapy when a therapist wishes she or he had said 'Let's map what is going on between us just now'. We are quite good at spotting patterns in retrospect. Hindsight really is a wonderful thing. It is a familiar lament that I can see clearly what was going wrong a few hours or days later, but I had no sense of it, there and then, in the thick of it. Hindsight comes from seeing something in a fresh light, stepping out of role, being away from the co-embodied moment, having space to see and understand another point of view. As in the various references to hover and shimmer, gaps, and links, our development of relational awareness of internal, mutual and social empathy is partly to arm ourselves with foresight to sense ruptures as they happen. We cannot have the foresight to know what we cannot see with hindsight. Mapping of the process in the room together should be done in the spirit of not knowing what it will bring. If we trust some of the unconscious processes in the spontaneous work of mapping, then something akin to 'immediate insight' may take the place of hindsight.

Shyness about 'here and now' feelings

In most cultures we are a bit shy talking about the relationship between us for fear of it distracting from the task in hand, or putting us on the spot, and threatening the relationship. This applies more so in the therapy room. We fear being exposed and embarrassed or embarrassing the other person. So, we steer round the interpersonal elephant in the room. Therapists stick to their manuals and clients stick to their story. Therapists fear getting it wrong. Clients fear being the problem. Such avoidance may work in everyday life, but in therapy talking in the here and now about what is happening between us is a major mechanism in the process of change. Talking directly and openly can bring us into the overlap of transference patterns arising from us working together. A readiness for, and a routine of, stopping and reflecting on the here and now needs establishing. This is where the process of mapping can help.

Map the moment

The following guidelines offer the client and therapist help in establishing a routine of stopping and talking about the process and building this up as a resource for when any major difficulties or transference processes arise. There will be times when the client feels that what is happening right now is not helping, and it would be good if we could talk about it. Or the client feels that in some way, a pattern of relating, which is rooted in the past and is a source of personal difficulty, is playing out now with the therapist. The client, or the therapist, might have been sensing something is stuck, or something has changed for the better but is not acknowledged.

> ### Weekly check-in: how are we working just now?
> It can help, each week, to spend a few minutes mapping out our pattern of working together, as it is, at present. It allows us to check out what is helping or hindering, where our attention is focused, and, what we might be not noticing, or neglecting as well as what we are doing well. Patterns and stories in our lives may have their parallels in the therapy relationship between us. If we can talk about what is helping or hindering us, it may make it easier to see opportunities or challenges for you and us, more generally in the therapy. To help this, we can map a moment together →

of making progress, getting stuck or feeling misunderstood. We should keep in mind the 'one third rule' which suggests that one third of what is going on is coming from patterns of mine, one third from patterns of yours and one third to do with the system or context around us.

To do this, we sit side-by-side, take a blank sheet of paper, and map out (see hopes and fears template below) the words or phrases for:

- What we have been seeking to do?
- What we have been doing well?
- What we have been avoiding or ignoring?
- What has gone badly, or we fear going badly?

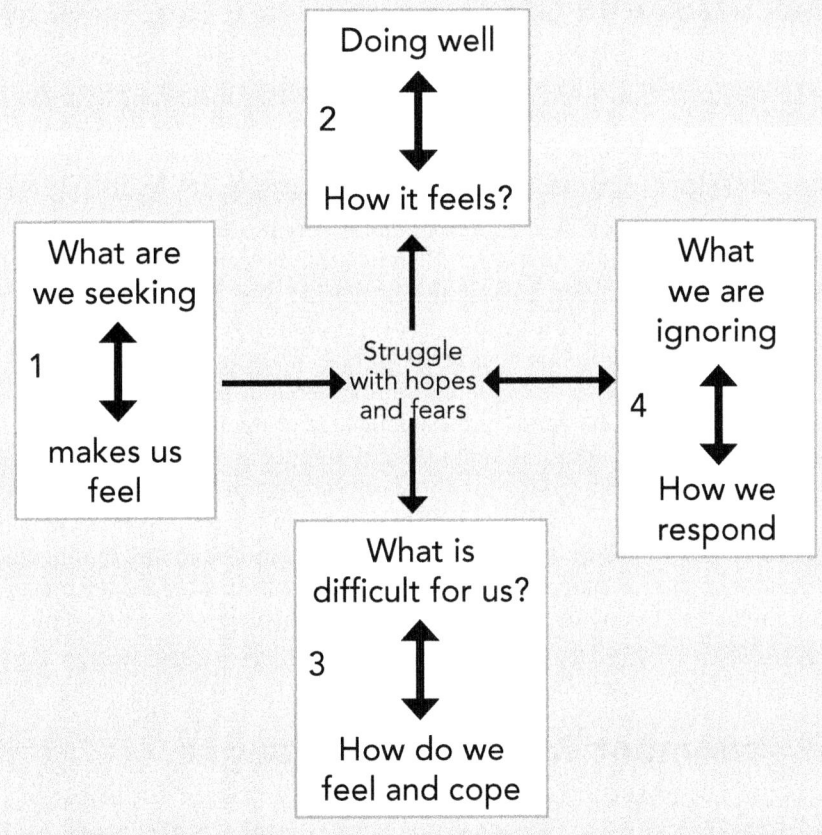

In looking at the map in response to these questions, the background questions should also be: 'Are we talking about what matters?' and 'Where are we on the map just now/then?'

We want to try to avoid blame, or shame, in checking how we are progressing. It is quite likely that doing well with some things will involve neglecting others. We need some time to see what comes up in this exercise. It may that be one or both of us will see a new angle.

From session-to-session, the therapist will keep these weekly 'check-in' maps. Over the whole run of sessions, they may offer a useful guide to how the therapeutic and helping relationship has developed. It creates a familiarity with talking about the helping relationship. As it becomes a routine part of the sessions, these maps can help talk about an important aspect of work that is easy to neglect and may be hard to raise. The best time to do this mapping would be halfway through a session. It might not always feel right, but it is best not to leave it to the very end of the session, because things might unexpectedly come up and this reflective task can then be overlooked.

It is happening here

When we use reciprocal roles to map our stories and experience, we often enact them. Talking of them brings the patterns of relating and associated feelings and memories alive with varying degrees of force and awareness. If the therapist is receptive and the therapy is transference-friendly, then such replay is an opportunity for deeper understanding.

In the middle of mapping a pattern of distressing recollections on paper, a client tells his therapist, as an aside when talking of how he coped with neglect in childhood, that he was always playing the comedian. As he recalls this, he makes a funny face and says: 'You have got to laugh'. And then he laughs. The therapist smiles with him. The trauma of which they were talking is suddenly being managed in a familiar way. The client had laughed off his distress again in the immediacy of the therapy. Mapping out reciprocal roles alongside these shimmering moments, helps hover with both the distress and the laughing off the statement. Such interactions are fleeting and easily overlooked. Micro-mapping the process in these moments creates a fresh sensitivity and awareness. In referring to the value of such moments in mapping one therapist (Rene Coffey, 2020, personal communication), having experienced process mapping for the first time, called them 'windows on immediacy'.

The moment when Michael laughs

Similarly, in an initial session with Michael I asked 'What if this therapy was really helpful and it was all that you could have wished for? What will we have done and what would be different?'. Michael laughed and said he could not imagine anyone being helpful. I smiled and gently said 'I wonder why not? Why did you laugh?'.

'Well I cannot imagine anyone bothering with me.'

'Am I bothering with you?'

'Yes, you are. It's shocking.' He laughs again.

I put the words 'shocking' and 'bothering with' and 'laughing' spread out on different bits of the sheet of paper. The gentle question, 'Why did you laugh?' brought the relationship between us into the conversation. Putting the words down on paper held the moment open in the room between us in the here and now. As a therapist I do not want to be directly challenging. Implicitly there could be an accusatory voice saying to Michael 'take yourself seriously'. Or a maternal voice, 'Let me bother with you. Let me be bothered by you'. The message from putting the words on the map was a statement of therapeutic intent to see if we could take the relationship seriously. Later, Michael reflected that his humour and his laughter keeps people away and keeps control of the emotional tone of his feelings but not this time.

Such little pauses in the here and now are valuable and don't have to add up to a big reveal. They can be healthy moments in the building of an alliance. There will be plenty of times of difficulty and rupture in sessions and enactment that are deep and difficult. Mapping the little moments of connection can be good preparation for talking about the bigger more difficult moments.

Entangling and disentangling

Karen Horney (1945) vividly described therapy as a repeated process of helping the client find a more sincere or wholehearted way of relating. Her humanistic stance is enriched by a psychoanalytic and relational view of the way we move towards or compliantly or aggressively move away or against ourselves and others. In the 1940s, she pioneered a way of thinking about our narcissistic, projective and externalising ways of coping with inner conflicts. Over and over again she describes in what she sees as the neurosis of our times the patterns of getting entangled and seeking to understand the 'tangle' and work out ways to therapeutically disentangle client and therapist, past and present and all the other dimensions of relating from each other.

> *'Most of us who live in this difficult civilisation are caught in the conflicts described here and need all the help we can get. Though severe neuroses belong in the hands of experts, I still believe that with untiring effort we can ourselves go a long way toward disentangling our own conflicts.'*

(Horney, 1945, page 8)

It is an idea developed more fully in the therapy room by Safran (2000) with his word 'disembedding' in his work on negotiating the therapeutic alliance.

As in the figure below, it is a reasonable description of the everyday life of a helping relationship that we get entangled in each other's' roles and states and take time to disentangle ourselves.

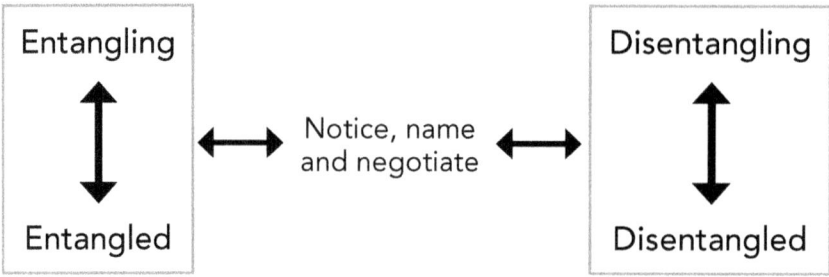

Mapping helps this powerful therapeutic process be visible and shared. It allows the tangles to be navigated and the knots to be untied more clearly because some of their features are on the map. It is the act of disentangling the patterns into a more visible, negotiable, sequence of feeling, thinking, action and consequence from the one end or other of a reciprocal role. It is a therapeutic process that is more helpfully visible with a map. Similarly separating out differently sourced and toned reciprocal roles from the entangled memory of them all in childhood (see Silvia's example in the next section) is a process of raising awareness. In the process of disentangling, client and therapist build negotiating skills.

Silvia's example of disentangling several childhood roles

Midway through session eight Silvia said 'I can't do this. It is too demanding'. The feeling of it being 'too demanding' was linked to how she felt about recognising a pattern of excessive concern for her children away at university. In her therapy letter we had written about the parallel between Silvia's attitude to her own children and her mother's attitude towards Silvia as a child. It had been wrapped up in one entangled, mix of reciprocal roles that had started innocently enough with her description of her mother as **doting** and she and her sisters as **doted** upon. However, seeing the word 'doting' on paper, had triggered a flurry of other words. We were shimmering between her memory of her mother and her reflections on herself now with her absent, almost grown up children. A reciprocal role from the past of '**Demanding** for achievement and for updates on progress' to which Silvia reciprocated by **'anxiously striving'**. There were **'threats of blame'** and Silvia responding (she now realised as the mapping progressed), by feeling loved but **guilty and bad**.

It all felt overwhelming (then as a child, out there with her children and in the moment in the therapy room) and Silvia worried that she in being 'doting' was being 'overwhelming' to her own children. As Silvia talked of these feelings, I had added them around the **doting to doted** reciprocal role on paper. The whole bundle was tied up in a knot of entangled feelings by her mother promising true adoration and approval if all demands could be

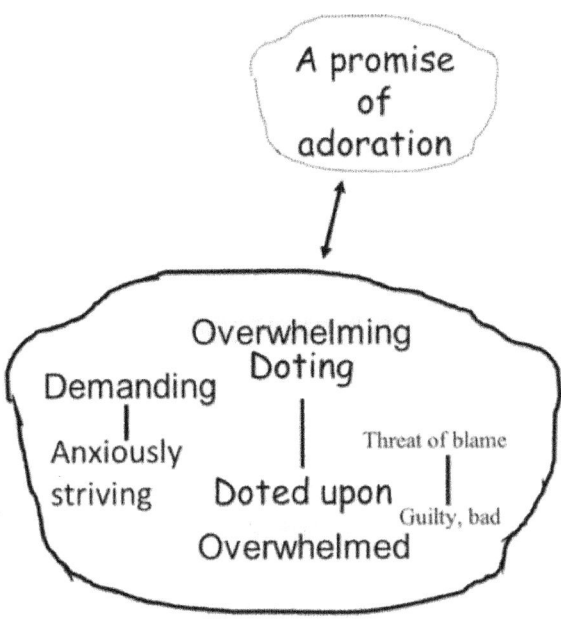

met. Representing their entangled, timeless experience on paper as in the figure to the side was upsetting. As Silvia said it was accurate for her both then, in the past with her mother, and now with her children. I had suggested disentangling the reciprocations, since they had different roles. Maybe if we could tease them out, we could see where to push for change – softening some role responses and sorting what belonged in the past with her and her mother, what was in the present with her children and what was being activated in the room with us.

In writing about it, we had called it 'the all-in-one mothering, a dance with no steps'. I only dimly sensed that her and my efforts to do well and show she was being looked after might mean that this trans-generational pattern was also active between us. We had ideas about how to spot it but had not touched upon it for some time, either through avoidance or from focusing on other patterns. Silvia's mother was 'after all such a good mother' and Silvia too was 'such a good mother'. Her children repeatedly told her so. In addition, and in an exact parallel, Silvia was being such a 'good client'.

What we missed was how entangled all these reciprocations were inside her. Now this pattern was in the room expressed to me indirectly and to herself so fully. The immediate pain was in wanting the approval for doing the therapy well and feelings of guilt, blame and striving were all entangled with this.

With a fresh sheet of paper, we teased out all the reciprocations separately. As in the map below, there was a doting to loved and giving love back' (1). There was a valuing to valued place (5) and a feared place of being rejected that never materialised. Suddenly her father's absence found a space on the paper. He seemed to ignore and be scornful of all this loving and striving. We wondered if the dad's absence was a silent rejection working within this orchestration. There was a feeling of guilt and blame that was now disentangled. Teasing them out on paper and the shared process of disentangling them had an abundance of therapeutic moments across the different parts of her life past and present. There was a recognition of the quite varied interactions with her daughters. There was a deeper realisation of the unwarranted but silently present fear of rejection by the children that led to sticking to the knotted entanglement of reciprocations.

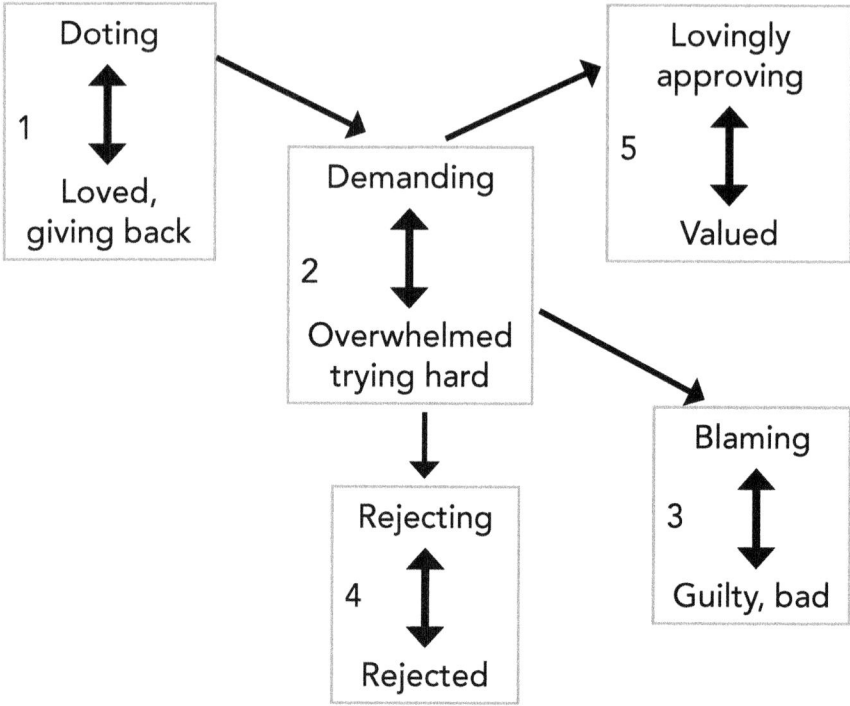

We talked through our experiences of making this disentangling map with great intensity and engagement. Above all, the process of separating patterns and roles out on paper seemed to loosen ties within Silvia. She did want approval from me, and she felt she was trying hard. As her co-worker, with the map I also wanted approval from her. I also was trying hard. We could see that my contributions of approval and co-working, like all the varied ways of interaction which she had with her daughters, were hard to let stand and be appreciated. They were so quickly colonised by the entangled patterns of relating on the map. We needed to stop and give each other credit and this was a easier to do with tangible evidence between us. At some point I felt a scorn for what we were doing. We were trying so hard and yet feeling bad about our efforts but who is there blaming us?

Without the aid of the disentangling work with the map, we could not have picked up the configuration of the transference or stayed in it and worked it through. This emotional state of mind (and unresolved part of herself) was between us in the room. It felt as if the therapy was swamping her with conditional care and affection and demands like her mum. Silvia was trying to be a good mum to the therapy. By untying the knots and teasing out the steps, something surprising came into view. The scornful and absent dad was also an unspoken and unnoticed threat in our relationship in the therapy. We summarised it like this: 'If we are not entangled with all this caring and striving, we will be scornfully deserving of being abandoned'. We laughed at the idea of both feeling useless despite trying so hard.

Silvia said 'My mother was never loving without being demanding. I was never loved without also feeling obliging, dependent and guilty until I rebelled. And by then the damage was done. I carried this entanglement with me. But I didn't realise the entanglement was a protection against an unspoken feared place of being scornfully rejected'.

Once we had put her father's scorn and her own fear of rejection on the map, the other places could be navigated and felt looser and more distinctive.

Name the dance, don't blame or shame the dancer

Silvia's example leads to one of the central ideas of creating a transference-friendly environment. It is captured by the phrase *'name the dance, don't blame the dancer'*. It is a change of pronoun from 'you 'to 'we'. Rather than 'what are you doing to me?' it becomes 'I wonder how **we** are in this dance of patterns?'. Rather than the accusative tense of 'what are you doing to yourself?' it becomes 'what are we doing here together?' By naming the 'dance' of feelings and behaviours that both 'dancers' are engaged in, it becomes a shared process and can be thought about without attributing blame or giving rise to shame. Elements of blame and shame may still arise, but they will emerge from the joint map and should not be buried in the foundations of the therapy.

The idea of dance stresses therapy as a joint activity that pushes and pulls us into different relationships with each other. We need to notice and name the dance before we can negotiate our choice of action. Our patterns of relating, especially our more personal and informal ones, are based on implicit procedural knowledge and ways of reciprocating laid down in our earliest years of life. This procedural knowledge is something we can become more, kindly and actively, aware of through mapping. It is what Jean Knox describes in her book *Self-Agency in Psychotherapy* (as co-embodied knowing that is implicitly mapped from the motor parts of our brain.

> 'A mother and infant may achieve a semi-stable state of turn taking in their interaction, a pattern of experience that if reliably and regularly repeated becomes a pattern of expectancy, or a template for future relationships.'

(Knox, 2011, page 39)

The metaphor of therapy as a dance wherein there is simultaneously a more deliberative process of making moves across the dance floor and a more intuitive trusting in the rhythm of the footwork. When we stop and reflect on our patterns of helping, it is an opportunity to see the link between our more explicit and chosen responses and those that automatically kick in, like the steps to a dance learnt years ago, even before we had the words with which to name and map it.

Doing with not doing to or for

The quality of doing the therapy *with* the client creates a sense of openly sharing responsibility. Ian Kerr in his extensive contribution to the development of the CAT approach pointed out the importance of 'doing with' (Ryle and Kerr, 2002, 2020). There will be time when the client feels therapy is being done to them. Or the therapist feels impelled to do the therapy for the client. There will be other times when for fear of doing for or doing to the client, the therapist does nothing at all. The therapist may not know what to do and feel helpless and stuck. Naturally enough, the times of doing for, or doing to, or not doing at all are likely to be animated by a transference pattern. As in the section below entitled the 'thirds rule' (page 99) the transference pressure may be coming from the client, the therapist, or the system in which they are located.

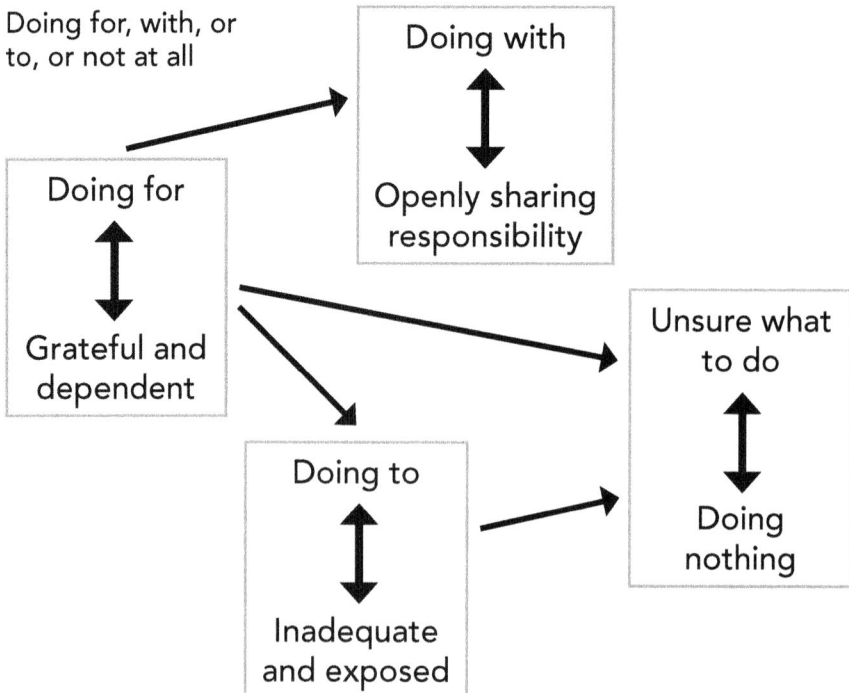

As in the map above, it is easy to do therapy *for* someone and elicit the feeling of **grateful dependence**. Or do therapy to someone in the manner of a medical treatment. The psychological risk is that a client then feels accused, exposed or de-skilled to the point of them having to be dependent on a wise other for change to be sustained. In response a client might retreat into not knowing what to do, feeling inadequate and waiting for direction. Any therapist will have moments of shimmering and shifting between these positions. It is right at times to do things for a client. It is appropriate for clients to ask for things to be done for them. It is equally right to take a 'doing to' stance on certain tasks. The point of thinking along these lines to see that the default position in the therapy, and in helping relationships, is the side-by-side 'doing with' position.

The map making triangle

Mapping is a very particular kind of enactment magnet. If therapist or client invest their feelings of criticism, admiration, compliance, contempt or rebellion onto the piece of paper in front of them and not directly onto each other, then a 'triangle of attention' ('me, you and the map') is created through which feelings and thoughts can more easily be approached and explored. Strong feelings or opinions are not entirely projected onto you, or introjected into me, but mediated by the therapy mapping space. There is less likelihood of extreme, therapy-threatening enactment of idealisation, blame or shame. Or at least there is more chance to work alongside these patterns when they arise. There is more chance with a map of naming powerful, therapy-threatening enactments in a non-judgemental and reality testing way. There is more chance to sit in the triangle of space between me, you and the tasks and goals of therapy and say 'I wonder where we are on the map' when what we mean is I wonder where are in the middle of all these feelings.

Then and now

When we are talking, we turn to a time 'then' in the past or in the future to make sense of what is happening now. The interplay between different times and different kinds of time is one of the richest parts of the arts in film, theatre and literature. Some of the patterns of repetition and the variations between past and present can be complex and the role of the process of mapping is to make it easier to travel within and between the time zones of our memories and stories. The past is always present in the therapy.

- It is a source of reference. If I look back, is this how I always did things?
- And it is a source of meaning. Why and am I like this? How did I respond then?

- And it is a source of repetition. Here I go again.

All of these are part of the texture of time in therapy. We cover up the past with dreams of the future. Mapping the past invites a need to map the future. How I would like or expect to be replaces how I was as the theme of map making.

The past is often present in ways that we don't immediately realise. Herein lies the rich and powerful processes of transference whether from the client or the therapist or the surrounding system.

The patterns of repetitions of our early relationships into the present situation have a timeless eternal quality. I learnt to be the way I am a long time ago and I have just kept it and carried it with me. One great value of mapping out a reciprocal role is that it can be talked through and tracked in a timeless way. It may have a resonance over several generations. Working with a map of a present story and the people in it may suddenly make a connection with an earlier relationship in life. The mapping process is always seeking to be a loose template. A space for analogies that link stories past, present and future. This loose template effect of the mapping activity is picked up at the back of the mind and other remembered times and places click into it or resonate with it. For more ways of thinking about time and place in therapy (see page 142 in the chapter on relational awareness). Also, time is the implicit theme to part three of the book as the beginning, middle and end of therapy is considered.

Transference awareness

A CAT and relational psychoanalytic approach to transference needs mapping to make it visible and workable therapeutically. Except for those readers familiar with a psychoanalytic perspective, the word transference may trigger wariness. What does it mean? What am I supposed to do with it? Is it a good thing or a bad thing? Whose transference is it?

Many therapists and therapy models acknowledge the importance of transference but then struggle to know what to do with it. This book views transference as one of the dimensions of relational awareness. As others, including Ryle (2006), have noted, in its normal manifestations it is everywhere and part of the fabric of all our interactions.

The first rule of transference is: don't mystify it. Transference is normal and affects every type of therapy. It can enhance the work of therapy. Transference is the carrying over into the relationship with the therapist of patterns of relating that are characteristic of difficult, or unresolved, patterns of relating from elsewhere. Transference is feelings on the move and sometimes in limbo. They are out there in the interpersonal and social space between us. They are looking for a home or an owner. The role of therapy is to offer these wandering feelings temporary housing and shelter in the therapy relationship and to work out where they came from and give them new meaning and direction.

The emphasis in working with transference is on 'we'. There is a legacy from psychoanalysis that carries over into other models such as CAT, whereby transference and the dynamics of the therapy relationship are discussed in a tone which is potentially accusative. In this manner the therapist might say, 'You are angry with me', or 'You are treating me like your father'. In process mapping the preferred voice and form of address is 'we'. Pointing to the map the compassionate and curious question is 'Can we explore what we are doing just now?'.

Mapping a therapeutic conversation takes us to the heart of psychoanalytic thinking. We create a transference-friendly space that is open to enactments and the carrying over of patterns of relating from one time, story and context to another. The following are the main components of transference that are brought alive in and played out through the therapy relationship.

Client transference
This is transference from the client into the therapy relationship with varying degrees of intensity and compulsion, or awareness. It involves pushing onto the therapy relationship and into the therapist (projecting) one or both ends of a reciprocal role. It is an unconscious process on the part of the client which may be unsettling, gratifying, or disturbing. An example is Silvia eliciting from the therapist the obliging and striving reciprocation to her demanding role. The force behind transference is a search to make a relationship visible and real and to see an orchestration of a familiar pattern. It is always a snag in CAT terms because it seeks relational awareness but defends against it at the same time.

Therapist transference
These come from the therapist's ways of relating, with varying degrees of intensity, compulsion and awareness, similarly to the client as in the definition above. Silvia also wanted to be the one who was striving and worrying in response to a demanding person and the efforts (experienced as demanding) of the therapist felt like a step in that direction. The therapist was both likely to try hard and not see a demanding side in his personal disposition and therefore in his personal transference.

Elicited counter-transference responses
Pushed onto and/or pulled from the therapist by the force of the client's transferences (see detailed example below of where is the anger). Equally the therapist's personal response may be pulled by what the client is eliciting. As in the tangle between demanding and obliging reciprocal roles with Silvia and the therapist it is a mix of transference, countertransference, and personal transference from the therapist.

The configuration of these transference patterns may be coloured by professional roles. (Freud and the early Freudians assumed the therapist would have analysed all his or her transferences and would only be a blank screen, or open space for the client's projections). Currently, it is more accepted that both client and therapist will have their patterns of transference playing out in the therapy room. The challenge for the therapist is to sort out the personal transference stemming exclusively from him or her, and the elicited counter-transference coming from the client but being felt by the therapist, as below. The privileged position and special duty of the therapist is to see the snag they are being pulled into by the client and make moves to map it out side-by-side with curiosity and compassion as something we 'might be doing just now which we can learn from and avoid.

Push and pull of system and professional responses

These are entangled in the expectations of the therapy and its limits of time and purpose. In this context the idea of the 'thirds' rule can be a helpful guide (see page 99). It is likely that one third of what is going on is coming from the client, one third coming from the therapist personally and one third from the model. For example, the client may be feeling forlorn and wanting to be looked after but expecting to be rejected. The therapist may be wanting to be caring and kind and reciprocate by looking after the client and denying the risk of rejection that the client feels. Meanwhile the system in the name of the manager may be putting pressure on the therapist or helper to limit the work and bring it to a close which would activate the client's expectation of rejection and destroy their feeling of being looked after. In using the idea of reciprocal roles such complex orchestrations can be better opened-up and understood and made visible with a process map.

Top and bottom of the reciprocal role

Transference in therapy could be by projecting into and/or identifying with the bottom end of the reciprocal role or identifying with and reciprocating through the top end of the reciprocal role. For example, Ryle (2006) describes:

- **An identifying counter transference:** such as one in which therapist feels sympathy for and solidarity with the hurt or harmed 'bottom end' of a key role in the client's development. This is the more likely response from any helper to the more 'wounded child' end of the reciprocal role. For example, for the therapist to say to Silvia 'your mother was so demanding and conditionally loving'. Whilst such a response is normal, to unreservedly respond or collude like this might miss the transference dynamic. The client needs to see their own internal version of the top end of a harmful or abusive reciprocal role to be able to change and awareness of this depends upon awareness of, and friendliness to, the transference dynamics. As in discovering the hidden scorn from her father, we need to map out and sit with the orchestration of childhood roles and relationships.

- **A reciprocating transference:** would respond to the client consciously or unconsciously from the top end of the reciprocal role or be perceived as doing so by the client. Therapists may be more reluctant to see their part in this. For example, the caring therapist may be reluctant to admit the service demands to end help is going to feel rejecting by the client.

All the above
All of the above play in and off each other in good or bad orchestrations, linking patterns from the past to events in the present and the tone and feel of the therapy. The value of such awareness is in accord with the rich heritage of psychoanalytic practice in all its varieties. If the interplay of an unconscious pattern in the therapy can be named and sincerely owned, it can then be linked to unresolved powerful childhood patterns. This helps in strengthening self-awareness, relational awareness and integrity. CAT goes further than some psychoanalytic approaches in linking such transference awareness work to the problem-solving patterns and personal development of the client through activities such as mapping and writing. On a personal note I cannot conceive how to work with the, often, complex dynamics of transference without a shared map and mapping relationship as a guide.

Mapping transference – 'where is the anger dance'

In this illustration of transference (as a form of projective identification), it is important to think of the emotions as being as much in the relationship as in the person. Remember transference is feelings in limbo in search of a home. The aim is to name the dance first without blaming or shaming the dancer. In the dance someone is feeling anger but does not want to know it or show it. The feared effect of anger or reciprocation to anger is also hidden or dissociated. It cannot be named because it cannot be thought, and it cannot be felt explicitly because it cannot be thought. But the anger is in the air and in the relational space between the two people.

To enter in this complex but all too common process let's imagine an insightful client saying the following long quote.

> 'I am afraid to feel angry because it feels dangerous and will bring out other feelings of fear and guilt. To protect myself from directly experiencing the anger, I act as if the anger is in you. The anger is there but it is not mine. In fact, I would happily go so far as to say it is nothing to do with me. I transfer (which is to say project) the anger on to you (mildly/intensely or tightly/loosely) and then - whatever you do back - I will read anger into it. Even if you are very nice to me, or you ignore me, I will think that anger is behind whatever you are doing. I might reciprocate in various ways to

your anger by identifying with it by being sympathetic, by being critical, by being a bystander. I might identify with 'your' anger as it allows me to have a manageable dose of the anger without having responsibility for it. All these variations of procedures for identifying with 'your' anger (you might be getting angry by now anyway) are my reciprocating or identifying transference. Depending on the intensity, tightness and direction of the projection, I must hide my feelings, for fear of 'your' anger.

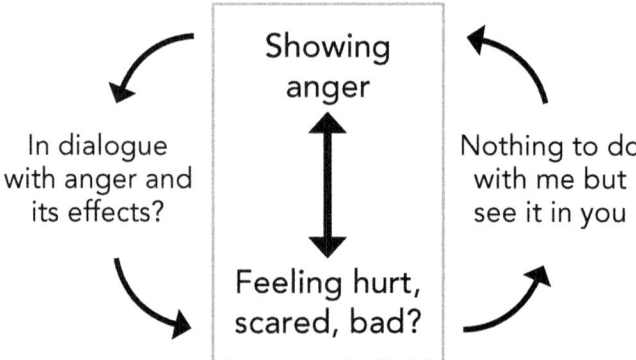

The whole angry interaction described above is a form of projective identification from the client. The therapeutic potential is that the therapist can tolerate and understand the projection of the anger. It needs a transference-friendly climate in the room that can regulate the dose of transference such that it can be noticed, named and negotiated. The capacity to do this will vary with the therapy model, the therapy setting and therapist. It is helped by freshly and freely mapping out what might be going on as a sequence of reciprocal roles. If we can make the interaction visible and less intense, we can begin to negotiate with it in ways that allow us to shimmer and hover, with ownership of anger, and the orchestra of emotions around it. Such dynamic and restorative work is too complex to manage without the helping hand of processing transference with a map.

In the best of ways, we use each other to discover, heal and repair our difficult emotions. Philip Bromberg puts it like this.

> '*I offered the view that the mind's fundamental ability to shift between different self-states without losing self-continuity makes it possible for someone to use another's self-states as part of their own. I suggested that this process of self-state borrowing can also manifest itself within and between a reader and an author and is what makes certain authors not just an author but your author.*'

(Bromberg, 1998, page 169)

Early learning stories

A good way to learn about transference, short of having your own psychodynamic or transference-focused therapy such as CAT, is to work with a partner to map out a school story that each of you remember from around the age of seven, eight or nine years old. It needs to be a story that you are happy to share and remember. As you tell the story over a ten-minute period your partner sits beside you and maps out the key words and joins in (conversational mapping style) to get hold of the key relationships and patterns of interaction in the story. Every so often, you recap with each other how the story telling is going using the map as a source of reference. When the map is complete and the early learning story is brought back to life, it is very common to see a pattern in the story that is still in play today. The school story may be very different to current events but the pattern on the map is the same for both. The mechanism of transference is revealed through this process.

The 'thirds rule'

When working with complex feelings which are entangled in the therapy relationship there is a risk of all the responsibility being loaded onto the client or taken on by the therapist. Or equally it may be placed on the system. Put simply in the face of complex dynamics and unresolved stories someone or something must take the blame and have the responsibility. The idea of the one third rule came up from working therapeutically with groups and using mapping in reflective practice with teams. The rule challenges us not put all the blame on the system or on the client or on ourselves. It is likely to be a mix of these and something arising from the relationships and interactions between people, treatment and settings. It is never exactly one third me, one third you and one third the system but it is not far off that in many cases. Having the idea in mind helps work against the natural tendency to totalise feelings of blame and guilt all in one direction. Instead we should wonder at the relational dynamics at play.

The working together checklist[1]

Working together with the tools, tasks and transferences of therapy needs an ability to mix and match the qualities of relating listed below. They are qualities that are looked for and shared between therapist and client within themselves and with each other. Hopefully, the therapist will have the awareness and training to lead the way but often the client will be the one

---

1. In running a course for ten years for supervisor training we evolved this checklist of skills in working together therapeutically. It has gone through many iterations in consultation with trainees. An earlier version was developed with Jane Stephens for which many thanks.

List of qualities we are doing or not doing	Rate 0-5 stars	
	Just now	Overall
1. Inviting, initiating, engaging, accepting		
2. Listening, noting, recapping, negotiating		
3. Receiving, holding, containing, waiting and pacing		
4. Feeling with, empathy for, participating		
5. Playing, expressing, improvising, allowing mess		
6. Voicing, exploring, trying out, challenging, discovering		
7. Being real, immediate, brave, honest and vulnerable		
8. Gathering, picturing, integrating linking, sorting		
9. Repeating, replaying and reliving patterns of interaction		
10. Staying in role, setting limits, maintaining boundaries		
11. Ending, feeling loss, moving on, looking ahead		
12. Wondering, playing, going beyond, transcending, imagining		

who shifts between responses or sees a gap to be filled. The more versatile the movement in and out of these qualities of relating on the list the more likely that relationally aware therapy and an alliance around the transference is taking place. It may help in reflecting on progress in a therapy to go through the list alone or together.

Patterns to notice, name and negotiate

In therapy we can find ourselves caught up in patterns of relating that need noticing, naming, and negotiating to work well together. Each of the following items are talking points for deeper discussion. There are no correct behaviours or good answers. What matters is a compassionate discussion led by curiosity. The list can help us talk about our immediate experience inside a therapy or helping relationship which is easy to neglect or bypass. It can help build a transference friendly approach. Any of the items on the list can be mapped out.

1. We hold back and miss out for fear of being too involved.
2. We want approval but are afraid to ask for fear of criticism or lack of response.

3. We might avoid being challenging and assertive for fear of being too much.
4. We are being open and sincere which builds trust and confidence.
5. We are not shy of talking about getting things wrong or being disappointed.
6. We keep quiet or just agree, when we don't understand, for fear of looking stupid.
7. We share pride and delight when something good happens.
8. We think it would be okay to be vulnerable and stuck sometimes.
9. We can be too serious and not allow ourselves to play with ideas.
10. We would like one of us to be more assertive but fear being controlling or directive.

A relational ethics of working together

Process mapping brings an ethical awareness of working together therapeutically. All models of therapy and all the supporting professions have codes of ethics and standards of professional practice. These elaborate on the original medical oath to do no harm. Ethical practice is self-evidently important. However, there is a tendency to view the code of ethics as a dutiful requirement rather than a living and breathing dynamic in the therapy. As if only bad and flawed people are unethical whereas it might be more relationally aware to think that we are all at risk of losing sight of ethical practice despite our best intentions. This is especially true when a key mechanism of therapeutic change is the interpersonal relationship between therapist and client.

The requirement is to keep professional boundaries and be aware of threats to these boundaries. Working self-consciously with patterns of relating is always going to test professional and personal boundaries. The under-involved therapist (what am I hiding from?) needs to be as aware of the ethical framework as much as the over-involved therapist (where are we being led?). Therapists need to talk to each other about their vulnerabilities, their mistakes, their dislikes and their idealisations. They need to reference these against the ethical requirements of their professional body and approach but equally they need to use their own personal judgement. The relational demands can be intense. How much do we care? How much should we care? How much should we intrude? How much have we got to give? How much are we missing?

In any therapy there will be moments of transference driven enactment that potentially challenges the ethical framework. Occasionally these will be flagrant and need supervision and investigation but more routinely they will be unsettling and confusing and need supervision and negotiation to recognise, apologise for and repair them. Good and bad practice need disentangling, without practitioners being overly defensive. Being sensitive to the risks is good for safe practice and is good for positive therapeutic practice.

Conclusions

The difference between conversational mapping in general as described in **Chapter 1** and the process mapping described in this chapter is that mapping the therapy process is a conversation about us in the therapy relationship. Mapping as a process makes the push and pull of the relationship more visible. As one client said, 'when we are talking about the map, we are also talking about the therapy'. The early sketching together is giving birth to something other than words on paper. It is gently teaching, a therapeutic attitude. The mapping process becomes a proxy for the therapy process.

Mapping the process in the room depends on and grows from skills in conversational, relationship and narrative mapping detailed in the preceding chapters. From a conversational mapping point of view, it is a conversation about us. From a relationship mapping perspective, the relationship in the room will carry elements of and links to ways of relating in the past and current everyday life for both client and therapist. Being able to map how we are relating right now will bring added life to all the other ways of mapping. From a narrative mapping point of view, it is the story of 'our' therapy relationship.

Chapter 5: Learning to map and talk

Introduction

This chapter offers guidance and exercises on how to learn to map in the various ways described so far in the book. It describes mindful mapping as a daily practice. It picks up on themes common to training in this approach such as mapper anxiety and speed supervision. There is a list of prompt questions that can help with the process of mapping.

Mindful mapping: ten minutes daily practice

Once a day take some time to sit down with pen and paper and have some private thinking time for yourself. Mapping takes time to become skilled in. Just like learning to play the piano or learning to drive, it requires some practice but once achieved can operate in the background. While mapping with friends and colleagues is one obvious way of practicing, mapping alone can be a resource for self-reflection. Here are some notes on what to do.

- Find some private time and space to sit at a table or with a drawing pad on your knee.

- Reflect on what has been going on for you that could be mapped out and reviewed. Perhaps a moment or an incident will come to mind in which you played a role or witnessed.

- If nothing comes to mind, then make a list at the side of the paper of some of the routine events of the day from brushing teeth to making phone calls. Put down some of the 'doing words' that come to mind as your stance in relation to these activities such as hurrying, patient, frustrated.

- Choose one that interests you and start where it starts, which is to say, map on paper the words that highlight what you recall.

- Put contrasting lines of action (doing), impact (feeling) and response (managing or coping) in different 'spread out' places on the paper. Use the template below to tease out hopes and fears, what you wanted, really, really wanted, what you achieved and didn't want and where you hid or got stuck. If you are mapping something that mostly involved others you are mapping from their point of view.

- You may be thinking, as you map, that it was you, or others, doing the doing, or both.

- As you put down the doing and feeling words you may add to them to enrich them or 'colour them in' with more detailed adverbs.
- Keep in mind that the words on paper are showing the links but are like pieces of the jigsaw puzzle waiting for you to 'free associate' further links to add as steps towards some narrative coherence.
- The test of these few minutes of mapping is: does it help you reflect? Do you make connections? Do you see another point of view? Does the link between the actions and the feelings make sense?
- Don't evaluate the quality of the map but the quality of the inner dialogue you are having with yourself.
- You can stop mapping as soon as your thoughts are flowing. Follow your own feelings and memories as they arise. Very quickly you may make a link that otherwise would not occur to you.
- Before you finish with one sketch go around it again with your pen or finger and see if any new connections come up. Circle words that matter, add lines and arrows where you see links.

'Hide and seek with hopes and fears'

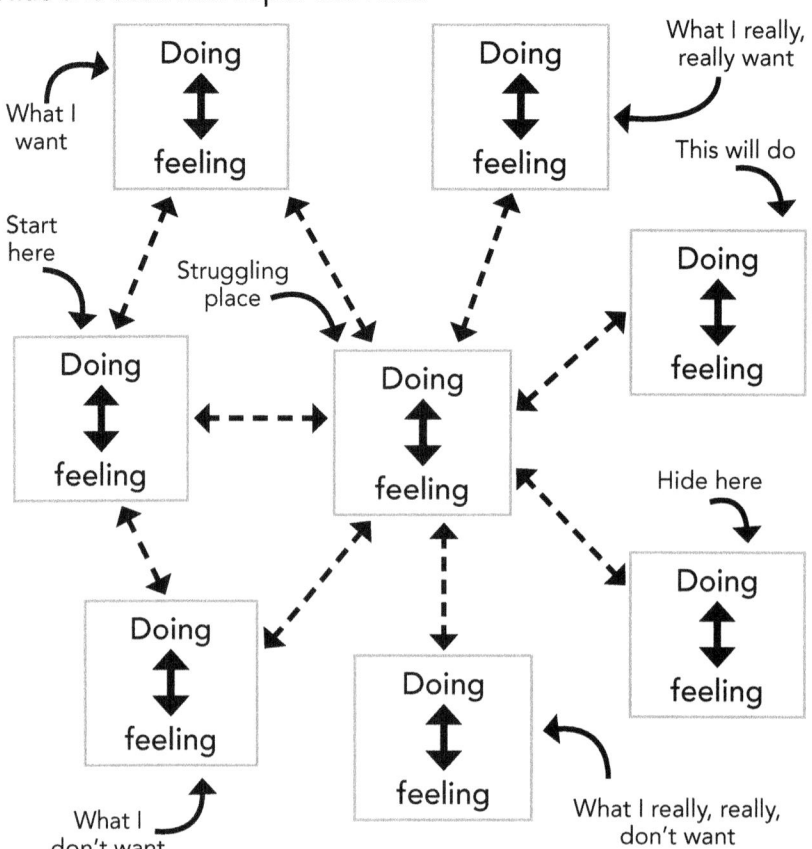

- If you have time it will serve well to write a sentence or two in the form of a short 'note to self' summarising what you have got from the map.
- Keep the map somewhere safe. Or if it is too personal, and has done its reflective work, dispose of it.
- The gain you are looking for in doing this routinely is a gain in mapping skills, and motivation to use mapping, but also in spotting patterns of interaction within you, and between you and others, when you are not mapping. The overall gain is an increase in relational awareness of how your life is orchestrated and re orchestrated moment to moment by you and others and the society around you.

Mapper anxiety

Anxiety is to be expected when learning to map given the unscripted, uncertain, and open process. 'Mapper anxiety' arises from the conflict between wanting to show competence and get the mapping right and wanting to work openly together with moments of mess and uncertainty. Mapper anxiety is partly like the anxiety which accompanies learning any new skill. However, another part of mapper anxiety for the professional person is a pressure to be expert to know what is going on. The best response to this anxiety is to tolerate it and mitigate it by reaching out to the client or the group that is being facilitated by mapping and assume that the process of mapping can only be as good as the partnership it generates. In this sense mapper anxiety needs to be reframed as a 'collaboration' anxiety not being able to find the right pace or pathway to mapping side-by-side. It was Bion (1961) who reportedly said if there are not two anxious people in the therapy room then therapy is not happening.

Mapping can also be the vehicle for carrying and locating anxiety which may belong elsewhere. It is the anxiety about fulfilling a role. Can I be helpful? Will I understand? The push and pull of these general anxieties about the purpose and process of therapy may be more exposed when mapping but they can also be more fruitfully contained and expressed with the aid of map making relationship.

Finally, another part of mapper anxiety is fundamental to the whole process. The ideas of hovering, shimmering and constructive dithering have been introduced in **Chapter 1**. In brief this means tolerating the mixed feelings that are simultaneously in the air about a memory, a story or event. This goes in with the mixed feeling about being understood. Or feeling exposed on the edge of connecting new meanings across gaps in understanding.
A helpful map will bring hidden patterns into view and invite links that otherwise might not be made. When we are on the threshold of discovering something new there will always be ambivalence. This is the challenge of therapy and it is a healthy, shared source of anxiety.

Learning to notice, name and negotiate

An important element of therapy is to enable the client to both speak freely but also to notice both how they are speaking and what they are speaking about. This is the double dialogue of process and content. Noticing is the first step in developing reflective capacity. Our biggest problem is that when we notice something about ourselves linked to what we are speaking about, we feel a reaction such as delight, shame, doubt, or inferiority (or superiority). The noticing is coloured by regard to our self-image, or our expectations of what others, such as the therapist, will think. The aim in therapy with a map is to encourage an open, curious, and compassionate form of noticing that can consider how the words are chosen, feelings are named and described. These general qualities of therapy are the moments of hovering, shimmering and constructive dithering described earlier. Mapping as detailed in this book encourages them as a self-consciously shared experience.

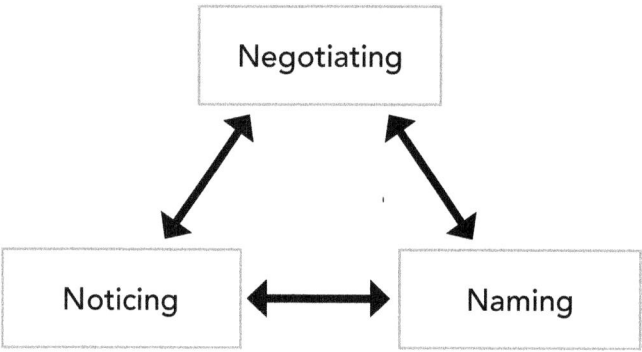

It is a dynamic three-way relationship whereby how we negotiate what we name changes what we notice. It invites reflection on what we give attention to. Do we need consciously directed attention to notice something? Or does that only come when it is named? For example, we may be out chatting on a summer's evening and though it is getting cooler and we are getting cold, we don't notice it until we shiver. In the flow of a therapy conversation we are listening with the aid of the mapping and recapping process to these 'shiver' moments as much as the words inked out on the paper. In retrospect we may realise our bodies, our senses, our unconscious ways of knowing may have been making sense of something for some time.

Managing the maps

The process of mapping needs to feel well managed around the edges. There may be several sketches. Some of these will have fragments of interactions on them, perhaps with a sentence or two summarising the emerging pattern.

All the bits of paper will be dated with initials or client code. Some will have a tag label of a phrase or sentence that captures what the map is of or about. Some maps are of the moment and just for the moment. They can be disposed of confidentially straight away. Agreeing to do this is, in itself, an interesting therapeutic choice. Indeed, the process of tidying up and sorting out which bits of mapping and writing are for keeping or copying is a part of the therapeutic process.

Most likely there will be one main map that is beginning to feel like it is capturing the focus of therapy. It might link sketches of childhood experience with sketches of the present. It might capture the main problem patterns. It might identity hopes and fears in the present and point to echoes in the past. There may be some exits, and alternative patterns marked on the map.

The working out of what to do with maps and writing is indicative of the ownership of the work of the therapy. The default position is that the therapist will take responsibility for keeping a folder of the work. The client may also develop a folder of work and should be encouraged to do so. This includes tidying, clarifying, and revisiting maps and writing through the therapy to maximise their ownership over their own journey.

For therapists in the public sector, their work system's rules will apply and if electronic records are being kept then brief summary notes of the mapping work, though not necessarily photos of the maps, can be kept. It is quite common for client and therapist to use their phones to photo maps made and writing that is drafted. In the 'Mapping tools Key' box below is a key to some of the ways that symbols can be used to improve the flow and visual effect of the map.

Mapping items from the psychotherapy file or the 'helper's dance list'

The psychotherapy file is a key tool in the development of cognitive analytic therapy. It is discussed more in **Chapter 9** on page 185. One way of practising mapping and getting to know CAT in a hands-on way through the psychotherapy file is to download and print off a copy. It is available at www.acat.me.uk or www.internationalcat.org/tools/file. Learn to use the psychotherapy file by making a map, either of a single item, or of the shift between one or more items, or combination of states, as listed at the end. Then write short summaries, no longer than a paragraph, of the pattern on the map. Mapping skills will develop, and the use of the file will become familiar. In addition, a relational way of working will be cultivated. Similarly download a copy of the 'helper's dance list' and pick out one or more items that might now or once did apply to you and see if you can map out the pattern. The list is available at www.mapandtalk.com

Chapter 5: Learning to map and talk

Mapping Tools Key

? = Unexplored area
→ = link between words
→→→ = sequence of links
E/R = either or dilemma
If/then = if this then that dilemma
↔ = reciprocal relationships
√ = word that comes up several stories
◯| = two positions that depend on each other reciprocally
◯ = circle round words that have a common feel
T = Trap
S = Snag

D = Dilemma
S-S = Self to self relationship
O-S = Other to self
S-O = Self to or pulled from others
∿ = line linking different positions, roles or states.
✦ = combination of unmanageable feelings derived from trauma
⚑ = flag up key role players in reciprocal roles e.g. Dad, job

Learning to be your own therapist

One goal is to hand over the role of therapist to the client. Ultimately the client knows more about their therapeutic needs and their ways of avoiding and sabotaging meeting these needs than the therapist can ever do. The client, moment by moment, is being guided to be their own therapist. By the end of therapy the role of therapist is handed over to the client. (As an aside this is a good argument for mixing individual and group CAT so that participants learn to be therapists for each other)

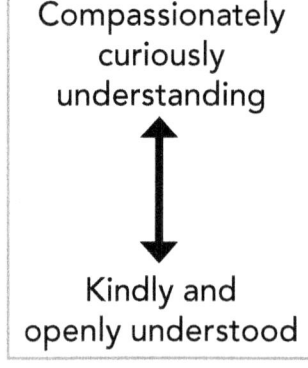

Compassionately curiously understanding
↕
Kindly and openly understood

In Ryle's (1994) paper therapy is described as a process of education and discovery together rather than persuasion. The aim is to help the client develop a therapeutic and compassionate attitude to themselves in their day-to-day lives, or at least in moments of reflection. This involves a reciprocal role relationship with one's self, one's problems and the world around which is open, curious, compassionate, and kind. Few of us had enough of this quality of relating in childhood (some had nothing like this). It can be summarised as constructively compassionately and carefully seeking shared understanding, and the reciprocal role is feeling cared for and understood in a kind and thoughtful way.

The common educational goal of all therapies by one means or another is developing space for this reciprocal role and seeing its presence in varying ways earlier on in life (a grandparent, a teacher, a hobby) and cultivating it through various procedures. One might say of CAT that it is not so much the education that is internalised but more the educational relationship.

In becoming their own therapist, the client is engaging the therapeutic relationship as a relationship they can author within themselves, with their problems and symptoms, with people that matter to them and the world around them. Therapy in this light is more like a course of learning and should end as soon as, but no sooner than, the client has learnt to be their own therapist.

Mapping my 'multiple me's'

This exercise can help make the interaction amongst the many sides of someone's life more visible. It is something that can be done alone, or with a partner, or in therapy. The client starts putting down on a big piece of paper, haphazardly about the page, all the key trigger words or images that capture the things going on in their life. Putting down trigger phrases may call out a response that takes them back in time or to another side of their life. The exercise is to keep paying attention to the reciprocations and responses to these trigger phrases. For example, putting down a phrase like 'coping with debts', might trigger a thought about living with no money as a child. Draw a line between these two and write on it a word or phrase that captures the link that is made. This might evoke a thought of being hard-done-by or self-reliant.

Or, as another example someone might put down the phrase 'going out on Fridays with friends' and this might trigger a thought about not being happy in their job during the rest of the week. The continuing call and response between people and things, is tracked as they fill the page. It may highlight a variety of reciprocations, each and all of which are parts of the plurality of ways of being that person. The process of response and reciprocation is kept in mind by saying yes to links that the person wants to explore and no thank you to links that are not wanted currently. In this process it is always important to be ready to tolerate and be curious about gaps in shared understanding, gaps in the process of remembering and gaps in self-knowledge.

As the variety of phrases (and sides to self) spreads out on the paper, draw lines linking them and add phrases that describe the relational qualities of such a link. You might find some of the responses are accusatory or critical or praising and triumphant. Others may be tender, or shrugging off, or dismissive. Keep in mind the notion of a dialogue between people and ideas. Put a ring around those items that cluster. Reciprocal roles may begin to take shape as might some of the patterns connecting them. Come back to it after a few days and explore what you missed. Some things are kept out of dialogue or get only the faintest call and response. Others are quite dominant. The aim is to get into a dialogue with the different sides of your life and how they shape your life-space now. They may show connections between ideas and people or between different periods of your life.

The 'learning to map' point of the exercise, as well as being personally engaging, is to see that key words spread out on paper already set in motion links and patterns of feeling, thinking and relating. Awareness of the simplicity and power of the exercise can help work in this way with clients. It can serve as an early mapping activity in a CAT therapy bringing up disavowed feelings or pointing to aspects that might be chosen to be kept out of dialogue for the time being. It may serve as a stepping-stone to a more typical reciprocal role diagram and help to describe desired, chronically endured, dissociated, and dreaded states. See also life story maps and multiple self-state maps on page 182 and letters to part of me on page 122.

Speed supervision

Mapping is best learnt in a form of speed supervision (Potter, 2014) whereby lots of quick and messy mapping is done in changing pairs to get a hands-on sense of the potential of the technique and the remarkable way we can draw out patterns of understanding from the most messy and ill-conceived maps.

Speed supervision is based on mapping and talking with one supervisor for ten minutes and then taking a jointly mapped out summary of the conversation to a second supervisor to elaborate further for another ten minutes before reporting back to the first person for five or ten minutes. It needs a group (eight to twenty in number) of supervisees willing to take turns in supervising and being supervised, an hour or two of time, tables to work at, plenty of A3 paper and pens and a facilitator experienced in teaching and managing the application of cognitive analytic therapy (CAT) maps in this way. The focus of the supervision starts with a specific moment or issue and the push and pull of factors affecting it. These ten steps help scaffold and contain the experience of speed supervision.

1. **See it being done:** like most shared activity – cooking, sport, dancing – it helps to see it being done before having a go. Speed supervision groups need a facilitator and the first job is to demonstrate mapping and talking with a colleague or willing participant.
2. **Be among others:** making a map and talking with others around seems to be contagious, and each pair senses the general mood of engagement, curiosity and openness and applies it to themselves.
3. **Allocate roles:** get in pairs, sit side-by-side, allocate roles and make introductions, work out who is the teller of the story or supervisee and who is the map maker – the one who mostly puts pen to paper and takes

the role of active listener or supervisor. They will reverse roles later when the whole exercise is repeated.

4. **Think of a moment or situation needing supervision:** the person taking the role of supervisee thinks of a recent moment in their work which they would value discussing. It is useful to focus in on the detail as it is very likely that the map of the moment will generalise to other stories and the wider situation.

5. **Start talking and start mapping:** As the supervisee begins describing what happened (how they and others felt; what they saw or assumed would happen), the other person maps out the key words (circling the important ones, putting similar ones closer together and the different or opposing ones far apart). The mapping is no more than a rough sketch of the links between key positions, feelings, events, and ideas underlying the discussion. It provides a scaffolding to track and develop a shared understanding as they talk. It fosters a different form and quality of listening which keeps more than one narrative thread in dialogue at the same time. It encourages empathy and perspective taking.

6. **The facilitator** goes about watching the work in progress (a bit like a primary school teacher) or joins in if there are odd numbers. They are ready to step in to help if people are getting stuck or not staying with the task. After ten minutes the facilitator calls them to halt, allows a minute to tidy up the maps a little and say thank you to each other for the work they have briefly done together. This is the cue for the one who has been in the supervisor role, and been holding the lead responsibility for making the map, to give the map as a gift to the one who has been supervised who then stands up and moves round clockwise to the next available supervisor.

7. **In the second pairing** and the second round of speed supervision, the person seeking supervision retells the same story but this time with the aid of the map and with the recent experience in mind. The supervisee is now in a subtly different dialogue with themselves. As they retell the story, it will be three stories interwoven: the story of the work situation and the story of the last ten minutes of supervision with the map and the story of the immediate moment of being in the process of giving a new account. The map comes alive with new perspectives and might be modified with additions. The activity invites responsibility and ownership of ideas. It tempts the person to be in a shimmering or hovering dialogue with themselves and their work rather than closing off to a rehearsed position or narrowing down to one issue.

8. **After a further ten minutes**, the facilitator as time keeper gently but firmly brings the pairs to a stop, invites them to spend a minute reviewing how they have done, to say thank you and goodbye, and go back with their map and any additions to the first person who supervised them.

9. **The final ten minutes back with the first person involves** looking at the diagram together and discussing any new developments. The supervision pair go over the diagram and review what has been learnt or understood so far. It can be useful at this point to talk about what might be taken away from the supervision experience or what might be patterns to focus on as a way of improving recognition or finding ways of changing.
10. **Reviewing the exercise in the big group is the final step. It requires** making it clear that soon the exercise will be repeated, reversing the roles of supervisee and supervisor in the pairs. This general time for review is important for hearing different experiences of the speed supervision and indicating that there is no one way of doing it. It may be useful to further demonstrate the mapping and talking process. Key issues may be to stress the need to let go of perfectionist or controlling and expert tendencies. At the end of the general discussion it can work to invite the pairs to review their experience for a further few minutes. Over the years a measure of relational awareness (RAM) and relational mapping experience has been developed and both are available at www.mapandtalk.com/ram

Finally, the whole process is repeated with the initial roles of supervisee and supervisor being reversed. Each round takes twenty-five to thirty minutes depending on the timekeeper and the size of the group and wider allocation of time. It is important to pace things so that there can be group discussion. The focus of the group discussion may move between lessons in and about the content of the supervision, the process of supervision or the skill in mapping.

Three-way mapping exercise

One variation on speed supervision is the following three-way mapping exercise. It is a very tangible way of linking the mapping of stories and mapping the process in the therapy room. One person describes their problems or case material, one person is helping by mapping the story as therapist or supervisor and one person is watching and making a process map of the conversation as it unfolds. The one mapping the problems is making a narrative map of the story being told. The one mapping the process is tracking the changing twists and turns of the session in a chain of reciprocal roles. After ten minutes the mapper recaps their understanding of the story being told by the first person telling the story. The third person in the process observing role shares their map and thoughts of how the discussion went. All three people then review the benefits and challenges of working with two kinds of mapping as a step to integrating the process with the content. It is a rich exercise in building awareness of how easy it is for content to swamp process, which is to say what the story is about dominates attention and distracts it from how the story is being told, shared and given meaning. By holding the different focuses of attention of the two kinds of mapping there is an open space to see the interplay between content and process.

Prompt questions to aid map and talk

The following questions highlight the conversational process of mapping and the way in which simple questions can help movement between topics and positions. Mapping is designed as a minimally intrusive process helping the flow and movement of thought, feeling and discussion in different directions.

Prompts to start the mapping

- What words describe working well together?
- What words describe when things are going wrong?
- What adverbs would bring that verb alive?
- What words describe the way things are avoided?
- What is the ideal place on the map, the stuck place, the feared place?
- Where is there a continuous struggle between success and failure on the map?
- Where is the hidden or forgotten place on the map?

Prompt questions to link words on the map

- Which of these words act together? (circle them as you ask)
- How does this word link to that word? (pointing to the words)
- When here what kind of awareness is there? (put one hand on each place)
- What is the hidden feeling word behind that word?
- Is there is no link between these two words? (draw a line to mark the gap)
- Is there a sequence of words that make these links into a pattern?

Questions to help reflect on the process

- What feelings does that word arouse?
- Is there a pattern emerging?
- Are we talking about things in the best way?
- Are we talking about what matters?
- Where are you/we on the map?
- What is the messiest part of the map?
- What is the clearest part of the map?
- Do we need to make a map of how we are working together right now?

Conclusion

The focus of this chapter has been on learning to map. The actual experience is always messier, and more disorderly than the kinds of descriptions offered in these pages. The skill of mapping comes from routine practice. There are links to training in the process of mapping both online and face-to-face at www.mapandtalk.com/events there are details of training in Cognitive Analytic Therapy at various levels from introductory onwards at www.acat.me.uk/training and www.internationalcat.org. The latter has links to national associations and training programmes in different countries.

Chapter 6: Writing and the therapeutic voice

Introduction

This chapter describes the therapeutic use of writing and the voice in combination. There are many ways of combining these activities and the reader who gives them a try will find variations of their own. One aim of the chapter is to encourage a willingness to experiment with forms of writing, speaking, and voicing alongside the process of mapping and talking. The chapter concludes with a map of one of the world's most popular poems and lessons from poetry in the way we work with the written and spoken word in therapy.

Writing therapeutically reviewed

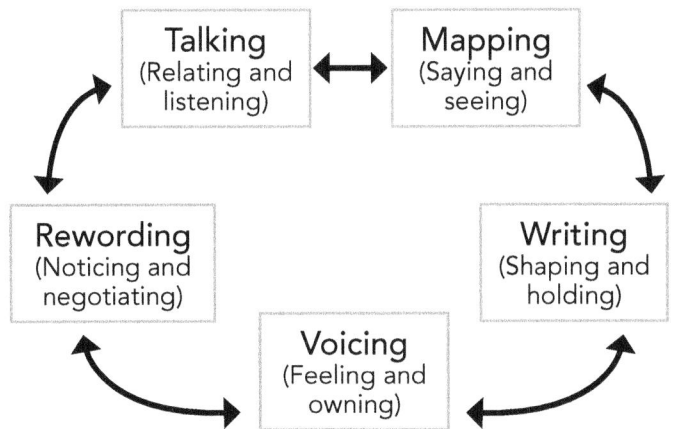

The focus of therapy with a map has been the spreading out of words on paper in a non-linear way. The aim has been to hover and shimmer between contrasting and conflicting ideas and emotions with the map as the scaffolding or frame. It is a mutually creative process as depicted in the above diagram showing the flow from talking to mapping, to writing, voicing and rewording. Voicing is the emotional gateway between brain and body, head and heart, self and other, individual and society. When, where, how and why we dare open our mouths and give our voices their freedom is the key to therapeutic healing and understanding.

In the evolution of the modern mind, the process of writing by hand with pen and paper is one of our most recent and most versatile forms of communicating. We might doubt our ancestors could foresee the impact it would have on the workings of trade, ideas and governance. It has greatly enhanced the second 'brain' of culture and society. It may now be a dying or specialist art. And yet we have barely begun exploring its creative potential. It is timely for the therapist to explore creativity in its therapeutic use.

Writing consumes a fair amount of the time of therapists. There are referral letters and court reports. Most therapist keep process notes, whether paper or electronic, and make entries into records of one kind or other. Training as a therapist involves writing up case notes and case studies. As indicated by Forrester (2016) writing up client's stories as cases is central to psychoanalysis. He puts the question as to whether truth is superseded by eloquence for example in the power of Freud's case studies. Writing notes is an analogical space where the therapy with the client can be replayed and worked out off stage. There is the question from literary theory of the reliable narrator (Booth, 1991). Is the therapist writing notes to show evidence of a record of work done in case of scrutiny? Do we write longer notes when we are feeling vulnerable? Or do we hide our anxieties from the potential scrutiny of a colleague by not noting something in the hope it goes unnoticed? Does the writing help discover or impose an order on what is being processed? Does our writing change when we are disappointed with the client or admiring of them? For the client what personal or creative writing are they doing?

Alongside case studies is diary keeping in the form of more personally reflective notes. There is an element in diary keeping of writing for self-discovery. This has the spontaneity akin to mapping and has echoes of journaling and other forms of expressive writing. These have been widely explored in various approaches to psychotherapy and counselling (Bolton et al, 2004; Pennebaker, 2016). Such writing might greatly help the therapy and is best judged as private to the client or the therapist.

Exploratory writing needs to be fast and spontaneous and without memory or desire. One CAT therapist (Ceara Geoghegan, personal communication) succinctly described her reflective writing as 'flow and edit'. In that sense the layering of levels of reflection through exploratory writing is a means of building insight. We write for ten minutes. Read through what we have written and then write specific reflections on that. We read through again and then write even more specific reflections on our reflections. It is the writer's equivalent of recapping with the map. The spontaneous flow and the thoughtful edit need each other.

Writing of this kind is enriched by reading back to self. It should feel free of editorial scrutiny. Or rather, as Freud (1912) brilliantly discovered (in encouraging free association), that it is in the hesitations and the censorship of thoughts that the important relational and transference dynamics are revealed. Such writing should include a stream of thought without regard to whom it is being addressed. This may only be clear as it is being read out. The second or third reading of a piece of spontaneous writing may bring new connections about the content and the process of writing it. However once written and out there the ideas and feelings may feel worth cherishing. For fear of leaving something lying around a quick way of storing such writing and symbolically keeping it in mind is to photograph it with a phone and then dispose of the paper copy.

Some therapists keep notes with the writing of the reformulation letter in mind. To do this in the freshest way it makes sense to write a sentence or a paragraph as it occurs, straight away in the manner of a letter to the client as if a component of the final product. This can be done side-by-side with the client or on reflection soon after the session while the feelings and resonance with key words is still fresh. Such writing has other functions which are richly explored in the therapy literature (Bolton, 2004).

The cognitive analytic letter writing tradition

Therapeutic writing in CAT, such as the reformulation and goodbye letters, are considered in detail in Part 3 of this book. Here their curious and accidental development is reflected upon as an example of the creative and organic development of innovations in therapy. Before there was the current version of a CAT reformulation letter there was a prose description in the first-person pronoun of the client. It was written empathically by the therapist and summarised the link between current problematic patterns and their origins in early relationships.

Before this there were simple weekly rating sheets which contained a brief description of the target problems and the patterns which support them. These were no more than a sentence long. For example: 'You want to be loved but fear making demands so opt for a quiet life which leaves you being ignored and makes you angry which you are sure, if you express it, will confirm you as unlovable'. Such single sentence formulations were powerful in their directness and brevity. They were readily negotiated and owned or disowned by the client. However, they begged the question; from where or whom did you learn this pattern?

Annalee Curran, the first chair of the Association of Cognitive Analytic Therapy, remembers the steps towards a full prose description of the reformulation process. Annalee describes scribbling on the single rating sheet a tiny worded summary of the origins of current problem patterns. The shared wording of such patterns led to a need for more open and extensive writing that could be discussed and revised in the session. Annalee remembers that in one early supervision group someone used a separate sheet of paper to write out both the target problem on the rating sheet and the history behind it. Someone else then said you had better add a sentence about how it might show up in the therapy relationship. This sheet quickly grew into a description, written by the therapist for the client, but in the first-person voice of the client. The therapeutic benefit of reading out and revising this prose description together was soon apparent. It was not long before this was supplemented by a goodbye letter reviewing the work of the therapy.

In that the therapist was doing the writing for the client, it then became the convention to write it as an interpersonal letter from the therapist to the client. There are challenges in the address of the voicing whichever way it is done. If written by the therapist writing as the client, it might feel patronising. If written as an interpersonal address from therapist to client, it might feel accusing, as if, I the therapist, know more about you than you do. The happy medium is a multi-voiced co-created letter, where the use of 'we' is as prevalent as the use of 'you' or 'me'. It is a dialogic letter with the process of composition designed to be as therapeutic as the final act of reading it out and handing it over.

The risk in the move to a lengthier and more elaborate letter was that it takes more effort to get right, hold in mind and work through. Clients can be grateful for, fulfilled by, or in awe of the effort involved in creating two or three sides of typed script. It may feel like guess work or interpretation at times. It works best as a very early draft to bring thinking together. In such a case it needs to be addressing simultaneously what we did, what you said, how I felt, what they didn't do. Writing of this kind can stretch the therapist's resources and sometimes the effort is not born out by the reward. The value may be that it helps the therapist clarify their thoughts. Equally for clients, who have never been listened to, and whose thinking about themselves has never been valued, the experience of a written account of their thinking, their formulations and their past suffering and hopes for the future, can be deeply validating.

What matters is that the letter is centred on the target problem patterns that are the intended focus of therapy. The aim is to help the client be better at self-observation of the enactment of these patterns in their lives, both within themselves and with others. One step in this direction has been the proposal from Alison Jenaway (2011) for the client to write their own reformulation letter in response to that of the therapist. The methods of writing the reformulation letter is considered in detail in **Chapter 10** and the goodbye letters in **Chapter 11**.

In a recent article Mikael Leiman (2019) noted that self-observation around the focused description of one or two key patterns may be lost in the longer letter writing and the more complex maps and diagrams.

The reformulation letter is a vital part of the whole therapy. The mapping process can help develop a recognition of the patterns and their history and locate the evocative and memorable words and turns of phrase. The work of mapping and writing bits of understanding from the map can help bring attention to the relationship in the therapy room. With experience therapists will vary their approach according to the needs of the client and mix mapping and writing as fits the work before them.

The reformulation letter as a piece of writing has become the hall mark of CAT therapy but it is a big ask of therapist and client. It is part of the purpose of this chapter to look at whether the benefits of the reformulation letter and the therapy map can be prepared for, or sometimes appropriately substituted for by more modest acts of writing.

Whilst the emphasis in CAT has been on the reformulation letter as a product and as a guiding document for shaping the therapy, it has also always been a tool to draw attention to the working relationship and to help a therapeutic alliance develop. It is writing as a therapeutic process that is most in mind in the following section.

Therapeutic innovations in writing

Therapy with a map also means working side-by side creatively as client and therapist with pen and paper. It would be odd if such co-creativity did not also involve innovations in the use of writing. There are many situations during a therapy session when writing together can add another dimension to the therapy. This can work with either the therapist being the 'secretary' writing out the client's words. Or the client being the writer and being helped with phrasing and focus by the therapist. All the time the dynamics of the activity and the push and pull of transference patterns are as much the focus of attention as the material of the writing.

Innovation has involved a move away from writing or mapping as a product and giving more attention to writing and mapping as therapeutic tools in a live and interpersonal therapeutic process. Client and therapist can be side-by-side at a computer screen composing and editing or at a table writing with pen and paper.

In a presentation to the international CAT conference in Nottingham in 2017 a group of therapists presented a summary of innovations in writing now available in reformulation (Amleh *et al*, 2020). They introduced various ideas for in-session writing such as dear therapy letters, therapeutic sentences and templates for the reformulation letter. This was linked to the use of the voice therapeutically in writing. It feeds into and draws upon some the following suggestions for the active and collaborative use of writing that can supplement the work with a map.

Writing our patterns from the map

This involves a few sentences to fill out the words summarised on the map. The more linear flow of writing may make detailed connections, show feelings, or restore memories that otherwise would not come to mind. The writing can be done by the therapist in large font in the manner of a target pattern or the application of a pattern to a specific aspect of the client's current life. Reading out and checking over the writing as it is written gives it therapeutic immediacy, depth and ownership.

Writing a protective sentence

This is hold something recognised but not yet resolved. There are moments of first encounters with distress and vulnerability in therapy that can be held in mind with a protective sentence. Marie-Anne Bernardy has worked with this in her therapy (2020). The client or therapist writes it down on a piece of paper for the client to take away. The client then has it as a transitional link to the therapy. It offers something on paper to nurture a capacity for reflection when the distressing situation threatens to reoccur.

Similarly, a compassionate, perspective taking or validating sentence can be written out. Its strength is in its simplicity and its sense of shared ownership inside and outside the therapy. It is a token or reminder of the therapy. For example, 'When I am beginning to feel panicky, take a step back and reassure myself that I have coped with this so many times and nothing worse will happen'.

Kind words of acceptance

This is in relation to feelings of being stuck in the therapy, or recollections of a state of helplessness or powerlessness. In line with Marsha Linehan's (1993) idea of radical acceptance, it can be empowering to write down and read out words that are kind in the face of frustration, helplessness, or rage at a difficult situation. This can work to value just sitting with feelings of helplessness and not letting them slide into feeling useless in general. Or it can be validating to remember a moment of pride in achievement. For example. 'You did well, you trusted your own opinion and voice and that put you in a new relationship with your problems'.

Breakthrough moments

The pattern that produces a breakthrough is as important as the pattern behind a setback. Breakthrough moments are those moments in therapy of heightened awareness and attention when something has been sorted or understood. These are moments of seeing a way forward, seeing a perspective, and experimenting with the loosening and changing of a pattern. Writing a validating sentence or two to one's self is one part of staying with or harvesting these moments such that more meaning can subsequently be drawn from them.

Memorable juxtapositions

The process of mapping can generate some memorable phrases. They are often one that elicits a counter position such as 'out of the frying pan into the fire' or 'brilliant or doomed'. A map can be made up of nothing more than two strikingly contrasting phrases juxtaposed. 'Either I am flying, or I am stuck in the mud.' When the therapist is mapping such phrases, it should be noted down at opposing ends of the sheet of paper. They point to a dilemma with each option being a trap. Subsequently they can be therapeutically puzzled over to see what meanings lie around or beneath them. Or what second thoughts and feelings arise. One client called them front and back of t-shirt phrases. They can be a hook for a longer, more considered piece of in-session writing with deeper and more complex reflections.

Discovery writing

This is also called journaling and its key feature is writing as a means to be in an open dialogue with our thoughts and feelings. The emphasis on discovery is the quality of free association and not knowing what links, words and phrases are going to come up. It adds value to such writing to limit the writing time to no more than ten minutes, to write spontaneously and free from constraint of anyone judging what is written. There is additional value in reading it out in therapy, to yourself, or a trusted companion, and listening for the way the voicing of what is written changes.

Writing a paragraph for each pattern on the map

In drawing out a pattern of coping the following template can be a guide to thinking relationally by filling in the unique pattern in the dotted area.

> 'When feeling this...... I want ......or need...... and then appraise my options as..........., and end up with the belief or idea.........., which in consequence, take me to the role of feeling or doing the following...... Which helps .... and/or hinders as follows.....'

This links to the therapeutic use of writing and the idea of the target problem procedures in **Chapter 9** page 186. In the case of a childhood pattern being compulsively replayed in the present, there is scope to see if the relational context to the pattern has changed. Whereas as a child it felt shameful to cry, now it might not be how others would respond. The reciprocal roles written out in full prose form on paper can help achieve a clarity about the orchestration of patterns of response in the limiting world of childhood. It is easier to look the relational and emotional origins of powerful and harmful core beliefs in the eye if they are out on paper. It is easier to see different angles and see what is in the past. They may be part of a pattern that once learnt in relation to a powerful other person have now become second nature or part of identity and personality.

'Dear therapy' letters

This is an innovation that has elements of all of the above and offers stepping-stones to the larger task of the reformulation letter. The idea is to take opportunities to write a letter which is not to self or to the client but to the therapy. This is partly to take away the personal and direct form of address in the letter.

The 'dear therapy' letter can be a helpful and engaging way of looking at what is happening in the therapy room in the present. It is a way of fishing for hidden patterns or shaking the transference tree. For example, if the therapy is struggling, consider saying: 'let's stop for ten minutes and each write and read out a short letter to the therapy as it is for us just now'. Once written, the letters are read out in turn and used to discuss how they validate or point to ways of refocusing the therapy. It is likely to bring us into the present, democratise the relationship and help us negotiate the direction of therapy. Such letters can be very useful after a few sessions as a precursor to, and rehearsal for, the reformulation letter. They can also help at times in the middle of therapy when the focus is getting crowded with too much to do or the direction of therapy is feeling somewhat lost. A dear therapy letter could be agreed upon as homework.

A letter to a part of me in time or place

Similarly to a dear therapy letter, letters can be written to a specific moment or aspect of self. For example, one client described herself as coming from a family of 'hardened weary worriers' who never let up. Within a few minutes of saying the phrase, the client could not remember it and only by going over the note on the map between us could it be contemplated for its relational meaning. Such phrases, if noted and remembered can offer an opening to untangle and untie the knots of mixed feeling that have become too tied up in one state. The client wrote this short letter in the session to the hardened weary worriers phrase.

> *Dear hardened, weary worriers*
>
> *I am from generations of hard-working women. I was feeling bruised by your hardness but in retrospect now, as I look at the words and stay with them, I see there are good reasons for being hard mothers and grandmothers, because if you relaxed or softened you would not so easily survive. The snag was not in you but the world around you. You were weary with worry every day, but you could not let yourselves falter. It is easier to accept this in words out on paper than half-formulated inside me. Now I can see and say it, I can accept you lived as best that you could in the circumstances, and I can say that though your hardness limited and hurt me I can forgive you. I have gained in my career by carrying your hardness and stubbornness with me, but I have also in the easier times found softness.*

In this case, the hard and weary worrying was a state of mind that carried across generations. Just letting writing flow around the words opens a discussion of how they got condensed into one phrase and one thought. The family history of the phrase was mapped out which led to discussions of financial hardship in childhood and the class background of both parents. There did not seem enough opportunities to get work and yet the client's parents kept trying. The worrying was a response to feelings of shame and self-blame from within the extended family. We are the poor relatives – the hopeless ones. As, additional phrases, such as 'blamed as the hopeless ones' and phrases that were accusative like 'opportunities galore' got spread out on the map the worrying took on a new colour. It was not worrying just about money but also about shame.

The special feature of letters to part of me is that it is writing that is a directed or personally addressed form of writing. It is from someone to someone, something or somewhere. The power and art of the framing of the letter is in the precise linking of who it is from and to whom or what it is addressed. Am I writing from my heart or my teenage self? Am I writing from the day I was injured in an accident or from the exam room in secondary school? Or the birth of child? In the same instance of identifying where I am writing from there is the arc of 'who am I writing to?'. Am I writing to my future self, to a lost loved one, to the day I left home?

The hallmark of these letters is their handwritten, spontaneous, free associative and healing quality. At any point in the therapy something may stand out as a focus of address. Writing of this kind always brings transference in its wake. It links to the dialogue between different sides of me and multiple self-states (page 182)

> **Dear teenage years:** *I am writing to my wild teenage years but also in the wake of the letter I am writing to my parents.*
>
> **Dear broken leg:** *I am writing to my promising football career that was cut short when I broke a leg but also I am writing to give voice to my unvoiced sadness, not just of the loss of football hopes, but also because at the same time I lost my father when my parents divorced.*

'Dear homeland' letters

Another form of letter along the same lines are 'dear homeland' letters. These letters address childhood but not directly to home or family but the locality and the neighbourhood and its geography. Dear homeland letters highlight how many of us have migrated far away from a place of origin. Even if we have stayed 'at home' the place and time of childhood was very different to how it is now. The homeland letters are surprising in the dialogue they generate between local and cosmopolitan views and the feelings of transition, loss and return that they bring together. It is a form of indirect address in that by not going head-to-head with the past but addressing it indirectly, more feelings and memories come into a manageable focus. Try writing a spontaneous letter to a place you grew up: the street, the estate, the town centre, or surrounding hills etc. Some people have found it powerful to then write a letter back from the street, or country, or homeland place. A dialogue, and voices across the gaps and divides between past and present, is potentially discovered.

Writing for the therapeutic voice

We hear our voice with our own critical or sympathetic ear. More of us are self-conscious, shy, uncertain or critical of our voices. Being self-conscious is potentially an asset if it can help us listen to the emotional cadence of our own and others' voices as we speak. We know the imminent change in emotional response (happier, sadder, angrier) by change in tone and pitch of the voice.

When reading aloud we read too quickly. Or drift away from our feelings about what is being read. If the therapist does not feel for their voice, their words will never leave the page and reach the client. If the client doesn't experience the therapeutic importance of 'giving voice to their words' their words may connect cognitively but not emotionally. If the therapy is not 'voice friendly' the client and therapist will not know their voice enough to understand when it hesitates or races between noticing a feeling or idea and naming it. The emotional potential of the therapy may be limited. The challenge is to write with the voice in mind.

The tradition in CAT has been to read the reformulation and goodbye letters outloud. The attraction to the letter form in CAT was that it put the voice into the therapy. The reading out as a therapeutic mechanism can be overlooked in the face of the pressure to focus on the accuracy of the content.

Voicing

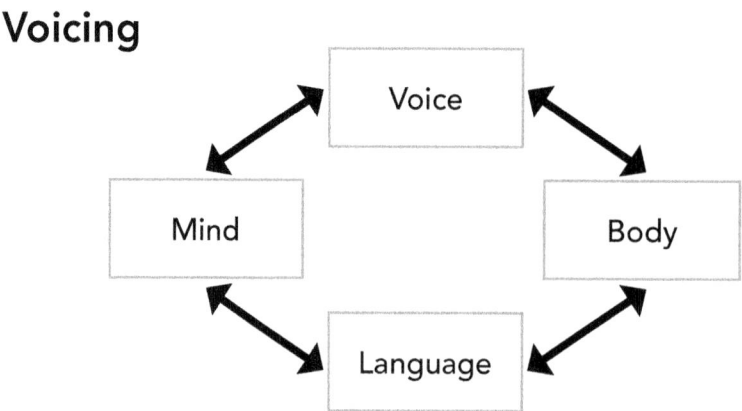

Giving voice to what has been written is another kind of therapeutic tool. The voice works as the gateway to sensory and communicative potentialities, with its sensitivity to context (am I entitled to speak?) to interpersonal relationships (how am I speaking and how are we listening?)

to the body and its sensory resources (can I hold it together to speak from my heart, with my head, with my breath?), with my identity (accent, social position, education and intelligence).

The voice speeds up and slows down, flows and hesitates, rises and falls in and out of dialogue with all that is within and around it. When we tell and re-tell stories of our life experiences, we are giving voice from a different position each time and with a different potential to remember and reconnect with cherished, disavowed or unformulated experiences. The voice vibrates with the feelings for and against this or that emotion or idea. Writing that is written to be voiced is different to writing that is not written with this purpose in mind. Reading out therapeutic writing offers an opportunity to be in contact with the interplay of what is written and how it is spoken. The voice may touch thoughts and feelings that lie beyond or beneath what is being read out. The voice may shimmer and hover over specific words, which in the moments of their expression have added power, resonance and therapeutic possibilities. It is always a good question to ask how reading out felt and which sentences or words were challenging or freeing.

When writing is read out by the therapist, it can have a different quality of voicing to that associated with the earlier therapeutic conversation. The voicing is more deliberate, more staged, has more of an 'addressing' quality. It is us giving voice to our understanding. It has a quality of 'me' self-consciously saying this to 'you' now. It is an invitation to the client to feel the emotions and ideas evoked by the writing in a different, more resonant and connected way. Often CAT therapists 'bypass' the exposure and anxiety of giving voice to what they have written and read in a more guarded professional tone as if only the verbal aspects of the voicing matter and the vocal aspects can be ignored.

The voicing of the letter is an invitation to re-vocalise; to hear familiar life experience in a different voice and to take the opportunity to reword, revisit and further 'reformulate' the reformulation. It is an act of bringing implicit knowing (Stern, 2010) to a more explicit and conscious level of knowing. This may overlap with bits of dissociated memory and emotion finding a place in the narrative of the reformulation. It brings the mapping and the writing alive in the room emotionally in a co-embodied, multi-sensory space of voicing, hearing and seeing words come alive and then linger in the memory.

How I hear myself is different to how I feel I am heard, which in turn is different again to how the listener hears me. The voice as depicted in the two-dimensional figure below is in and out of dialogue with an inner and outer hearing of the voice. Giving voice in a therapeutic way would have movement around the four quadrants. These are: top right: being in dialogue and voicing ideas and feelings outwardly with an interpersonal focus. Top left: being in dialogue with an inner voice or voices and being reflective. Bottom left: being thrown into a ruminative space where there are inner voices, but they seem out of dialogue with each other and poorly orchestrated or attuned. Bottom right: a kind of outward going voice that is hectoring or lecturing and 'talking at' because it is out of dialogue in the interpersonal or social spaces from which talking arises.

Writing out-loud mediates the inner voice outer voice dialogue

Geraldine's unexpected booming voice

Geraldine recalled a small detail of her usually mild-mannered and shy father. When answering the phone, he would give his number and say with an untypical boom in his voice 'To whom am I speaking?'. Her grandfather, her father's father, had been a very confident man with a superior and secure middle-class background of entitlement. Geraldine's father had much less confidence and lived and worked far away from the safe confines of this class heritage. Geraldine had inherited this quietness and a hidden social anxiety. She had grown up with a very different accent from another part of the country. With a mixed feeling of tears and astonishment she added that she could never answer the phone like that. We proposed writing and reading out a short sentence or two to this fleeting, booming voice as a fragment of relating from another time and place. We decided she might try imitating her father's booming voice just as a small experiment as she read out her letter. Her letter read as follows.

> *'Dear booming voice*
>
> *When announcing yourself to strangers, you are making a show. You don't need to shout. It is okay to be polite and mild. You will still be heard. You will still have things of value to say.'*

Geraldine was surprised when she read this out loud. She immediately added in writing, speaking as she wrote.

> *'I realise now that you are a pretender. A voice from another age. My dad, and I after him, have carried a sense of shame that we cannot give out the booming voice. Though we speak well in mild and sensible ways, we carry the 'shouty' sense of that booming voice as somehow superior. Loud is confident and quiet is shy. But no, I think not. I will boom now just for once to let the boom out, [Geraldine booms and smiles] but I will no longer feel that I have to speak in the invisible shadow of the greater worth and esteem which is claimed by the booming voice. You [speaking of her voice] of course, will not shut up. There will always be loud people who, through joy or entitlement, have a need to boom. But I won't carry that script in my head anymore. And I will speak with my dad about it and be curious about his view of booming voices among his class and generation of men and women and those of his father.'*

At times subsequently in the sessions, Geraldine mimicked her grandfather's booming and upper-class voice. As her voice boomed in a somewhat mocking way it freed up another voice which was the overlooked abandoned part of her saying 'Listen to me, let's stop the cover up'. Some weeks later Geraldine reported a surprising phenomenon. She felt she was generally talking louder and more assertively as if her voice and accent had been freed up.

Wandering lonely as a cloud

The interplay between mapping, writing and giving voice to words on paper is most evident in poetry. Why poetry and not prose? According to the novelist Ali Smith, because in poetry we expect more of the words (2012). It is this expectation of words to be held, in high, deep and playful regard that is needed in therapy. Perhaps a definition of poetry might be words written down and then voiced with reflective, sincere and serious intent. By this definition, this book about therapy with a map is a book about the art of poetry with a map.

The Nobel Prize winning poet Seamus Heaney (1995, page 9), in talking of redress of poetry cites the journal of the Greek poet Seferis (1974) saying of 'poetry being strong enough to help'. It can be the job of the therapist and the client to make words 'strong enough to help'. In his book, Heaney explores the richness of words and the struggle for a poetic imagination that make them work. As psychotherapists we don't seek the power and elegance of poetry but sometimes, we find it, unexpectedly in the words that come from the conversation between therapist and client. The use of words in therapy does not aim to be poetic in the grand sense. Nor does it seek eloquent turns of phrase, but as client and therapist work together with the raw language of experience there are moments of poetic elevation of words that are made rich by their local ownership in that moment. They are as good as the tears, smiles, cringes, and insight that come from them. Indeed because of the unique, personally crafted intimacy of the experience of words in therapy they may often exceed the power of poetry.

> ### I wandered Lonely as a Cloud by William Wordsworth
>
> I wondered **lonely** as a cloud
> That floats on high o'er vales and hills,
> When all at once I saw a **crowd**,
> A host, of golden daffodils;
> Beside the lake, beneath the trees,
> Fluttering and **dancing** in the breeze.
>
> Continuous as the stars that shine,
> And twinkle on the milky way,
> They **stretched** in never-ending line
> Along the margin of a bay;
> Ten thousand saw I at a glance,
> **Tossing their heads in sprightly dance.**
>
> The waves beside them danced; but they
> Out-did the sparkling waves in glee;
> A poet could **not but be** gay,
> In such a jocund company;
> I gazed – and gazed – but **little thought**
> What **wealth** the show to me had brought;
>
> For oft, when on my couch I lie
> In **vacant or in pensive mood**,
> They flash upon that **inward eye**
> Which is the bliss of solitude;
> And then my heart with pleasure fills,
> And **dances** with the daffodils.

To conclude this chapter there are lessons, hopefully, in mapping one of the world's most popular poems (Wordsworth, 1807) and seeing what its mix of inner and outer voice tells us about words and writing in therapy. Wordsworth's poem has a lightness and simplicity. Yet it contains more subtlety and complexity than it is credited for as an evocation of the interplay between imagination, memory and activity linked to the transference and return of feelings. His poetic workspace is the same as his reflective space. He is wandering both on foot and in mind. He is lonely and perhaps self-absorbed until an external sight takes him out of himself.

Incidentally, his original first line according to legend was, 'I wandered lonely as a cow'. But his sister Dorothy suggested that would not ring out so well and offered the idea of wandering lonely as a cloud instead. The cloud image allows him to project on to it a solitude (perhaps not the same for the cow) and a perspective from where beauty can be seen.

On the map below, the poem moves us from lonely (1) to a desired place of floating on high (2). This is what the narrator wants, because it lifts and connects him to what he really, really wants which is to be dancing

Chapter 6: Writing and the therapeutic voice

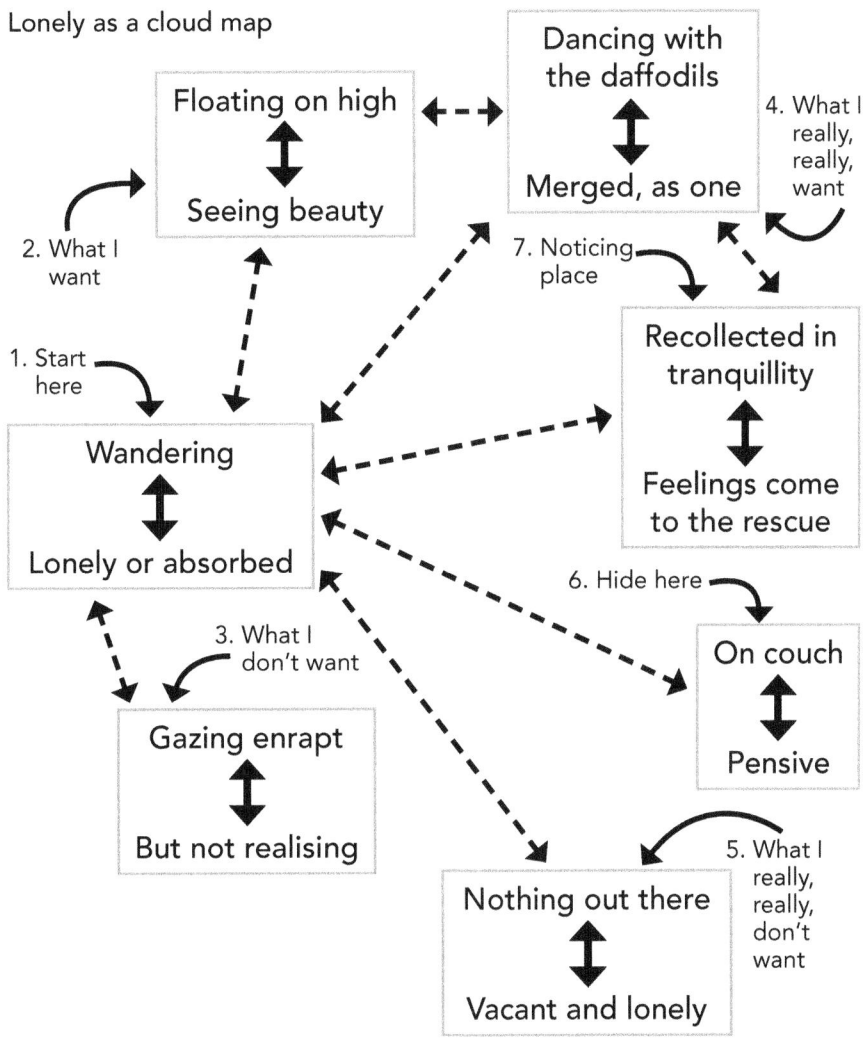

Lonely as a cloud map

with the daffodils (4). This evokes a feeling of merger and in the image of 'dancing', the daffodils are personified (tossing their heads in sprightly dance). He could lose his loneliness and be part of the crowd. Is this an image of embodied merger and of being at one with nature? Or psychological merger and being at one with life and people dancing? It is a shimmering point of ambiguity. Such an idealised and dream place may be more rapture than reflection and risks him gazing and enrapt but not realising what he wants (3 on the map). What the poem shows Wordsworth doesn't want is 'gazing but with little thought' (or awareness) of what was happening inside him in a more enduring way. This might be the unwanted and feared place that comes with wandering alone (5 on the map). Without the activity of poetic work with words and the hovering and shimmering of the poet's imagination, Wordsworth would not have had the tools to externalise his inward eye. The wandering is a wandering in dialogue between an inner and outer world. In the language of contemporary neuroscience, he is re-consolidating his memories to good effect.

Being vacant and feeling pensive (6 on the map) has its risks and its value. For Wordsworth the key point (and for us his educational moment) comes with the:

> *'for oft, when on my couch I lie in vacant or in pensive mood, they flash upon that inward eye which is the bliss of solitude. And then my heart with pleasure fills, and dances with the daffodils.'*

Here in the poem and in the recollection, he is moving to his dream place point (4) from point (6) on the map (vacant and pensive), being perhaps at risk of nothing being out there (5). The map highlights his connection of two states simultaneously orchestrated in his mind: the desired joining with the daffodils in memory whilst recollecting in tranquillity. To quote Wordsworth directly from the prelude:

> *'Poetry is the spontaneous overflow of powerful feelings: it takes its origin from emotion recollected in tranquillity: the emotion is contemplated till, by a species of reaction, the tranquillity gradually disappears, and an emotion, kindred to that which was before the subject of contemplation is gradually produced, and does itself exist in the mind.'* (Wordsworth, 1802).

Conclusion

This chapter has touched on a big topic and reached across from the world of therapy to the many forms of creative, poetic and literary writing. Writing in contemporary society is in transition. Handwriting and the frequent 'postal' letter writing of a generation or two ago may well be a dying art. In its place, a brand-new distinction has arisen between formal writing of the school room, the academy and the office and the informal writing of emails and social media. McCulloch, (2019) in her recent book exploring the new rules of language arising from the internet, celebrates this new informal style of language. She argues that it has a surprising richness and nuance. What this chapter has sought to address is not so much the style of the written word, whether formal or informal, old fashioned or modern but the work of uncovering and discovering the meanings and feelings between the lines and in the spaces between words. It is through this deconstructive and re-orchestrating activity that relational awareness and a healing narrative can find its therapeutic voice.

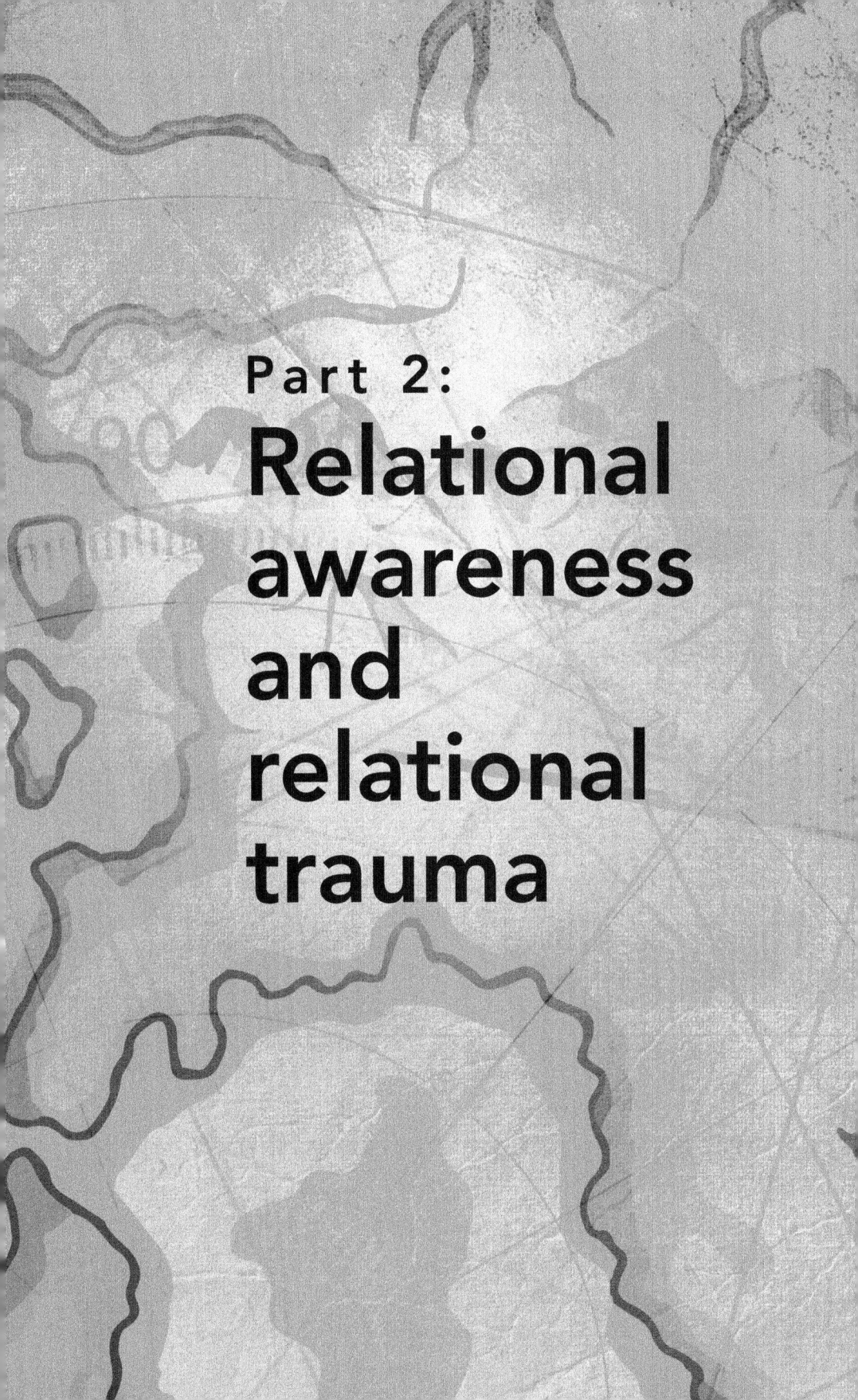

Part 2:
Relational awareness and relational trauma

Chapter 7: Relational awareness

'Only connect! That was the whole of her sermon. Only connect the prose and the passion, and both will be exalted, and human love will be seen at its height.'

(E.M. Forster, Howards End)

Introduction

This chapter introduces and defines relational awareness as the imaginative and intellectual framework for the activities and methods described in this book. It explores some of the qualities and dimensions of relational awareness and introduces a grid of nine elements from which a questionnaire has been derived (Potter & Bonfield, 2020). The chapter explores the idea of relational awareness as a response to next decade of the 21st century. The author is aware that for some readers the mix of ideas will be unusual, and they are evidence of the start of an ongoing journey of enquiry into a new paradigm rather than its completion. The chapter introduces the idea of 'chronotopes', 'the four stories of therapy', 'gappiness' and the impact of a narcissistic use of ideas in our private and public forums for shared thinking. It links these concepts to the way we go in and out of awareness with our bodies, minds, and each other. It gives a central role to the immediacy of interpersonal awareness and concludes that relational awareness is something we might develop through the varieties of shared activity described in this book.

What is relational awareness?

Relational awareness is an active, dynamic intelligence that we co-create. It is an orchestration within, between and around us of qualities of intellectual, emotional, expressive, and assertive engagement. The main qualities such as hovering, shimmering, mapping, and storying, rewording and restorying, processing and negotiating have already been discussed in part one of the book and are applied in part three of the book.

It is the awareness we yearn for, in trying to orchestrate and manage ourselves in the twenty first century individually and collectively. Trauma based on interpersonal abuse and neglect and traumatising social systems based on gender, ethnicity and 'race', generation, ability, or class can limit, damage, restrict or deny our relational awareness.

The qualities of relational awareness work simultaneously in and across many dimensions of interaction which can be clustered as follows:

- **Within us** we have a world of mind, brain, and sensory connections in and through our bodies, along with the memories and stories we carry forward from the past into the present and the future. It is a dynamic world inside us with the push and pull of unconscious and conscious processes acting intentionally and automatically.
- **Between us** we have the space of an interpersonal encounter through shared behaviour, role reciprocations and the orchestration of meeting person-to-person in search of meaning, validation, and care.
- **Around us** we have the groups, the joint activity of language, the shared stories, power dynamics, cultures, and institutions of society in a simultaneously local and global context.

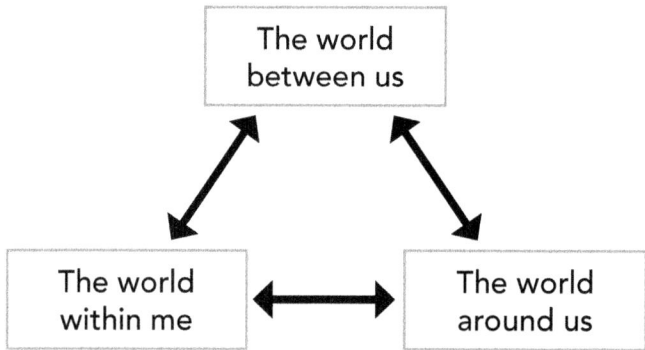

There is another world which might be framed as the world beyond us with its connotations of collective, artistic, transpersonal, and spiritual meaning. This is a topic for consideration by others but there is a quality of relational awareness that is more than the sum of its parts. It offers a dialogic imagination and points to a pragmatic philosophy emerging from the world of psychotherapy. It draws upon the interplay of ideas from psychoanalysis and other models of psychotherapy, infant and child development, social psychology, cultural theory, neurosciences and the wider post-modern and feminist perspectives of the humanities, contemporary philosophy, and politics. The intellectual challenge of these influences can be held in view and given a practical voice with the process of mapping and the conceptual tools of cognitive analytic therapy.

Qualities and dimensions of relational awareness

In the preceding chapters some of the qualities that bring about relational awareness in the process of mapping have been described. These are now restated in summary form in interaction with the dimensions of relating internally, interpersonally, and contextually summarised above. The interaction between these qualities and dimensions creates a grid of nine elements of relational awareness. We have used this grid as a template for developing a measure of relational awareness consisting of eighteen items (www.mapandtalk.com/ram/).

The table below shows the nine elements inside the grid. They make up a 'palette' of colours or 'orchestra' of instruments for being in dialogue with relational awareness. They imply movement and connection between points of view and positions. They support the ability to be in the space between self and others, inner and outer awareness, closed and open thinking. They allow an interplay of time and place between past, present, and future.

A table of the main dimensions of relational awareness and the key qualities that help in its development, orchestration and expression	Dimensions of relational awareness		
	Within us: internal self	Between us: interpersonal	Around us: contextually
Hover and think Making links, seeing patterns or finding gaps between thoughts, beliefs and ideas, between picture and detail, now and then, here and there.	1. Reflection and self understanding	2. Dialogue and debate in sharing ideas	3. Curiosity about values, systems and societies
Shimmer and feel Tolerating the anxiety of mixed emotions, hopes and fears, uncertainty and ambivalence; with empathy, sincerity, commitment, courage and sensitivity.	4. Ambivalence and authenticity	5. Empathy and involvement	6. Feel the diversity and power of us and them
Participate and do By choosing to do things together sharing responsibility and leadership with self-control and expression that is in role and enabling.	7. Managing self in relation to a given role and task	8. Co-creative work and activity	9. Consenting to ways of leading, being led and organised

(Left axis label: Qualities of relational awareness)

1. **Reflection and self-understanding:** being able to hold in mind the orchestration of different ideas, life stories and points of view with compassion and curiosity. Seeing links between past, present and future, exercising personal judgement.

2. **Dialogue and debate in sharing ideas:** ability to negotiate and navigate each other's views and beliefs and find a relationship to fit mutual tasks and duties and create new ways of working as much as valuing what is already being done. Helping each other author and own life stories.
3. **Curiosity about values systems and societies:** The resources, capacity and support to keep making sense of the complex world around in the context of diverse lives, cultures, fixed and changing structures of social and economic power. Ability to discern ideology and propaganda from thought and theory and see self and others in and out of role in society.
4. **Ambivalence and Authenticity:** A capacity to accept, assert and value truths within us whilst tolerating ambivalence and the simultaneous presence of contrasting and conflicting feelings. A sensitivity to the push and pull of feelings with others through their resonance within us.
5. **Empathy and Involvement:** The capacity to share involvement and interact appropriately with each other's feelings without being swayed into one state of mind for long unless it is jointly chosen and navigated. A feeling for changes in mood and moment, harmony and disorder. A curiosity about the retelling and the re-orchestration of each other's life stories.
6. **Feel the diversity and power of us and them:** A feeling for and openness to cultures and society in a global context wherein multi-local and universal forces and themes interact. Compassion and curiosity for what is felt to be fair and not fair based on the ability to put oneself in the shoes of others in the world without losing a personal identity or depriving others of a freedom of identity. A sense of the historical imprint of patterns of oppression on the life of groups and institutions across generations.
7. **Managing self in relation to a given role and task:** The ability to choose and act, to do things with a mix of self-restraint and expression in a way that orchestrates the parts, the roles and the whole sense of you as a person. Knowing when to hide self behind a role or allow self to manage by appearances.
8. **Co-creative work and activity:** being flexible and inventive and able to act together to make and sustain a working relationship. Recognising and valuing the process and story of this shared labour and productivity. Being inventive and delighting in seeing something jointly achieved and mutually attributed.
9. **Consenting to ways of leading, being led and organised:** knowledge of leadership and organisational roles, and how to participate as leader or follower in and out of role, formally or informally. A capacity for a democracy of ideas and feelings in co-operation with others and systems in society. A culture of mutual aid in helping each other contribute and be part of a wider organisation.

The continuously changing orchestration and re-orchestration of these nine elements in one specific time and place, role and state of mind is the business of relational awareness. Some are out of awareness, or orchestrated in partial, fragmented, or dissociated ways arising from individual and collective trauma or neglect. The shared activity of mapping helps see the limiting and enabling orchestrations of the past and present and bring the qualities of relational awareness to help understand and heal them.

A talent for the 21st century

Different eras evoke different kinds of consciousness. There may have been a time some generations ago when our relationships; within, between and around us, were simpler and more direct. We were born, lived our allotted life span within one culture and society, with one status and role in a one-dimensional world. Of course, there were dislocations and times when the world was turned upside down and migrations led to new perspectives. But on the whole, we had less need of the mediation of relational awareness because there was no place called outside that we could look in from. There was mostly only one horizon. Now, we are faced with complexities evoked by the nine elements of relational awareness in the table above. They are harder to hold in mind alone without shared thinking and the resources of mapping. We are all mediators now in a global world of multiple horizons. We swap between looking in as outsiders and looking out as insiders whilst also doing the same with our inner lives. Such conversations with ourselves and the world around us are the baby steps in orchestrating our lives. We are very dependent upon the openness of the parenting, schooling, and informal and institutional culture around us. Even at the best it is a complex and anxious process. The closed and fixed horizons of the past are now offered cheaply and deceptively by pundits and politicians as a nostalgic and populist refuge from this new complexity.

Today's world is a multi-relational world. There is a basic shift in the power dynamics within and between cultures and societies. The end of western colonialism and patriarchy, the environmental crisis, changing life expectancy and increased freedom of intimate expression and self-discovery combine to create a more exposed, acutely self-conscious, or saturated sense of self. From one viewpoint, we are at the end of a grand narrative of patriarchy, progress and exploitation with its twists and turns between authoritarianism and exploitation, rebellion, and creativity. From another view, we are approaching the point where computers may outsmart us and either make us free of labour or redundant of role. From another view, climate change and climate denial on a global scale sum up our incapacity to be relationally aware beyond our immediate local world.

In the face of this complexity, we are in between eras. To borrow from Nietzsche: we are no longer, but not yet. No longer in denial, not yet woken. No longer ruled by patriarchy but not yet in an open, mutually enriching, pluralistic relationship with gendering and being gendered. We are no longer in an industrial but not yet in a post-industrial work culture. We are no longer in climate denial but not yet fully engaged. Or no longer locally tied to a monoculture, but not yet both local, multi-local and cosmopolitan. We are no longer governable within nations but not yet governed by stable and accountable, global institutions. This experience of being uncertain in transitional times shows up increasingly in the therapy room.

Philosophically our transitional situation finds helpful voices in aspects of post-modernism, feminism and theories of social justice and empowerment. Jane Flax (1990) in her marking out of the similarities and differences between psychoanalysis, feminism and post-modernism finds a world hovering between grand narratives. She offers a philosophical opening to the kind of dialogic and flexible thinking touched upon in this book. Flax argues that the transitional state of global societies: *'generates problems that some philosophies seem to acknowledge and confront better than others. In our time these problems include issues of self, gender, knowledge, and power. Certain philosophies best present and represent "our own time apprehended in thought". Like dreams, they allow us insight into the primary process of our age'* (Flax, 1990, page 14).

Flax draws upon psychoanalysis, feminist theories and postmodern philosophies as 'the modes of thought for transitional times'. Her words capture the multi-directional nature of the relational imagination we need. Since she wrote that we seem to be receding further from a capacity to measure up to her challenge.

Several decades before Flax, Karen Horney (1945), offered a framework free of Freud's oedipal conflict to look at how we negotiate a relationship within ourselves based on our awareness of our entanglement with others. In her work, she opened a bridge between psychoanalysis, feminism and humanistic psychology and an accessible relational language for the therapist and the client. Some decades later, Ruth Josselson (1995) gave a broad and integrative account of object relations theory and attachment theory. She takes the reader through the range of ways of navigating the interpersonal space between us. Her writing gave texture and a palette of needs and desires ranging from holding, yearning, inspiring to validation and embeddedness. Josselson offers an account that helps us see the multiple subtle ways we navigate a meeting of minds alongside a meeting of bodies in the earliest years of our lives. She locates the qualities of relational awareness in the interpersonal space between us.

In his final book *'To Have or To Be'* Eric Fromm (1978) draws together a lifetime's intellectual endeavour and clinical practice by setting two narratives of future life against each other. He writes of an alienating consumerist culture of 'having' been set against a culture, or social character of 'being'. For Fromm, being is what we might see as a relational and humanistic approach to life. He talks of needing a new frame or 'orientation' for living in this modern world before we destroy it. This orientation lies at the heart of our taken-for-granted identity or, as he calls it, our 'social character'. His book is concerned with mapping out the social and radical humanism of such an orientation. It needs a map of life that is founded upon an inner cohesion or integrity but also a willingness to discover and negotiate as the map evolves. Eric Fromm writes that:

'Without a map of our natural and social world – a picture of the world and of one's place in it that is structured and has inner cohesion – human beings would be confused and unable to act purposefully and consistently, for there would be no way of orienting oneself, of finding a fixed point that permits one to organise all the impressions that impinge on each individual. ……….. Even if the map is wrong, it fulfils its psychological function.'

(Fromm, Page 137)

This basic shift in orientation requires more time to map, negotiate and navigate than most of us have available. We need a primary forum to give it attention. Each age generates its own 'forum spaces' where ideas are exchanged and policed, rendered okay, ideological or subversive. The church, or the carnival was the forum space for medieval times. The school room or the shop floor was the forum space for the industrial age. The lab or the art room for the modern age. The therapy room is one of the forum spaces for the transitional age between local and global lives.

The Polish writer Olga Tokarczuk, on being awarded the Nobel Prize for 2018 at a delayed ceremony in 2019, gave this relational and narrative view of the world in her acceptance lecture.

'The world is a fabric we weave daily on the great looms of information, discussions, films, books, gossip, little anecdotes. Today the purview of these looms is enormous—thanks to the internet, almost everyone can take place in the process, taking responsibility and not, lovingly and hatefully, for better and for worse. When this story changes, so does the world. In this sense, the world is made of words.'

She writes about the struggle to write in the first person, to tell our own stories and not have them storied for us. Her acceptance speech is worth reading (Tokarczuk, 2019). She is saying that we need the relational and narrative imagination to live in the transitional space, to tolerate the ambivalence and negotiate the complexity. We long to simplify. We are vulnerable to the ideological simplifiers. Olga Tokarczuk goes on to say:

> 'We lack the language, we lack the points of view, the metaphors, the myths and new fables. Yet we do see frequent attempts to harness rusty, anachronistic narratives that cannot fit the future to imaginaries of the future, no doubt on the assumption that an old something is better than a new nothing, or trying in this way to deal with the limitations of our own horizons. In a word, we lack new ways of telling the story of the world.'

In this speech, Tokarczuk captures the uncertain, wide open transitional space. Jane Flax referred to this, Karen Horney sees us neurotically entangled in this space, and Eric Fromm proposes we now need new maps to find a new outlook. Ruth Josselson shows us the roots of an interpersonal imagination in our early years that needs honouring if we are to develop the relational awareness that will be strong enough to help. Tokarczuk gives voice to the challenge.

These representative writers and many, many more with their mix of psychoanalytic imagination, dialogism, humanism and social justice offer a framework for thinking and feeling together with a map that might help us find our way in life in the next decades of the 21st century.

We need help staying with the complexity without getting overwhelmed or lost. Can therapy with a map help? Can it play a role in helping us share our stories and find a renewed confidence in truth seeking? Can mapping and writing contribute to developing our talents for the twenty first century? Or at least finding out what those talents might be? An answer may be in the following sections.

Four stories

Relational awareness arises from the capacity to hold four kinds of therapeutic story telling open to and apart from each other. In bullet points these are introduced as:

- the formulation story (what is wrong?)
- the healing story (what will make me better?)
- the present story (what is happening in my life now?)
- and the past story (what were my earlier years like?).

These four stories can easily be merged, hijacked one by the other reducing their diversity of focus to one. For example, the meaning of the present story can be reduced to a repetition of patterns from the stories of the past. Or the healing story arises like a simple prescription from the formulation story. They need holding apart from, and open to each other like different kinds of paint on the painter's palette or different instruments in the composer's orchestration.

As summarised in the diagram below the different elements of storytelling and formulating can focus in different combinations. When a new client begins therapy, they tend to start with stories about the present. This may be a story of current distress or difficulty, or of personal hopes and fears. The process of formulation may bring about a focus on solving personal problems (top left quadrant in the diagram). Alongside it, may be a help seeking story also in the present about trying this or that remedy or no longer being able to cope in a familiar way. These stories of the present have their shape and characters. Practitioners of relational and cognitive therapies such as CAT map them out with reciprocal roles, schemas, and procedures and so forth. They can be micro stories of an incident or moment (let me tell you what happened) and/or scale-up to macro life stories (this is a story of who I am in our kind of world).

<u>Four stories:</u> if held apart and open to each other, can touch and trace the gaps in self-knowledge making a therapeutic and healing narrative.

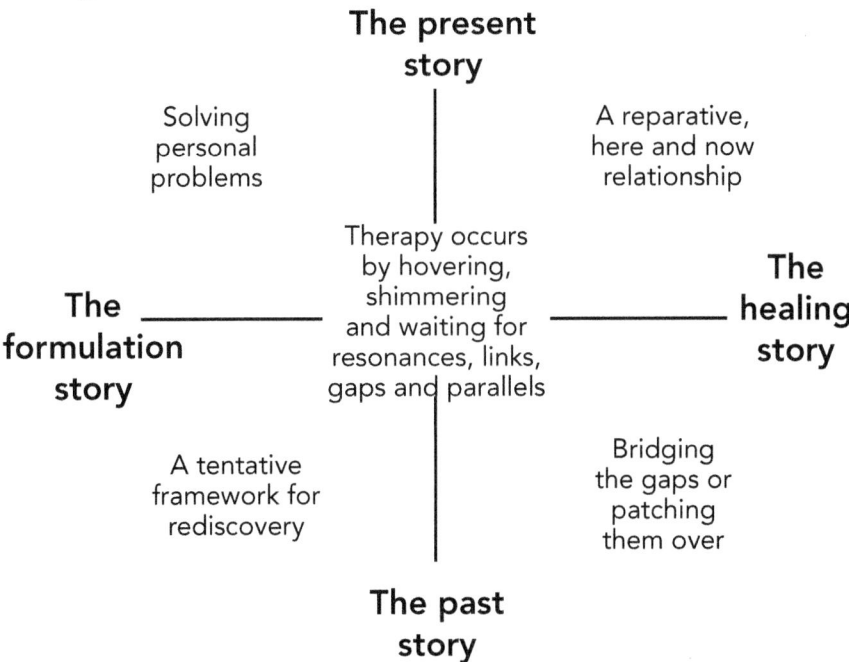

The client or therapist will turn attention at some point to the past and tell stories of the origin and formation of self. These stories also can be micro (the moment when my dad got arrested) or macro (the family's way life based on our religion). We listen to and map these stories and enable their fuller telling – often for the first time. In the process of doing this, we must be very careful not to simply assume that these stories carry in them the templates for the orchestration of life in the present. The past and the present are two distinct territories to be mapped out to see their unique orchestrations and patterns. Once we have them apart and in front of us, we should be mindful not to jump to conclusions. We must not fall into a psychoanalytic determinism that the patterns from stories in the past are the controlling and defining patterns of the present. That would be to colonise the client's unconscious with the therapist's templates.

As indicated in the diagram, the separation between past and present stories is on the vertical axis. There is a zone in the middle where they meet and as therapy develops a map of the interplay between past and present arises from waiting for resonances, links, and gaps to be remembered and voiced.

The horizontal axis distinguishes between the formulation or diagnostic story and the healing story. It is key to therapy to be clear that the formulation or diagnosis is not the treatment. Careful mapping and tracking of the stories now and then behind current difficulties can produce a good shared reformulation. This is the focus of the beginning of therapy as described in **Chapter 9**. But the reformulation is also setting out the lines of a treatment story, or healing narrative of how the process of recovery and change might take place. The healing narrative has an important component in and of itself. It may take on its own life and direction. Though anchored by the reformulation, it is a continuous process of reformulating and restorying. The end of therapy and the goodbye letters exchanged in the final sessions, as described in the final chapter of this book, are likely to be the true measure of a distinctive healing narrative linked to but apart from the reformulation story.

Clients as much as therapists might find this distinction between the four stories of therapy useful. Relational awareness is an attribute of being able to hover and shimmer in and among them.

Swimming with chronotopes and the times and places of our lives

Chronotope is Mikael Bakhtin's word. He was a young intellectual and classics' scholar at the time of the Russian revolution and miraculously survived the Stalinist purges. He lived into his seventies and throughout his life wrote about genres of writing and our relationship with language. He invites us into an open dialogue with literature, philosophy, and society without being tied to one time, one genre or one ideology. Bakhtin's ideas are interdisciplinary and open-ended. The reader with a philosophical leaning may find great clarification in the book on Bakhtin's work by Michael Holquist (Dialogism, 1990).

Chronotope is a wonderfully unsettling word. It joins 'Chronos', the Greek word for time, with 'topos', the word for space or place. In Greek mythology Chronos was the god of time and out of time came shape and a relationship with places. The idea of chronotope for Bakhtin was a device for seeing how we give locality, order and meaning to our sequences of experience and thereby shape them and gain a hold on them. Chronos, as the bringer of time, offers an orchestral awareness of past, present and future where before there was timelessness and chaos. Similarly, in our early development as toddlers we begin to order and share in orchestrations of time and place and map them in our memories. There are chronotopes of bath time, bedtime, nappy time, nursery time and cuddle time to mention a few and each is held and embodied differently. Before the infant can walk or talk, he or she is swimming among his or her small sea of baby chronotopes. It is from this mix of relational spaces that a narrative sense of self emerges. As one three-year-old said: 'In my house, I can sleep on my own now because I know where my family is'.

The idea of chronotopes helps us link the personal self and the collective world to our past, present, and future through a matrix of times and places. It is a device for thinking that frees our imagination and makes it relational.

Swimming through chronotopes is the capacity to live simultaneously in several times and places, with varying roles and ways of storying them. Our stories, or storying abilities, involve classifying one type of time and place (work) with another (home) and their associated qualities (good company, a boring evening, a trip away). Our memories guide us (this is one of those situations, I have been here before) and give us images and references to see what kind of time and place (chronotope) which we are in just now. A car journey might fit the 'road movie' chronotope or it might fit the 'school run' chronotope and while doing one we might imagine the other.

For Bakhtin, literature at different times in history had fixed ways of arranging the narrative sequences of time and place in comparison to the real time in the actual unfolding time of story. The narrative of time and place in a novel (and in the therapy room) breaks up and rearranges the actual sequence of events. Knowing how this is done is to have relational awareness of the chronotopes involved.

Bakhtin imagined that in the epic tales of ancient Greece there was an adventure chronotope and romance chronotopes with fixed rules for the shaping and sequencing of the story (see page 71 for the contrast between 'epic' and 'novelistic').

Here is an example. I am sitting on the underground train from Waterloo station to Stratford station in East London. I am in the time and space of the train. People all around me are in the same space and time as me but swimming in and out of their own chronotopes. To pass the time, I am reading the newspaper. A story about a pop star, not one from my generation. I am thinking of my time of music. Of earlier decades. The news story transports me to a memory of the era of punk music. Then I remember (why then?) I must buy some milk on the way home which triggers a memory of bottles of milk delivered to the door, childhood and my first home. I would love to swim deep into that memory and see and touch the milk bottles on the front doorstep. But it is a chronotope too far removed (from now and the present moment).

Most modern-day time is heavily institutionalised (or commodified as work time, leisure time, shopping time). The timetable is given to us and relatively fixed. Our chronotopic imagination is constrained. Even psychotherapy time is ritualised with its fifty-minute hour, its treatment protocols, its number of sessions prescribed by funding bodies. It is a challenge (or a relief), to live with the pressure of institutional time: the appointment to be kept, the other work to be done, the claims on time and space of peers and superiors. Time management is chronotope management.

It is a challenge to enter the local time of one session between client and therapist and leave the other chronotopes room to swim in and out. Most experienced therapists think they develop a knack for this. It has always been one of the central ideas of the humanistic tradition to give oneself wholeheartedly to the moment (Horney, 1946; Rogers, 1954; Stern 2004). It is well worth noticing when the surrounding weight of institutional time intrudes helpfully, or unhelpfully, on the, ideally free space of, therapy time.

It is a human achievement of the highest order to be 'swimming' (hovering and shimmering, delving and dithering) in and among the different and overlapping times and spaces of our lives. We cannot do it on our own. It helps to map and track the moments which we encounter to give them vitality and novelty.

Mind the gaps

It should be clear by now that relational awareness is neither a linear nor a smooth process. There are gaps in our stories, in our memories, and our skills in meeting our needs. These are gaps in our self-knowledge. They are gaps outside of time and place. These are gaps that are covered over and defended against. We sometimes live with them, as if they are not there. We do not know the un-lived life or the untold story. This aspect is explored further in considering the dissociative processes of trauma in the next chapter.

In her inventive and original book on Shakespeare's plays, Emma Smith (2019) talks of 'gappiness' which is to say, for example, the quality of gaps in our knowledge of Hamlet's motives, or the gaps in the stories around the characters in *A Midsummer Night's Dream*. In introducing the idea of gappiness not so much as a lack of something but as a quality, Emma Smith argues for an idea which is of relevance to therapy as much as to theatre. Her intention is to invite the reader into a new more open relationship with Shakespeare's work. It involves having a feeling for gaps. Smith starts by saying the playwright gives us so little about Hamlet's backstory. We think of the play as sacred and daunting literature (trapped in the chronotope of 'English Lit.' and teenage schooldays). We don't appreciate how much each director and each troop of actors fills the gaps by bringing context and colour to the story of the play. As the audience we too bring a capacity to fill in the gaps with our imagination. Or we compound the gaps in the meaning of the play with our gaps in responding. Smith turns our longing for narrative coherence on its head. We need to be open to the gaps and tolerate them. A good story is not a tidied story. Relational awareness is enhanced by our capacity to carry our gaps more knowingly with us.

Gappiness in Shakespeare points to the next mechanism of change arising from therapeutic mapping. It is the moments of saying and putting on map, 'I think there is a gap here'. Sometimes naming the gap makes it okay to not know. We don't mind the gap. It means not knowing is not a failure. There is art in not knowing. It is not an inadequacy. Finding gaps may be as good as making links.

Art works with gaps. For the visual artist, the gaps are between colours and shapes. For the instrumentalist in the orchestra the gaps are between trumpet and violin, between first and second violin between the one note and the next. Great music has this quality of each note being lived in a singular fashion at the same time as being part of a continuous flow. At an orchestral level, the musicians live and breathe this double dialogue between merger and separation of individual instrumental sounds. Great classical, choral, rock or jazz music is an expression of relational awareness at its pinnacle. It works in part by working the gaps.

Similarly, in a conversation there are gaps and jumps between stories, changes in tone from clear declamation to anxious muttering.

The process of mapping is a reconstructive one and for Ryle the idea was that the conscious and clearly remembered elements of a coping procedure once down on paper and out in the open can help shed light on the more hidden connections, thoughts and feelings. The blank spaces on the map have a role to play. They may point to the gaps in our lives and their recognition and acceptance. Where there is a sense of a gap, leave a question mark or a note to return there. The very act of leaving a question mark or pointing out a gap sets client and therapist thinking about what may be missing. The wish to fill the gap should be resisted as the links will come in time. A respect for our need to tolerate gappiness and be creative with it as a quality is a component of developing relational awareness in and among all the nine elements.

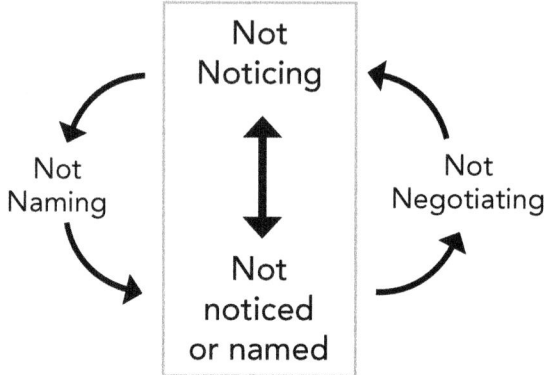

In and out of dialogue

Astronomers searching for extra-terrestrial life have the idea of a 'Goldilocks zone' in the 'just right' range of the distance of the planet from its sun. The story of Goldilocks is of a girl looking for shelter and whilst wandering in the forest she finds the house of the three bears and tries their food, chairs and beds in search of the experience that feels just right. For astronomers this is a zone where it is neither too hot nor too cold for life. Similarly, in therapy there is a 'therapeutic Goldilocks zone' where the therapy relationship has the right emotional temperature and the right level of openness, protection, and exposure. We go in and out dialogue with this zone all the time. The challenge is to notice and negotiate these movements in and out of dialogue and map and talk about how they arise. At times, the therapy conversation and relationship can be in the top left quadrant and too hot, close, and actively entangled, and yet out in the open and in dialogue. At other times it can be in the top right quadrant where there is dialogue and understanding on the map but the reflections on it are too detached and cool. Or there are times when being cool and detached coincides with a process of interaction which is hidden, not on the map and not negotiated. Perhaps the most painful place is to be emotionally hot and entangled combined with no reflective awareness or scope for negotiation as in the bottom left quadrant. We seek in therapy to be in the Goldilocks zone of being in dialogue both because of our shared resources of relational awareness and in search of it being extended. At times in any therapy as in any relationship we are likely to shimmer emotionally between these four quadrants.

The 'Goldilocks' zone of therapeutic dialogue

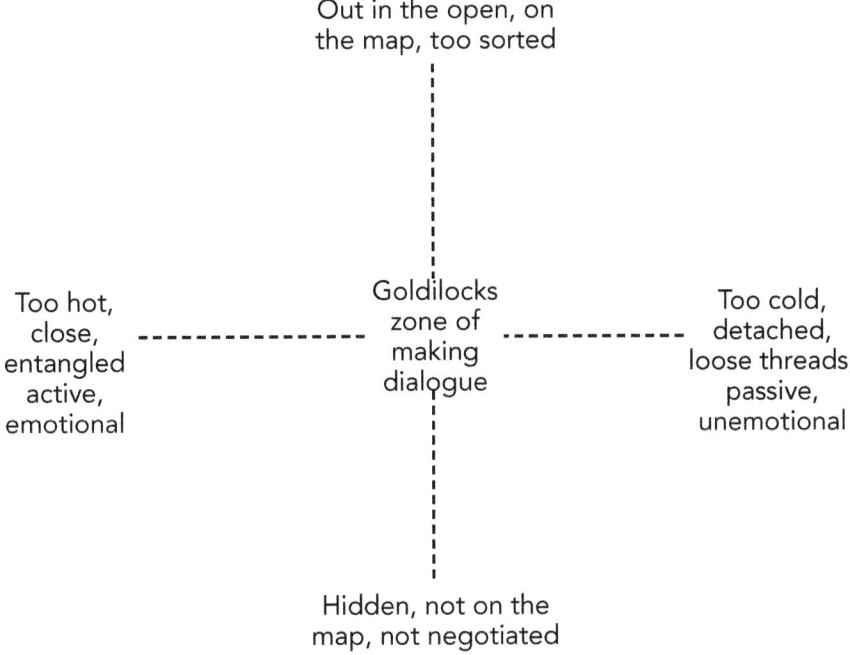

When the narcissism is in the idea

There are many ways of thinking about the interplay between personal knowledge and ideology. Therapy of all kinds might have in common the delicate struggle to loosen the ties of personal knowledge to ideology. One key theme of relevance to contemporary societies is the role played by, what here will be called, our narcissistic use of ideas. This is explained in the following notes and diagrams.

It takes a certain kind of society to make a thoughtful relationship between people. It is also through society that prejudiced and fixed ideas are formed and used. The challenge is to have some relational awareness of how social ideas and personal allegiance interact. A map might help. The map starts at point (1) with a curiosity to know what is going on in the face of complex and confusing ideas. Understandably we want things to be less confusing, complicated, and exposing. At such moments of cognitive uncertainty, we are vulnerable to people who rush forward to meet our request for knowledge by offering an appealing and tidy answer (2 on the map). In adopting the ideas which are offered, we risk submitting to overvaluing them, and over-identifying with the people allied to the ideas. This begins our narcissistic use of an idea.

In the Greek myth, Narcissus lost himself to the idea of his own image. He did not fall in love with himself but with an idea, an image projected by the gods before him. He wasted away and died because there was no room for other ideas such was the exclusive over-valuing of the idea in the still water reflected before him. In his narcissistic investment in the single idea he lost all capacity for dialogue with other people and their ideas and wasted away and died.

In contemporary society, individuals and groups are vulnerable to losing themselves through narcissistic over investment in an exclusive idea ('make our country great again', 'God is on our side', 'United for the cup'), or ideology which is further overvalued by social media. The price is not only rigid dependence on one idea (just like Narcissus in the myth) but a narrowing of thinking and connections that adds up to a loss of the relational awareness that flows from being in dialogue with multiple ideas.

Tracking the narcissistic use of an idea

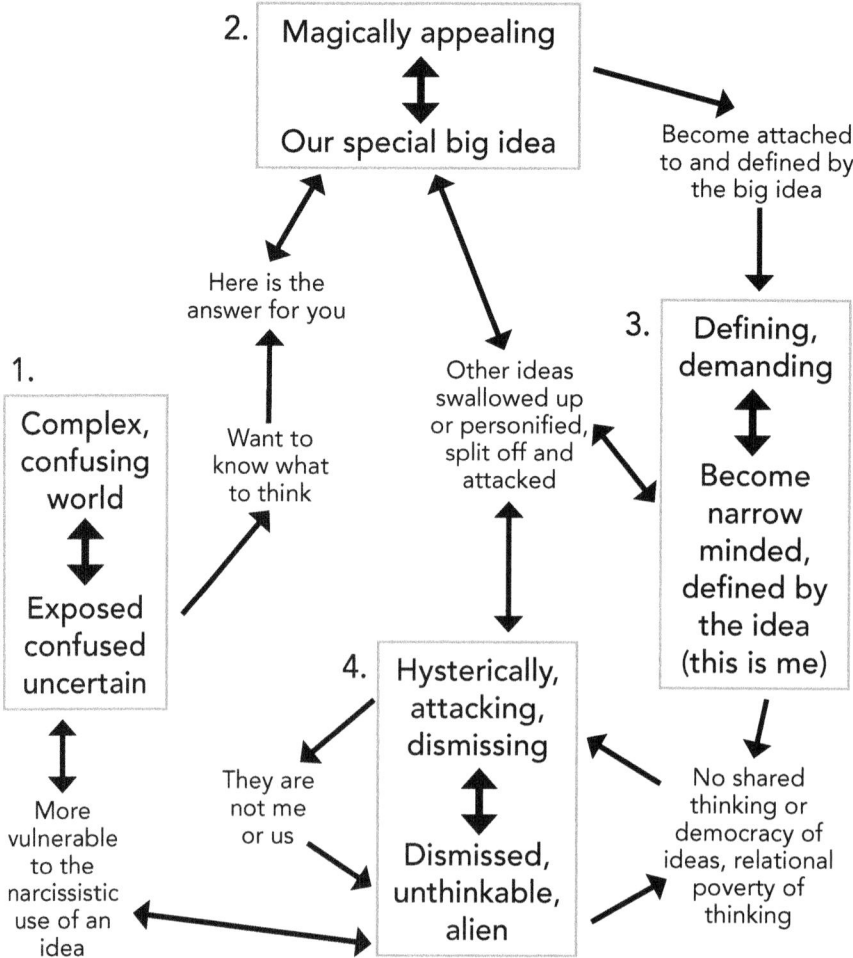

As in Box 3 thinking is defined and subordinated to the big idea in Box 2 in the diagram. Other ideas are swallowed up, personified to vilify them, or split off and the entire process of thinking is narrowed. This narcissism in an idea is okay if it is local in time and place such as the Saturday afternoon narcissism of 'United for the cup' or the 'honeymoon narcissism' of 'we are the most amazing couple'. The idea is temporarily bracketed away from reality. But if the narcissism of the idea becomes a dominant and exclusive part of an allegiance to and identity with a group then it can feel fragile and exposed. As protection the overvaluation of the idea must be matched by a deafness to competing ideas, and the groups that support them. Other ideas and their supporters are attacked (sometimes hysterically) and dismissed as a threat (box 4). This locks up and narrows our thinking further but also hurts us in relation to each other. We become aware of a stark reality: belong to the overvalued idea and feel included. Or be part of the devalued ideas and be excluded. The latter hurts the individual's capacity for relational imagination and the wider culture suffers from poverty of imagination and thinking. We become more confused and the system of narcissistic use of ideas locks us into an ever-stronger longing to be rescued by a big appealing idea (box 2).

Put another way, this loss of self and community to an idea is compounded by an external loss of connection with the wider world of ideas. In a process of selective attention and selective inattention (Sullivan, 1953; Barton, 1995), we cannot think outside the box in which the idea puts us. But this box is not just a box of ideas but a box of allegiances. The process of association (these ideas are me/us) is tightly bound up with an equally powerful process of dissociation (those ideas are not me/us). Those who attempt to think the unthinkable (dissociated ideas) are ridiculed or seen as stupid and put in an 'alien' box (4). All ideas are tarred by the narcissistic brush and either overvalued or devalued. The public and private result is a diminished capacity for debate and dialogue. Personalities, groups, organisational and political processes that are most suited to such a narcissistic climate of ideas tend to dominate. It is one of the contributions of psychotherapy to challenge this narcissistic pattern of relational thinking. Karen Horney in her book on 'Our Inner Conflicts' puts it well referring to us as 'he'.

> 'In contrast to authentic ideals, the idealised image has a static quality. It is not a goal toward whose attainment he strives but a fixed idea which he worships. Ideals have a dynamic quality; they arouse an incentive to approximate them; they are an indispensable and invaluable force for growth and development. The idealised image is a decided hindrance to growth because it either denies shortcomings or merely condemns them. Genuine ideals make for humility, the idealised image for arrogance.' (Horney, 1945; page 98)

The opposite of the narcissistic use of ideas is worth considering and mapping out. It is one of being in dialogue with ideas. As in the figure below the challenge to make sense of confusing and complicated reality and know where I stand is the same starting point as in the narcissism diagram.

In dialogue with ideas

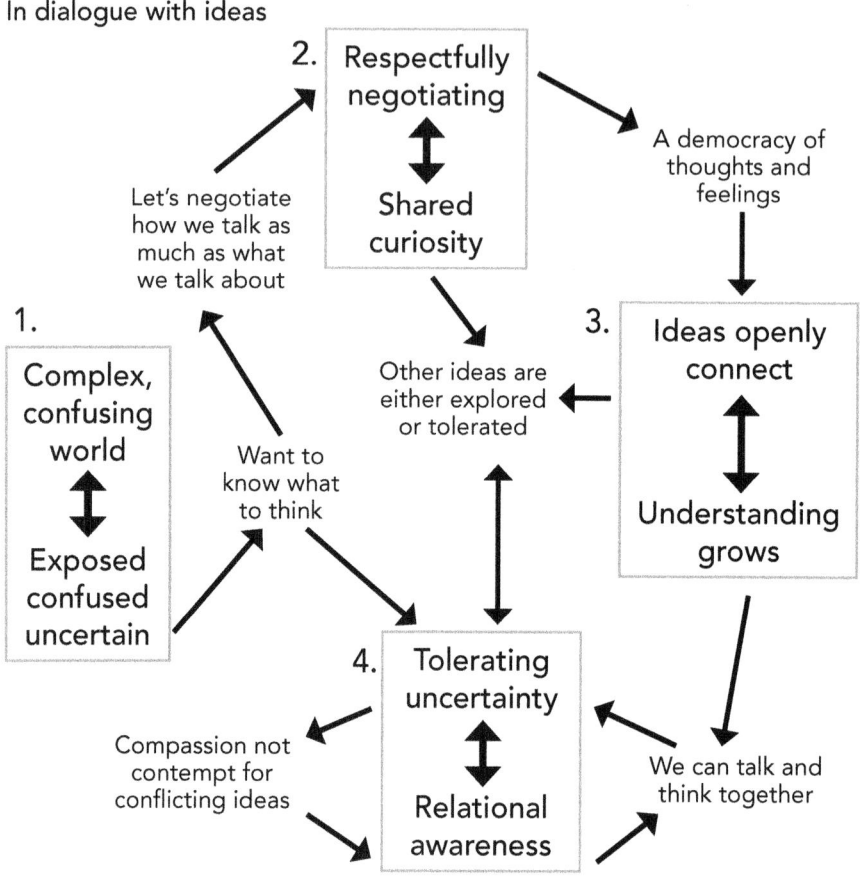

The difference is in the more relationally aware process all the way through the patterns and positions making up an open response. The offer (between box 1 and 2) is to negotiate and talk about how we deal with ideas as much as what the ideas are. By making how we share our thinking as important as what we think a shared curiosity and a democracy of thoughts and feelings is possible. Ideas connect and understanding grows and as a result uncertainty is tolerated and new or contrasting ideas are explored. A process of thinking together is re-established.

Relational awareness combines two 'brains'

Relational awareness is a meeting of two 'brains.' One brain is in our heads and that is the one we know about and is in the neuro-science textbooks.

The other brain is dispersed in the society around us in the fibre optics, in the libraries, in the school rooms, and, for better or worse, in the social media. There is a brain in our heads and a brain in society. The cognitive archaeologist Merlin Donald (2001), in his work on the long human evolution of the modern mind, implies that what has changed in the last 100,000 years of our development is, not at all a larger brain, (there has been no change in size) but a relationship between our brains and a bigger shared brain of the culture around us. The tools of human evolution – whether hand axes or words and stories, mediate the 'small' brain of the individual and the bigger brain of culture. It is a reciprocal relationship and produces what he calls a hybrid brain made up of mind and culture. It may be worth considering our scornful or complacent relationship with the big brain of society and culture and our over individualised exceptionalism (I know what I am doing and what I think) in relation to our own brains.

We cannot have the brain in our heads – it will not fire and wire as a human brain – without the social and cultural life around us. Our brains are primed to be adaptive, relational, dialogic. Not surprisingly the brain is an orchestral partner with the organs of our bodies and the organs of society. It works by combining and composing its left and right, top and bottom, old and new parts. Different bits of the brain seem able to stand in for each other.

The brain is relational and orchestral because it is a brain made up of different emotional sub systems or action tendencies (Panksepp, 2012). In this spirit of enquiry, there is a dialogic or relational view, in neuroscience that sees the brain itself as a multi-centred relational web with different centres and different potentials for orchestration and separation. Only an integrative approach that looks at the relational interplay between mind, brain, body, and culture will bring answers to the kinds of questions we ask in psychotherapy. Accordingly, it might be useful to think of the therapeutic mapping activity as an intermediate 'brain' space between us and the world around us.

A dialogue with our bodies

Our first experience of relational awareness is through co-embodied multi-sensory activity. We learn to think in minds by first 'thinking' in and with our bodies. In the intimate co-embodied spaces of infancy, we develop simple thinking narratives or 'maps' through the combination of our senses of sight, sound, touch and taste. Our bodies co-create relational stories as templates for interaction before we have the language and minds to relate. We do our first relational thinking through hovering and shimmering in co-creative, co-embodied imitation of others. It is the co-ordination of hands and eyes, sounds and smells that maps on to my brain and gives it the framework for thinking.

Part of our relational awareness comes through our bodies. We talk with our bodies, with heart or, at times, embarrassingly out of our backside. We first know the world through a dialogue between bodies. The early months of our lives are so intensely and deeply co-embodied we soon develop a rudimentary sense of mutuality, negotiation or even separateness. As our senses of touch, taste, sight and sound begin to work together, and the boundaries of skin become boundaries of self, we are on the long journey of giving meaning to the connection and separation of self from other.

Ekaterina Fotopoulou (2017) describes the first year of life as the formation of self-awareness through sensory integration. This astonishing process of becoming a being in the arms of another is echoed by a handful of infant researchers (Trevarthen, 2017; Stern, 2010) for whom the relational space, the interpersonal world and joint sensory activity is where humanity begins. The beginning of relational awareness comes through different senses interacting hearing and looking to where the noise comes from and then, touching, and tasting what is held. This goes with sensing an inside of the body interacting with an outside: taking in and pushing out. The infant's activities of cuddling, shuffling, and repositioning to find comfort are the beginnings of reciprocation and thereby of finding the boundary between self and others. They are in other words the beginnings of navigating, in 'baby' form the nine elements in the grid of relational awareness. It is from these beginnings that the later childhood and adult orchestrations develop. How they develop will be influenced by the relational dynamics of trauma and healing described in the next chapter.

The experience of this founding dialogue for being human is described in attachment behavioural terms by Bowlby (1965) and those who have developed his line of exploration (Ainsworth, 1965; Josselson, 1995). The mind yearns for what the body craves. The categories arising from Bowlby's work of secure, anxious and dismissing or disorganised attachment patterns have been influential and have face-validity for any therapist. From the viewpoint of negotiating and navigating relational awareness we need a more flexible framework. Ryle's reciprocal roles and the use of them in mapping offers to build on and combine the attachment theory thinking with the more contemporary intersubjective, co creativity and agency of Josselson (1995), Trevarthen (2017) and Stern (1985).

We never leave these first experiences behind. Our body carries them with us as its own early orchestration of 'baby steps'. So many writers have conveyed this psychoanalytic idea that we live in bodies shaped dynamically by our earliest years. To quote Heinz Kohut (Siegel, 2016) we never outgrow the symbolic and metaphorical need for 'mothers' milk'.

As richly described by Bessel Van der Kolk (2014), the body keeps the score of neglect and restriction. We integrate layers of relational awareness on top of the founding cognitive and emotional work of our bodies. Or through restriction, smothering, neglect or abuse we have gaps and holes and unresolved accounts of traumatic early experience. Our capacity to be aware of the word around us starts in our early interaction between baby mind and body.

Interpersonal awareness is pivotal

In the grid of qualities and dimensions at the beginning of this chapter, one of the three dimensions of relational awareness is interpersonal. There is a special relationship with those with whom we interact person to person with the whole of ourselves. In such moments we are in the multi-dialogue of relational awareness in relating simultaneously in role or in partial ways with each other's wider context in mind whilst encountering each other as one person to another. Our need for each other, our sensitivity to each other cannot be reduced to just one of the needs and tasks we work on together or the roles we occupy.

In line with Stephen Mitchell's clear account of relationality (2000), there are therapies and theories that make their distinctive focus just on behaviour, on emotional connectedness or role interactions or on meeting as two persons. However, therapy in all its varieties is one means or another to experience a high-level interpersonal trust and awareness. As clients we will struggle for this quality of 'being with'. The quality of the interpersonal meeting is genuine (Rogers, 1954), wholehearted (Horney, 1945). For Eric Fromm it was a component of the art of loving (Fromm, 1978) captured by his radical humanism. It is an awareness of the whole, not of the parts. It is in part a legacy of humanistic psychology that stressed not looking at behaviours in isolation or second-guessing unconscious motivation but to meet the whole person. For Meares it is the richness of knowing another person over time as an 'interpersonal duration' (2016). We meet and spend time together without knowing why we meet. It is a process of sincerity more than authenticity. It is at times fragile and elusive. An important aspect of this interpersonal awareness is the capacity for conversational intimacy described in **Chapter 1**. Training in interpersonal skills and human relations sometimes touches it but often may seem more like role play.

Relational awareness can be mistaken for or reduced to interpersonal awareness. The argument in this chapter is that interpersonal awareness is the crucible out of which relational awareness develops. Trainees in counselling and psychotherapy (and the helping and health professions more widely) might be forgiven for thinking that relational awareness begins and ends here. There are threats to interpersonal encounter by being too role bound but equally threats by losing sight of the context and the boundaries. Relational awareness is the capacity to negotiate interaction: not too role bound; not too interpersonal; not too group conforming; not too individual.

Orchestral awareness: agency, ownership, and authorship

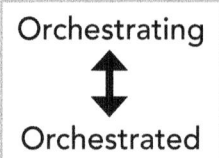

All the qualities, dimensions and elements of relational awareness work together like the instruments in an orchestra. Their combined effect is to offer an orchestral awareness. But where is the conductor's hidden hand? We need to open the hidden hand of orchestration up (as with holding open the four stories of therapy). By seeing orchestrating as the top end of a reciprocal role and being orchestrated as the felt experience we can open a gap between the orchestrating and the feeling of being orchestrated.

Our sense of self is orchestrated, well or badly, stage-by-stage of development, from the first year of life. Year-by-year, layer-upon-layer, we are orchestrated into first patterns of stimulus and response enabled or limited by the relational resources available to us. A parent holds us close. We begin to hold back and hold ourselves close. A seven-month-old baby hears a noise and turns to look and see the source of the noise. Hearing and seeing are orchestrated as a small unit of sensory, relational awareness for the first time. A later step is hearing a noise, imagining seeing (knowing) what it is and choosing not to turn and look. Making or breaking (leaving a gap) in the link between the senses is held in mind as a baby's building block of self-orchestration and relational intelligence. Touch, taste and smell are linked to co-ordination of our hands, arms and legs. Our whole bodies become a first experience of an embodied sense of self. Fotopoulou (2017) sums this up by viewing all the senses as engaged in joint work with increasing orchestration. They are the first experience of a sense of self. As detailed in the next chapter they are also tragically the first experiences for some of neglect, restriction and trauma.

Joint activity with others in the first year of life is also joining-up activity with self. Through my senses, I embody me. These experiences might be understood as chronotopes, the early co-sensory maps of the spaces and times in which we find ourselves and make our lives. At one year old, the toddler hears then sees a plane in the sky, and points and hears, and all but says 'jet'. At two years old the toddler sees a jet and thinks of the holiday chronotope.

Year-by-year the toddler-then-child grows and develops relational awareness and orchestrating capacity. So much depends on the attunement of others. The quality of this attunement, depends on the terms and games of language in the child's culture. How will the child be orchestrated, and positioned by language, or find their own voice, their own agency and powers of orchestration?

In putting the case for relational awareness being re-invigorated by the various forms of mapping in the preceding chapters, it is not a case for interpersonal sensitivity or social consciousness raising – much as they matter. It is a case for an orchestral agency or an ability to co-author a life with others. Jean Knox (2011) in her book on the developmental and neuroscience components of developing self-agency quotes Gallese, the Italian neuroscientist who proposes a central role for mirror neurons.

> *'Being a self depends on the acquired capacity to 1) recognise the existence of multiple frames of reference and 2) to put them in dynamic relation to each other by a continuous process of analogy and differentiation. [T]he emergence of the self can be seen as the adaptive tool able to give coherence to these interacting levels of representation.'*

(Gallese & Umilta 2002 page 37 quoted (page 100) in Knox, 2011)

It feels a fitting quote to make a bridge between the healthy and hopeful development of relational awareness in an open and just society and its damage and inhibition through individual and collective relational trauma which is the subject of the next chapter.

Conclusion

The chapter has speculated upon, and tried to reach, a wider sense of the qualities and dimensions of relational awareness. A grid of nine elements that add up to more, or less, relational awareness have been identified through a repeated process of observation and iteration of the mechanisms of change arising from relational mapping in the context of CAT theory and practice. These nine elements and the resulting relational awareness measure are described by Bonfield and Potter (2020) and the questionnaire is available to complete and use www.mapandtalk.com/ram/. A relational and orchestral awareness is what we need to be therapeutic and heal our emotional wounds in contemporary societies.

The chapter has touched on the psychological complexity of living in a simultaneously local and global society. We live with gaps in individual and collective knowledge and struggle to both participate and observe. We find ourselves, minute by minute, in the changing network of links and gaps between brains, bodies and minds and culture. The challenge is to develop, with others, a more distributed, orchestral and interpersonal awareness. This can be called relational awareness. Mapping helps us develop this awareness and is the key to developing a more therapeutic sense of self. The aim is to develop and share more flexible and open ways of negotiating with the world within us, between us and around us. It is an awareness that is multi-dimensional, multi-local (Taiye Selasi 2015), multi-layered with changing intensity, direction and intention. The qualities and dimensions of relational awareness are entry points into a relational matrix of the nine elements. It is for the poets, painters, artists, musicians, theologians, philosophers, and creators of new sub-cultures to show us the full and ever changing texture of this matrix.

Chapter 8: Relational healing

Introduction

This chapter explores the harm which is done by trauma in our early years to our capacity for relational awareness in adult life. It takes account of the preceding chapter in that healing trauma should bring gains in relational awareness. They are the two sides, one fearful and one hopeful, of the same coin. The chapter offers an interactive and developmental view of trauma. In the process, it identifies six areas of harm, which can be made more accessible therapeutically through mapping. Working with them helps develop a healing narrative as well as a formulation of problems and their origins. The six areas of harm are:

1. Unmet childhood needs.
2. Untried skills.
3. Hard to manage emotions.
4. High-cost coping patterns.
5. Divided sense of self.
6. Gaps in self-knowledge.

Specifying these six areas of harm reduces the overwhelming effect of thinking trauma is too complex to recover a sense of self. The roots in early harm and neglect are described for each of the topics and the limiting responses and consequences named. A path to healing and repair is proposed.

Trauma is a relational idea

Trauma is a relational concept (Howells, 2003) which offers an interconnected view of various kinds of hurt and damage (war, sexual violence, emotional neglect, child abuse, social deprivation) to our physical integrity and knowledge of ourselves (Howells, 2003; Herman, 1994). Relational trauma in early years directly hurts and shames but indirectly it limits and devalues human development. Trauma theory relates the specific pattern of hurt and abuse to restricted, broken or divisive ways of coping leading to gaps in self-knowledge.

As various writers affirm relational trauma needs relational repair (De Young, 2018). The active and collusive relational context to trauma has an impact on the body (Van der Kolk, 2014), the brain (Panksepp, 2012; Corrigan, 2018), our relationships and the mechanisms of healing and repair. Elizabeth Howell gives a thorough and wide-ranging account of the contribution of psychoanalytic and relational approaches (Howell, 2003). Her focus is on dissociation. She revives interest in the original ideas of trauma and dissociation by Pierre Janet. Donnel Stern (2003) in his description of unformulated experiences offers a framework for exploring gaps in self-knowledge at the heart of our sense of who we are. Russel Meares takes the view that '…the self will emerge in therapy in the same way that it emerges in child development' (Meares, page 154, 2016). He gives a sense of the double nature of the damage done by relational trauma by citing two categories. 'One related to the disruption of the development of self and the other to the recurrent intrusion of conscious and unconscious traumatic memories.'

The concept of developmental trauma is brought into sharper perspective by the turn towards a more dialogic and relational view of infant and child development (Stern, 2010; Trevarthen, 2017) and in the renewed interest in the overlap between neuroscience and psychoanalysis (Solms, 2015; Fotopoulou, 2017).

Sullivan (1953) and the relational turn in psychoanalysis in the United States (Bromberg, 1998; Horney, 1945; Mitchell, 2000; Stern, 2004) have also contributed much to seeing how trauma damages a sense of self. The pioneering work on a general concept of trauma (Judith Herman 1992) and the more recent work offering an integrative mind-brain-body view (Van der Kolk 2014) seem to tie in with the CAT way of thinking about multiple self-states and dissociation and the importance of mapping.

Cognitive analytic therapy gives a flexible framework for mapping the extent of damage to relational awareness and the possible paths to repair and healing. Ryle (1995, **Chapter 3**) talks of three levels of damage contributing to the experience of what he referred to reluctantly as borderline personality disorder. The first level is a narrow range of reciprocal roles. The price is a limited palette of ways of relating. The second level is badly orchestrating evaluative or judging reciprocal roles. An example might be a process of shaming and harshly criticizing of self for any show of vulnerability or need for care from others. The third level is limited reflective capacity leading to a diminished or damaged ability to orchestrate a coherent sense of self in the face of different states of mind.

As already mentioned, others give a perspective on the deeper understanding of effect of trauma from the viewpoint of new methods of work. Leading examples are the development of EMDR (Shapiro, 2018) and related methods that bypass the higher brain functions and touch the deeper non cognitive parts of the brain (Corrigan & Hull, 2018). Van den Hout (2012), offers a powerful exploration of how approaches such as EMDR might work by taxing working memory. He indicates that one key explanation may come from the simultaneous process of holding elements of the trauma in working memory and then making new distractive connections. It is a potential research question to see if the micro process, moment by moment, of shared mapping facilitates an interaction between working memory and the reconsolidation, softening or clearing of trauma memories.

Damage done by childhood trauma does not just hurt, shock and shame. It affects our cognitive and emotional development. It damages our growing sense of self and our relational skills in interacting with our inner worlds, with each other and the world around us. The damage is done to our delicate layering and expansion of relational awareness and self-knowledge. The damage is in the interplay with the living matrix of brain-body-mind-culture-persons-groups-institutions. The challenge of therapy is to contribute to ways of healing this damage. Mapping is one contribution to a relational, 'restorying' and re-orchestrating form of healing by indirectly offering a scaffolding for a range of interventions and directly by engaging mind, brain and body in reparative mechanisms.

Early relational trauma: an overview diagram

The following diagram shows how these aspects of damage interact in framing the orchestration of relational and developmental trauma. Inevitably to offer a relational overview there are necessary simplifications. The diagram starts at the left-hand side and the reciprocal role **Box 1: Engaging-to-engaged**. We are born ready and willing to engage and to be engaged in a shared, co-embodied experience. We anticipate and reach out for nourishment and care and soon learn to reciprocate and co-operate. We hope for, and mostly get, some well-attuned care, attention and stimulation.

The reciprocal to this is a good enough amount of security and responsiveness as in the reciprocal role **Box 2: Attuning-to-attuned and in dialogue**. By the end of the first months and year of life we are moving between Box 1 and 2 on the map taking both ends of the reciprocal roles. We are both engaging and engaged, attuning and attuned, active agent and willing or passive receiver. In the process, as evoked in the preceding chapter, we are developing a first sense of self through a delicate process of sensory integration of sound and sight, touch, taste and smell. What happens between us begins to happen in parallel within us. Our repertoire of ways of relating multiplies. All being well, we develop a healthy relational awareness.

At times, for all of us, there will be experiences of the bottom half the diagram in reciprocal role Boxes 3, 4 and 5. In the box **'Restricting-and-neglecting-to-unmet-needs'** at point 3, we will have unmet needs. We are primed to take in the good 'relational' stuff and tune out of the bad stuff. But there comes a point where the regularity and the intensity of the bad stuff takes the main role of providing secure attachment and we, following Fairbairn (Savege & Scharff, 2005), will attach and relate to a bad pattern rather than have no pattern to relate to at all.

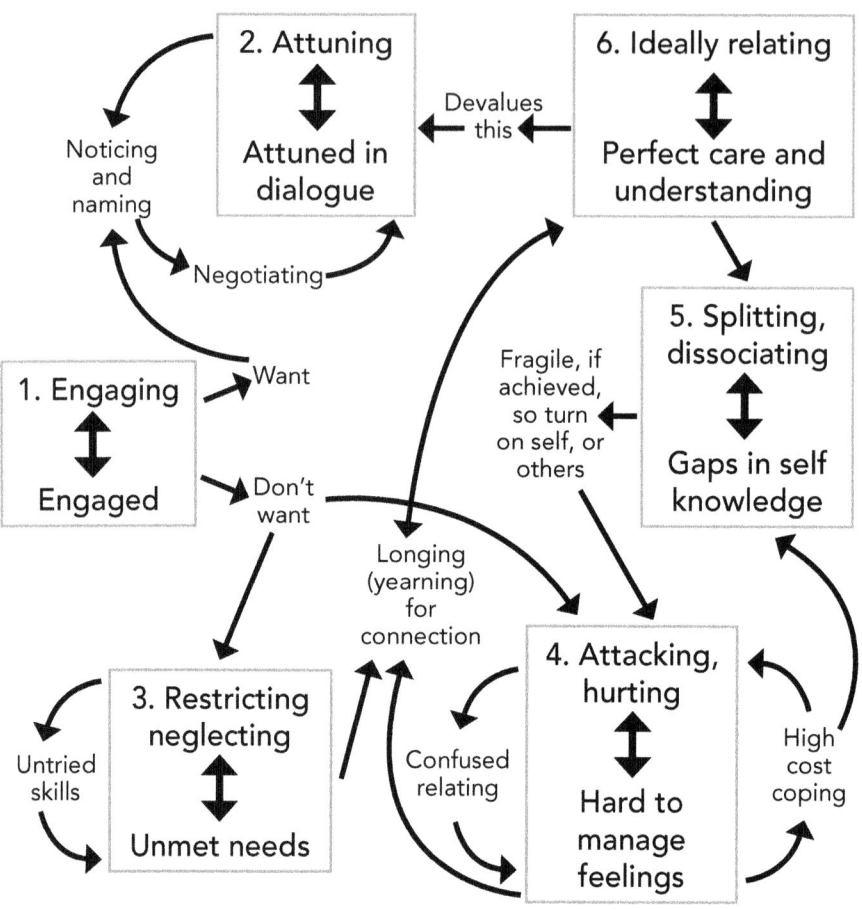

If restriction and neglect exceed the experience of attunement in this way, we will not flourish. Our limited environment will lead to untried skills in emotional expression and negotiation. The greater these unmet needs, the more we may yearn for **ideal care and perfect understanding** as depicted at point 6 at the top right of the diagram. This may well develop as a fantasy longing ('only in our dreams') which is rarely achieved but powerfully present in orchestrating an adult sense of self. It may, in turn, **devalue** the routine interaction of care in 1 and 2 as ordinary and not enough. Or we may grow up in an environment where loving care is overvalued and romanticised (we had 'wonderful' family holidays despite the rest of the year being one of careless neglect) and comes mixed with sudden reversals to restriction and abuse. Either way the ideal care is held as a fragile and yearned for. It is an unvisited, unreal place on the mental map of our lives. In all these developmental relationships we can be alternately at either end of the reciprocal role to ourselves and others.

Alongside this, we dread reciprocal Box 4 on the diagram: **Attacking-to-hard-to-manage-feelings**. Memories of what was felt in response to attack may be fragmented or unformulated. The fear, or hurt, may be overwhelming of our newly forming, cognitive and linguistic resources. Hard to manage feelings (4) call out for high-cost (emotionally and socially, inwardly, and outwardly) ways of coping, as indicated to the left of point 4 on the diagram. Our capacity to relate sincerely to others is confused despite our best intentions.

One specific high-cost way of coping is to gain control over attacking experience by becoming the attacker to self or others. The mixture of rigid patterns of coping, narrow ways of dealing with others and dissociation from unbearable emotions leads to gaps in self-knowledge. This links to **reciprocal role** Box 5 on the diagram, the splitting and dissociation which solidifies these gaps and may show up as several partially dissociated roles, social identities and self-states.

One key, final comment is needed in response to this overview diagram. To survive as children, we worked with the limited psychological resources available to us. These limited – and gap filling – methods of survival continue into adulthood but may also have become painfully adaptive. We may build a strong but narrow sense of achievement. Or we invest greatly in an identity of being the warrior, or the rescuer, which gives us esteem and reward. In this way gaps in self-knowledge may be well-hidden by the development of childhood and adolescent identity which is a 'cover' identity that only gives us a partial sense of being wholly in the world. Despite its limitations, its emotional costs and gaps in self-knowledge it is our identity solution. We are reluctant to let go of it.

These multiple processes of relational harm and attempts at healing will now be considered in more detail in each of the areas identified.

Unmet childhood needs

We all grow up with some of our childhood needs unmet. Our needs to be loved, guided, protected, inspired, or held and challenged are never going to be perfectly orchestrated. See the work of Heinz Kohut (Siegel, 2016) for a rich psychoanalytic formulation of meeting and failing to meet our needs to be cherished and valued on the one hand, and our need for an inspiring role model for charting our ambitions and achievements on the other hand.

The tools of mapping help us go back to the relational and painfully bare bones of childhood and add a compassionate observing eye. We are likely to meet strange combinations of roles, such as loving and criticising, idealising and neglecting, cherishing, and abusing, exciting and carelessly forgetting. Our need for a consistent space in which we can rehearse and learn how to negotiate our interactions is vital for a healing narrative. This view is richly developed by Ruth Josselson in her book the *Space Between Us* (1996).

An alternative title for this section might be ill-met needs. The needs may be met but in a way that is partial, random, teasing and unpredictable. Often clients at the first discussion of their unmet childhood needs recall their childhood care as seamless and that there was always something going on. Some needs are met and act as a cover story for the unmet needs, 'Look at what we have done for you'. Our unmet needs may be overlooked by the necessary and essential, habit of drawing on what was available – a kind of 'make do and mend' approach to meeting unmet needs. Unmet, or ill-met childhood needs, can be passed across generations. We may find our needs were met in line with our parents' reading of the culture at the time. In this way we might have been raised with an eye on the 'rear-view-mirror' to fit the values of a vanishing society with rules of gender, submission or faith that no longer work.

Our unmet needs may be met by surprising sources of care. One client found comfort in nature and the hills around where she lived. She developed a language of care for nature and indirectly for herself through the seasons and their changing responses to her needs. In a loveless world she found love between her and nature.

As mentioned earlier, Ruth Josselson talks of a 'yearning' as one aspect of managing the relational space between us. She has chapters on holding, tending, caring and passion. In combination they go a long way to mapping out the intimate dynamics of developing relational awareness. Relational trauma for her contributes to, or results from, a deficit in one or more of these dimensions of early relating. She writes of a longing for relatedness:

> *'In which people are destined always to want more connection with others than is possible, aching to overcome inescapable aloneness. In Freud's model anxiety calls up the need for defences. In Kohut's theory, narcissistic overexcitation is warded off. In this model, it is painful longing that we must keep out of consciousness lest it disrupt or undo us.'*

(Josselson, 1996, page 11)

Yearning is described by her as an impossible longing for a perfect and unattainable relationship. It stops us taking in the ordinary potential for intimacy, comfort and creativity in the relationships around us. Ruth Josselson was writing twenty-five years ago but her ideas are still innovative in reaching out from attachment theory and infant development to a more freely relational perspective.

In session three Jane brings in a list of her unmet childhood needs as requested at the end of the previous session. She apologises saying that, 'it is just bullet points.' She agrees to read it out. Her list is as follows:

- A need to be taken seriously and not teased – my dad not my mum.
- a need be fed consistently at mealtimes (she cries at this).
- A need for parents not to row and bicker all the time. She looks up and adds that it was awful. A need for friends my age – I was so lonely and isolated.

- A need to realise that I was not guided, not held, not loved.
- A need for less, much less intimidation.

Jane's list when she read it out was like poetry leaping from the page at her. Jane said she'd felt quite dry and detached in writing 'just bullet points.' Now, she adds, 'it feels full of emotion as if connecting with a bigger picture for the first time'.

It is an example of emotion rekindled, once recollected in tranquillity. Our childhood experience varies. Many of us have major unmet needs and, in some cases, have gone through experiences of tragic, unexpected or horrible neglect, control and disappointment. We carry the relational template of neglect (which is unique to us) into our adult lives and, rightly or wrongly, assume our unmet needs won't be met there any differently. Therapy is the space to find ways of rehearsing a change of expectation about our unmet needs.

Lucy Cutler, a psychologist based in Jersey, has made use of placing unmet childhood need at the beginning of mapping out the patterns of coping with the painful and hurt end of a reciprocal role. It invites the client to think positively about the care, or attention, which went unmet in childhood. This helps think about a pattern of seeking care from self or others that might now be expressed and responded to differently.

Untried skills

Alongside the adjustment to unmet childhood needs there are untried skills. We can only develop our own skills by association with the intimate habitat of people and culture around us. We won't know how to talk about our feelings as adults, if talking in such a way as children never happened or was derided as soft. We cannot express affection or tenderness if none is shown to us. If anger was never allowed, we are only going to have very restrictive skills in its expression and regulation.

We are likely to learn these skills in the style and tone of the way they were offered. If affection was always linked to obedience, we will be frightened to assert ourselves for fear of not being loved. We may always link affection and obedience. If frustration was always dealt with by arguing, blaming and violence, we may too easily resort to this as a way of coping, rather than a more balanced or varied response.

Untried skills can be marked out for rehearsal as exits from harmful patterns on the map, to new and healing behaviors. Mapping offers immediate access to one commonly untried meta-skill of compassion for, and kindness to self. If the absence of compassion and kindness can be noticed, and the elements of the compassionate or kind behavior can be practiced, then it can slowly become second nature and genuinely owned as a lasting part of me. This applies regardless of how false or superficial it may feel at first attempt, as in the example of the buying flowers on page 72.

Unmanageable emotions

Unmet needs give rise to untried skills creating a vicious circle of emotional deprivation and restricted relationships. Together they limit our emotional world in the closed system of childhood and family. It is all we know, and we may take it to be normal. Since life is not going to stop facing us with emotional demands, we are repeatedly faced with unmanageable emotions. As we meet the wider society and meet adults and peers with different emotional responses, we are confronted with our unmet needs and untried skills.

Ryle developed the idea that the bottom end of the reciprocal role could be understood along the lines of Mann's idea of chronically endured pain. James Mann (1973) devised a brief psychodynamic therapy that put the focus on addressing an emotional state of distress and stuckness as the single focus of therapy. This succinct formula for brief therapy is echoed by Luborsky's (1990) idea of a central therapeutic focus on a core relational conflict. In many ways they both echo the pioneering work of Karen Horney as depicted by her book *'Our Inner Conflicts'* (1945) which so vividly shows the emotional costs of hard to manage emotional conflicts.

There is a problem with learning to manage difficulties with emotions. The bias in mental health professions has been to focus more on a discourse of emotional individualism. Our feelings about anger, sadness, hope, pride, shame, happiness guilt and so forth are viewed as a personal problem to solve. In part they are individual problems. But at the same time, they are also symptoms of, and gateways to, our problems in relationships. The value of recapping together, of hovering and shimmer around a map is to see our conflicting mix of feelings in the context of social relationships. Healing the trauma of unmanageable feelings means no longer being alone with the emotions.

When mapping out hard to manage emotions there may be moments of silence or feeling stuck. It is no small feat to get back into dialogue with what has been driven out of dialogue for so long. The well-paced use of mapping, writing and voicing offers a supplementary medium alongside talking. Unmanageable feelings are often unmanageable in the memory of them at the time of trauma. In clearing the trauma memories using methods such as EMDR and, in seeing the historic personal context to the people and times involved in the trauma, the contrast with present times may be apparent. The coping strategy that seemed so necessary then may not feel so necessary now. The compulsion to repeat may feel less compulsive. Past feelings of fear and shame, once so overwhelming, may now be lessened enough to manage with kinder feelings towards self. Writing a letter addressed specifically and directly to the time of high trauma or to an unmanageable feeling may help gain movement and compassion for self and others, and the context of the original suffering.

High-cost coping

Many of the initial reasons for seeking help are because costly emotional coping patterns are causing symptoms of mental ill health, psychological distress, or trouble with relationships. Through the experience of unmet needs, untried skills and hard to manage emotions, we develop 'high-cost' ways of coping. A high-cost way of coping involves cutting off, isolating myself, depriving myself or switching between hurting myself and then hurting others in combination with patterns such as clinging, controlling, or abusing others emotionally or physically.

High cost ways of coping in response to early trauma, persist and become part of our identity. Phrases such as 'I don't make a fuss' or He is hot tempered' turn patterns of coping into character traits. They are taken to be second nature. Putting them out there on paper, in full interactive detail, talking over their early history, and current value can help distance ourselves from them (see page 209 for more detailed examples of working in this way). All the items in the psychotherapy file point to patterns of high-cost coping that are endured because they are familiar. They provide stability and identity despite their cost.

High cost ways of coping may fit in with the prevailing culture and appear normal, such as comfort eating, managing social anxiety with alcohol, drug use to build self-esteem or love addiction in search of the 'honeymoon high'. We are willing to pay the emotional price of high-cost ways of coping because they still work as survival and emergency procedures.

It is as if the threat that gave rise to them in childhood is still imminent. This is rarely the case. It is the re-play of the coping procedure that recreates a recurring, virtual relationship with the old trauma. If we can look at the relational roots of the pattern and link them fully to the details of the costly way of coping, we can begin to separate ourselves and our identity from them. Only a relational map can get us to the heart of this complexity without getting lost in the emotional intensity of the detail and rekindling the original trauma dynamics.

Gaps in self-knowledge

Gaps in self-knowledge are eloquently explored in the book by Donnel Stern entitled *Unformulated Experience* (2003). These gaps lead to a sense of self which is divided along the lines described by Harry Stack Sullivan (1955). He describes a split between an association with an emphatic sense of self – this is the good me – and that is the bad me on the one hand and a rejected

Loose or tight association and dissociation

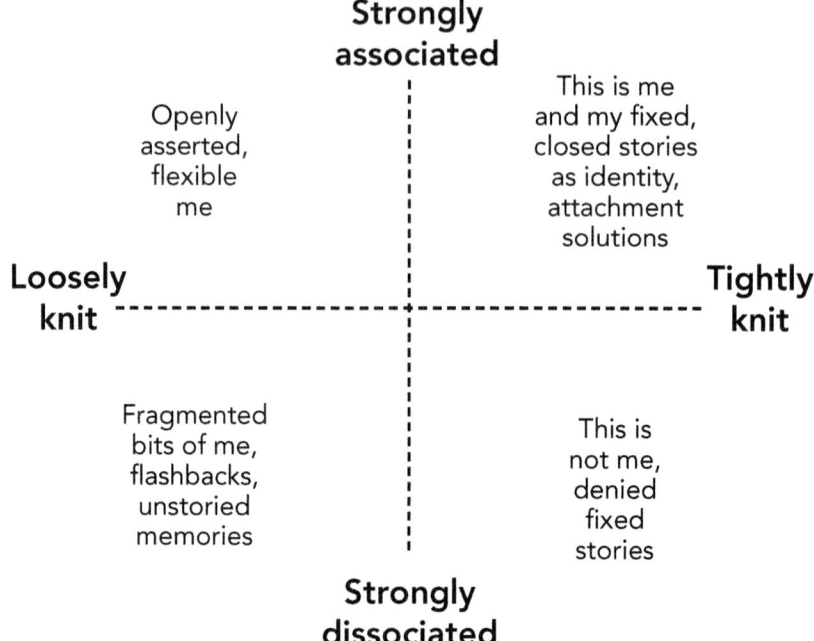

part – this is not me on the other hand. This prejudiced partition – between a strongly associated part of the self and a strongly dissociated part of the self – is a double move which goes someway to explain the overlapping dynamics of rigid social identity formation and narcissistic patterns of personality.

In the two-dimensional diagram above, one dimension tracks the degree of emotional connection and awareness. At one extreme is the strong dissociation from memories, roles, and feelings. At the other extreme are roles and attitudes that are strongly associated ideas about identity that are consciously held. The horizontal dimension extends between loosely and tightly knit. The word 'knit' refers to the way in which the dissociative or associative material is held or storied within the person and in their relational environment of people, cultures and institutions.

The top righthand corner is a place of fixed, strongly held identity and ideology. It is saying 'this is me'. It is a flag waving, tightly held identity and attachment solution. It may have a covering of narcissism for the individual and contempt for those not associated or included. The bottom right corner is similarly tightly knit but out of awareness and is dissociated or repressed. This, in the terms of Harry Stack Sullivan, is either 'bad me' or 'not me'. It may be expressed indirectly through projection onto others. The bottom left corner is loosely knit in the sense meant by Donnel Stern's idea of unformulated experience. These are fragments of trauma memory, discordant bits of powerful emotional experience that float about in memory unconsolidated or loosely consolidated. Finally, the top left-hand corner is the space of open dialogue and scope for relational thinking and awareness.

The preceding aspects of relational trauma leave gaps (for more on gaps and 'gappiness', see page 144) in our capacity to weave and work with our memories. Ryle, in adapting Vygotsky's social developmental model, said that 'What the child does not do today with another then they won't do on their own tomorrow'. Since we grow up in the limited bubble of our own childhood experience, we grow up with gaps which we cannot see. We know them in some deep sense but have no narrative to go with them. The cognitive analytic approach understands the reformulation process as a reorganizing of the personal memories and stories in a way that shows the dissociative gaps and the habitual, compulsive or addictive links that cover them over.

When we become aware of the gaps, we may be resistant to further understanding. 'Why would I want to know this? It is too painful, and too hard to see what might be done differently.' Recognizing gaps in meeting our childhood needs and realizing that we survived by costly ways of coping, requires a supportive and guiding framework for a more open dialogue. The sensitive use of mapping is one of the aids to such an approach.

Developing untried skills helps address unmet needs and manage hard to manage emotions which, in turn, helps address the gaps in self-knowledge. Somewhere deep in the self comes a memory, a fragment of feeling, a compulsion to react in a certain way without knowing why. If they can be put into words, they can feel like words without stories. Sometimes they show up in the spontaneous process of conversational mapping as random words on the paper that despite recapping and reworking don't seem connected but do have some emotional weight to them. I can say I am angry, but I don't know why because the story is missing.

Divided sense of self

Some trauma memories, and some gaps in development are outside of self-knowledge in a double move of simultaneously dissociating and moving away from one feeling and moving to associate self and identity, exclusively and powerfully, with another contrasting feeling. There is the example of Michael on page 46 is of shutting off from feelings of weakness (dissociation) to the point of not recognizing his vulnerability and fear by also seeking out and investing self in the state of mind and identity of being a 'hard man'.

One response to gaps in our knowledge is to live with a cover story (see earlier mentions page 73, 161) as the stoic survivor, heroic defender or outsider. These stories are our hiding place and offer protection at the cost of limiting our relational choices. They link to the idea of a divided and false self. For Winnicott (2016) the, so-called, false self is linked to a real or genuine self. Our cover stories and identities are just as real and were once very necessary for survival.

> *'In the cases on which my work is based there has been what I call a true self hidden, protected by a false self. This false self is no doubt an aspect of the true self. It hides and protects it, and it reacts to the adaptation failures and develops a pattern corresponding to the pattern of environmental failure. In this way the true self is not involved in the reacting, and so preserves a continuity of being. However, this hidden true self suffers an impoverishment that derives from lack of experience.'*
>
> (*'Clinical Varieties of Transference'*, 1955-56)

The role of the relational therapies such as CAT, and the approach to mapping and writing as proposed in this book, is to help see the emotionally costly ways of coping and orchestrating a more functioning sense of self in the face of trauma. The legacy of trauma is managed but at a price of a partial loss of self. For those, perhaps more people than is admitted, who cope and suffer in this way, a process of relational healing through retelling stories and reconsolidating memories is needed as much as a trauma memory clearing process as offered by approaches such as EMDR.

When abuse and hurt is explained and given open and negotiable meaning, we have more chance of recovering from the trauma. It has less psychological impact on our sense of self. In contrast, when abuse is accompanied by denial or misleading or contradictory stories, we are left confused and are exposed to a second layer of abuse to our capacity to make meaning, and test and retest the stories we tell of ourselves. Equally, when faced with abuse and neglect, we are less able to co-create a shared story. One way of understanding how gaps in our self-knowledge become fixed and sealed off comes from mapping the way in which we rely upon secure and guaranteed 'cover' stories about ourselves.

A healing narrative

Much of the work described by this book points to using CAT tools to create a healing narrative which promotes connection between the divided and disorganised stories of the self. A healing narrative is the sum of those moments recognising: unmet needs, trying untried skills, softening, or stepping out of, high cost ways of coping, and healing the wounds of unmanageable feelings. It is a process of beginning to weave new patterns of relational awareness across the gaps in self-knowledge and the divided elements of self.

Help comes in lots of little healing steps as adult life progresses. At the same time, harm is perpetuated by lots of little repetitions of the trauma derived patterns. The mapping, writing and talking process is useful in holding in mind the detail of these little steps for and against a freer, less divided sense of self.

A working assumption is that we have a powerful need for narrative coherence. Or to put this another way we find comfort and security in life-stories that hold and enable experience. We will settle for a narrow and limiting story if it is presented to us by a powerful other and offers closure. If my parents repeatedly tell me I am clumsy, or special, beautiful or lazy, then I will begin to tell myself the same. I will find coping strategies and identity solutions to complete the story. Such tightly imposed storying is at the heart of our culture; boys have 'boy-stories', girls have 'girl-stories'. With help we can learn the relational imagination to step in and out of stories in search of a healing narrative.

In the same way as EMDR (Shapiro, 2018), there are a handful of exciting new therapies that claim evidence that they can clear trauma memories (Corrigan & Hull, 2018) in the deeper parts of the brain where the relational and cognitive therapies have less reach. The proponents of these new therapies give good evidence of resolving trauma memories but do not take so much account of the legacy of lifelong coping strategies built to manage the early trauma woven into identity and personality. Whatever the specific moments and techniques of breakthrough in reducing the impact of trauma, they need to be woven together in a healing narrative that is owned and shared by client and therapist.

Conclusion

All cultures involve distressingly ordinary routines of trauma in their childrearing practices, in schooling, in gender formation and setting group against group. These collective sources of trauma link to personal experience of abuse and restriction. Mapping can help us see how personal and collective stories of trauma weave together. It can help us see where change is possible or where risk is greatest. It can create, in the therapy space, a level of relational awareness that helps develop a healing narrative. The larger goal of mapping is to develop a freer, more open relational and orchestral awareness. In the process, the client has the space to develop agency, ownership, and authorship over their lives. It offers more ability to be in dialogue within ourselves and with the people and the society around us.

When CAT talks about reformulation, it assumes the client will bring formulations to therapy (their own stories and personal theories about their lives and distress). The re-storying that flows with reformulation can be part of a healing narrative. How this is done is explored in the detail of **Part 3** of this book.

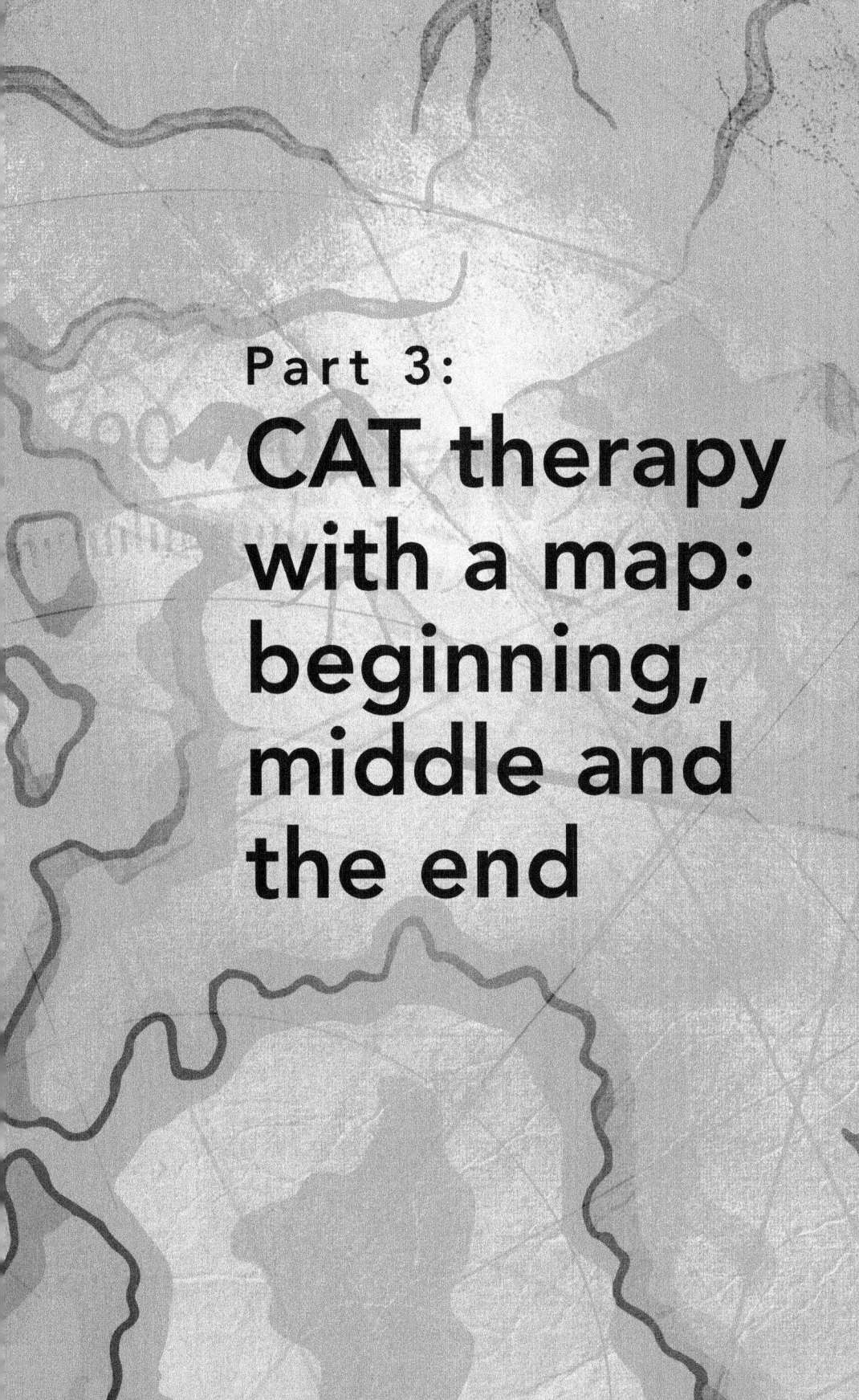

Part 3:
CAT therapy with a map: beginning, middle and the end

Chapter 9: Beginning therapy

Introduction

This is the first of three linked chapters which illustrate a cognitive analytic approach. The emphasis is on the co-creative work of the therapeutic relationship. It draws on the shared activities of mapping and writing covered in parts one and two of the book. It is about preparing for, and starting therapy, with a focus on the first few sessions concluding with a reformulation letter and therapy map. It considers responses to some of the common problems at the beginning of therapy. It is followed by chapter on what to do in the middle of therapy and one on the ending of therapy.

Before the therapy begins

Consideration needs to be given to the context and system around the therapy. How is the offer of therapy made visible? What message does it convey? How is the client helped to make a choice about therapy or not? What guidance or reassurance do they need about the mixed feelings they may have about seeking help?

Clients come to therapy in a variety of ways. They may self-refer, or may have been referred by a professional, friend or family member. They may come actively and willingly, or reluctantly and sceptical about the value of therapy. Or with shades of both.

Equally, the therapist prepares to meet a new client in a variety of ways. Her or his role as therapist may be mediated by a professional role in psychology, social work, psychiatry, occupational therapy, counselling, nursing and psychotherapy. They may be at the early stages of their career or new to a specific way of working or setting. Their workload may be heavy or manageable. The funding and organisational context may set limits on sessions or approach and may be inside or outside the institutional framework of healthcare.

Therapist and client need the organisation around the therapy 'space' to be relationally aware, transference friendly and supportive. In addition to the structure around the therapy, the therapeutic approach should also be explained conversationally in the first session but also through an accessible and readable description of the therapy context and approach.

The 'help-seeking' story

Every client brings to the first session a 'help-seeking' story which is worth knowing and is easily bypassed. It may indicate past helping relationships, the way systems have responded and how the client now feels about asking for and receiving help. How therapist and client join this help seeking story will shape their relationship.

What indirect evidence of the help-seeking story is there for the therapist? There may be records of previous therapy, referral notes and letters. There may be a pre-therapy phone discussion. This is well worth considering as it models an active and engaging approach to working together (Talmon 1990). The therapist can prepare by checking any preceding files but the greater opportunity to connect with the client will be in the first session around some version of the question. "What has brought you here?"

The help-seeking story may be very immediate, apparent and local because of a life-crisis, or it may have been rumbling as part of background thinking for some years. Most help-seeking stories capture a struggle between a failure to breakthrough to something in life or a fear of breaking down.

The apparent help-seeking story may mask one that is hidden or not yet formulated. There may be a story which has others involved. Or one that held true six months ago but has been lost by the length of time waiting for help. Patterns of relating and of transference that are likely to be played out in the therapy are likely to be embedded in the help-seeking story.

The therapist will also have their own help-seeking and help-avoiding history. They will bring their unconscious biases about who should seek help and how it should be done. Some therapists will be having therapy themselves at the same time as helping others. At the back of their minds, they may have their own mixed feelings about seeking more therapy for themselves. The therapist will be more available as a therapist if they are also mindful about their own past and present help-seeking stories. Therapists may prefer the protected role of 'giving help' to the vulnerable and exposing role of 'receiving help'. The therapist may admire, or envy, the 'courage and openness' of their client for seeking help. Or conversely may imagine in horror 'the helplessness and disorganisation of life' for which the client is seeking help.

Show don't tell

The rule most often given to creative writers is show don't tell. This may be good advice for therapy as well. There is value in telling a client what the therapy will be like, but a key part of the initial session is to show how therapy might work. One way is to micro-map bits of the help seeking story. One of the advantages of the shared therapeutic activities of writing and mapping is that the framework for a conversational therapy is tangible and visible.

The client can benefit from an active and open demonstration of what the therapy journey will be like. The therapist is hoping to help the client be a reliable narrator (Booth, 1991) of their lives and that the therapy will achieve a reliable narrative.

Sally had been waiting months for a therapy appointment. At times, she had got agitated about the wait and then, at other times, she had forgotten about the idea all together. When an appointment came, her first words to her partner were 'about bloody time'. She was surprised at her anger. It came with her into the first session and yet she was polite and mild-mannered during the first half of the session. When asked about the process of seeking help, the phrase 'about bloody time' came rushing to her mind. The therapist asked if it was okay, to put the phrase down on paper and said in a rather impulsive way 'I didn't realise you were cross. You have been so polite'. Sally retorted 'Well you'd better put "polite" down on the paper then'. Two emotions (compliant, polite and cross) both contrasting and set against each other had co-existed in Sally's help-seeking story. With the conflict on paper she and her therapist opened a wider discussion about what she wanted, how she had waited and what was okay to share and feel in the therapy room. They were making a bond (Bordin, 1979) helped by the activity of mapping in search of a focus for the therapy. The task at this stage centred around a capacity to be open to the expression and transference of feelings between them. Could they notice and name them without fully understanding them at this point?

Sally said 'Is this it then? Is this how it's going to go?' The therapist nodded and added 'I am so sorry you have had to wait so long. I am glad you have let me know how annoying it was at times.' A key quality of a conversational and relational therapy had been shown.

The client may not be used to being in a relationship which seeks to be open and curious about their own motives and expectations.

Talking about the help-seeking story offers a model of talking about the therapy relationship as it develops. It also helps to have out on the table between them some of the ambivalence and risks that might get in the way. One option is for client and therapist to spend five minutes half-way through the first or second session writing very short 'Dear therapy' welcome letters, which are then read out. The idea is to facilitate a bond around the forthcoming tasks and activities of therapy.

Dear therapy

You have just begun. I have made a big step is seeking you out but now I have mixed feelings. Will it take me places I don't want to go? Will it show me up as a bad person or naïve? Will I want care and not get it? Or will I get care and be embarrassed to accept it or vulnerable if I give myself in to the care. I don't want to feel stupid or lost, so I am hoping the therapy will be upfront and quite active. It has taken me a long time to make the first step. I am glad the therapist has told me a bit about their approach and who they are. It helps to feel there is an agreement to sign up to. Well here goes!

Sharing hope and warmth

Alongside exploration of the help-seeking story, it is the therapist's job to be hopeful and to look out for the client's strength and willingness to engage in the therapy. Getting hope, warmth and compassion on the map and in the room as part of the therapy is a key early task. Equally, acknowledging fears and doubts as to what might go wrong and who will then be to blame need naming and negotiating.

The therapist should discuss what makes the client feel optimistic that this therapy will help. Optimism is a mechanism of change. No doubt it protects the therapist from falling into despair, but it helps hold and care for the client in re-orchestrating the emotional parts of their lives. The voicing of past and present hurt and despair, the feelings of fear and anxiety or the owning of great dreams and forbidden desires are all shared in the hope that they can be understood and integrated into a whole picture.

Julie's story

Julie came to her first session on the back of a lot of encouragement to come and was quick to agree that she was sure therapy would, or could, be very helpful. She had heard accounts of how much it helped friends. However, at the heart of her help-seeking story was a snag that Julie did not think she would be very interesting. Until this was named and explored, her anxiety about not being interesting was blocking the path to working together. Julie carried the view into therapy that, of all her siblings, her parents regarded her as the 'low-drama, safe but boring' one. 'Low drama' was one of those words with the music of transference in it that could carry across several of her life stories. It was an early sign on paper for the 'shared memory' of the therapy, as it developed. It was pointing to a key childhood role that had now surfaced in the help-seeking relationship – would Julie be interesting or not? In the process of exploring this, the therapist seemed to enact his own pattern, transferred into this therapy, of being expressively interested and curious. He said, noting a look on her face, as he showed his enthusiasm to prove her self-image wrong: 'Am I being too positive?'

'Yes' she said, 'Aim lower. I can be interesting without resorting to high drama'. They smiled. 'Aim lower' went on the paper in the middle. 'High drama' went at the bottom of the sheet. 'Low drama, safe but boring' was at the top. Neither client nor therapist knew how the words related to the therapy. Later in the therapy when something important (and interesting) was being explored, she asked for that early sketch with 'aim low' written on it.

'You want to cross it out?'

'No, don't cross it out. I just want to add a phrase.' She added, in big bold letters 'Aim high but keep the low drama'. This example highlights how shared ownership of the tools of therapy is a stepping-stone to shared ownership of the therapy.

The therapy assessment

The key features of psychotherapy assessment are well covered elsewhere (Ryle & Kerr, 2020; 2002). There are assessment questionnaires, and psychotherapists and allied professions have training in how to gather a history and assess suitability for a specific approach to therapy. As an aid to assessment, it is worth trying out one or two sessions of mapping and writing described so far in this book. If done in a tentative, side-by-side way, it is not building up high expectations and can help get enough understanding together to make treatment choices or have ideas about appropriate care and support.

If the client is suffering from serious illness, is unstable in the use of drugs or alcohol to the extent that they cannot begin and sustain a reflective personal conversation, then any form of active therapeutic help is limited to a supportive, contextual, welfare and counselling approach. But someone who is hostile to thinking personally and psychologically, or who is suspicious and mistrusting, or grossly self-important and contemptuous, may through a gentle, preliminary, process of sketching out word maps begin to see the possibility of a therapeutic bond. It is the feeling of a capacity to work side-by-side, however faint or troubled, that is the litmus test for therapy and of working together therapeutically.

An assessment needs to have some rehearsal of what that therapy with this person, at this time, might be like. The assessment is two way. The practical barriers to therapy are easily overlooked. Can a client afford the travel costs? Will the winter nights put a client off evening appointments? It is worth asking what might get in the way of, or compete with, regular therapy sessions.

Getting the therapy going

The therapist might begin by saying: is it okay for me to ask a few questions? Or where do you want to start? One colleague after a pause begins with a gentle enquiry, 'What's up?' This is often a relief to the first-time client, as their worst fear is a lack of structure which will feel un-containing. The therapist does not want to fall into an interview mode of listening. There should be lots of points at which the therapist is inviting the client's point of view and second thoughts.

> **Dear therapy**
>
> *I was glad during our first session that you didn't just leave me to wriggle around looking for words. You got involved alongside me. You asked if it was okay to ask questions. You prompted me with your 'doodle' words on paper. You showed you were listening and gave me space to come in.*

All that has been said in part one and two of this book applies to getting the therapy going. It may be helped by moments of conversational mapping as both client and therapist find their way more fully inside a key life story. In the process the therapist will be having his or her own hopes and fears but will be seeking to create the conditions for a shared experience of moments of building relational awareness whilst seeking to solve personal problems.

Boundaries

Another central task in the initial session is to talk about the boundaries to the therapy.

Some features of therapeutic boundaries are obvious and should be guaranteed. The client needs to know what the service and individual therapy can offer and be given a broad outline of how the therapist proposes to work. A clear statement about confidentiality, if or how information will be shared or used, should be given, as should the process around a missed appointment or illness. The client needs to feel some sense of choice about opting in or out of the therapy, to share some responsibility for naming any difficulties with the therapy and identifying goals and evaluating progress.

Saying no to therapy may at times be also therapeutic and space should be given to thinking about this without fear that the offer of therapy will be withdrawn. Naming and negotiating routine boundaries, offers a rehearsal for later managing more subtle, or riskier, boundaries as therapy progresses.

Shared sensitivity to, and awareness of, boundaries is an important element of developing relational awareness. It is through micro moments of approaching or crossing boundaries and recognising and negotiating them that client and therapist meet and figure out an appropriate level of self-disclosure and intimacy. The therapist has the greater power and responsibility. However, in working with transference, it will become clear that recognising and making therapeutic use of personal and professional boundaries is a shared responsibility. There is further discussion of this topic in relation to transference and enactments in **Chapter 4** on process mapping (page 94).

Taking time

Clarity about the duration of therapy and the active and therapeutic use of time is more important that the amount of time taken. In general, it makes sense to initially contract the number and length of sessions at the start and then review and restate this as part of the reformulation.

Many therapies end before the agreed number of sessions have been completed and this should be kept in mind throughout. It is wise to discuss in advance how to negotiate the ending if the client cannot or does not want to continue. In some settings it might make sense to count every session as the final session in some small way (Talmon, 1990).

Reformulation shapes the therapy

Reading out a written reformulation letter and the sharing of a reformulation diagram or therapy map are the defining tasks of the beginning stage of therapy. The term reformulation implies that something already formulated is being reformulated. Existing thinking is being rethought and understood in new ways. Reformulation is a process as much as a product; it must retain a quality that is tentative and open to further reformulation. Both the letter and the therapy map are always presented as drafts for further revision.

The process of reformulation will not follow a linear, step-by-step path. Therapy is intended to be a co-creative relationship that allows space for moments that are novel, surprising and spontaneous. Indeed, a therapy without surprises won't be very therapeutic! The therapist brings some confidence in his or her ability to shape and orchestrate the therapy. This confidence may come in part from having a framework to follow and a scaffolding within which to explore and build therapeutic work.

Whatever is mapped out and written out in the session is followed by the therapist offering to go away and tidy up and organise everything they have shared and understood so far, into something which is clearer and more useful. This gives the therapist space to digest and process on their own. They may also use supervision. However, it is equally an option and potentially more transparently and efficiently of value to the therapy to do this sorting and sifting together with the client in the session. The path which is taken will depend on the needs of the client, the expertise and style of the therapist.

Background to the idea of reformulation

Knowing something about the background to the discovery of the idea of reformulation helps explain the very collaborative way it is practiced now. The idea of reformulation for Ryle arose from his work in pioneering outcome research (Ryle 1979). With his research hat on he came up with short general descriptions of a few sentences (later called target problem procedures) which were a clear focus to the intended work of therapy. By spelling these out there was a baseline of description against which progress in the therapy could be measured at the end. Only in re-reading the description of the therapy problems at the end was there any sense of progress or change for the better in them. If there was a good outcome to therapy or a mixed outcome, then reference to this initial description would be the point of reference for evaluation. Ryle was not initially doing this for the client but as an outcome research measure. However, his clients were soon interested in his research method as a direct aid to the therapy and idea of formulating one or more key themes in the first few sessions and evaluating progress during and at the end became the first element of therapeutic writing in CAT.

The working out of the key themes was aided by a list of common patterns Ryle had derived from reviewing his cases during the research process. These became the basis of the psychotherapy file (page 185) which works as a personal, self-research tool for the client. Ryle and CAT were not alone in creating a short reformulation at the beginning of therapy. Something very similar can be seen with the work of Lester Luborsky (1990) and the idea of the core conflictual relationship theme.

Focus and shape to the therapy

A sequence of therapy sessions, whether time-limited or part of longer series, cannot consider all aspects of the client's life. It needs a focus, and this is achieved through asking questions about the client's life history, sketching out initial client stories, mapping the moment together in therapy and using tools such as the psychotherapy file. The client and therapist are gaining an overall picture, spotting, and naming the problems that may eventually become the target of the therapy. These target problems are the general personal problems that are standing in the way of achieving the client's goals.

Begin where it begins

As mentioned elsewhere, one of Anthony Ryle often cited phrases in supervision was to 'push where it moves'. This implies that we should go where there is readiness and willingness to go and avoid getting into a head-to-head confrontation when resistance is encountered. Learning to work at change is helped by early progress.

The client might begin with an immediate life event that is troubling them or they have a memory or story from the past. Having talked about a safe entry-level topic, they may jump tracks quite early on and find themselves diving into describing an event which links to their main difficulty. Such diving moments need noting and naming. It is okay to dive, as long as we notice, and negotiate, the water being dived into and the way back to a safe depth.

It can be of value to 'follow the flow' of the therapy; it may show a new path. The client may make new links. Sometimes we go in directions that carry implicit meaning that is not yet clear to us.

Sketches

At the beginning of therapy, we need simple sketches of the roles played in a key life story. These sketches initiate the client and the therapist's educational and healing relationship as they begin to learn a therapeutic attitude and develop relational thinking. Sketches are not seeking to be the complete therapy map but arise from moments of mapping together. Links between words, which are not yet fully formulated, will have arrows pointing into a blank space with a question mark. These half-formulated sequences are as important as the clearly formulated ones. They encourage a process of reflection and joint working. They show something about the emerging working relationship.

Sketching out a story works on several levels at the same time. It helps trace out the target problems and patterns but also allows relational thinking and feeling to take place in a way that resonates between person and paper and from micro-story to macro-story.

One therapist in the first session with a sixteen-year-old girl made six small sketches for each of the main events in her current life. They were all on a separate sheet in a pile and the therapist (as the session neared the end) spread them out neatly on the table between them. As they contemplated them, the young woman said, spreading her hands across all the sketches across all the pieces of paper, 'These are all parts of me'. It was a first moment of overview for her of the different sides of her life and her emerging identity, with all its troubles and possibilities as a young woman. Being able to encompass her contrasting experiences on paper made it easier to integrate them in her head. The subsequent work of the therapy over several sessions was for her to begin to work out 'how to hold myself together as I move between them.' This integrative capacity for an overview orchestral awareness is likely to precede, and make easier, tackling the difficulties on any one of the sketches.

Life-story maps

In contrast to sketches a life-story map is the framework for gathering a history of their life side-by-side with the client. It needs a big sheet of paper, sometimes more than one session, or an extended session. The map will be multi-local,[1] to borrow the rich and freeing phrase from the author Taiye Selasi, with a dispersed variety of hub reciprocal roles highlighting the various positions and patterns of people and events in the client's life. Seeing the bigger picture across a lifetime and across generations might complement a genogram or stand in place of it as a relational guide to patterns of influence upon the client's current experience. In the chapter on narrative mapping there is a fuller description of life-story maps. They are not the same as a therapy map or diagrammatic reformulation detailed in forthcoming pages. They are not looking for answers but seeking to be in and alongside history and memory. They are messier and are meant to offer a shared experience between client and therapist of holding in mind, and seeing on paper, all that is involved in stories leading to the client's life now. As highlighted in the chapter on relational awareness, it is a process of seeing myself and my life experiences in memory and in place both 'here and there' and 'now and then' through eyes of significant people and moments.

Multiple 'states' maps

Some people may be so distressed and unstable in their moods and sense of self that they come into first therapeutic contact in a crisis. In their distress they switch quickly between different moods. One client (Joe) came to the therapy room door full of anger at being kept waiting and treated 'badly' at reception. Very quickly Joe, shifted to being upset and expecting to be abandoned and then shifted minutes later to expressing regret for outbursts and being apologetic, which led then to insistently demanding forgiveness. After this Joe's mood went quiet and Joe became very switched off and numb, at which point the cycle reactivated, and anger came to the fore and a sense of being entitled.

They were still both standing in the doorway. The helper (it does not matter if they were a social worker, a therapist, a nurse or a doctor) invited Joe into the room and led, and invited Joe to touch the blank sheet of paper on a flip chart stand at the front of the room. The helper said 'Look it might be useful for us to put some words down for all these feelings. If we could just see them out there (pointing to the paper) it might just give us some sense of what to do that would help'.

The activity of putting the words on the board slowed things down. After a while Joe was drawn to the array of hot words on paper each with a circle around it. The words were: 'angry', 'hurt' and 'upset', 'ignoring' 'demanding' and 'expecting', 'rejected', 'guilty' and 'apologetic'. They were spread out all over the flip chart paper. They could both touch them

---

1   Taiye Selasi, in her writing and a Ted talk in seeking to escape definition of where are you from found a richer narrative in seeing herself made up of multiple local experiences as in the phrase 'multi-local' www.ted.com/talks/dont_ask_where_i_m_from_

and were stand side-by-side in front of the writing as it was expressed and tracked and recapped.

As these words were surveyed, Joe became admiring of the helper trying to map out what was going on. The helper said. 'Don't admire me, admire the words we have put down on the flipchart where we can touch them and interact with them and see how the do or don't link up'. Joe said 'I have never seen all of me in one place. So often I feel all over the place. But here, at least on paper we have got it together'. The helper then asked if it would be okay to have a slower look at the words on the big sheet of paper. They were both thinking and had both been affected in different ways by the storm of feelings that had just swept in.

The helper added the phrase 'thinking time' to the word map and said that what they wanted with Joe was some 'thinking time' about all these powerful feelings. The map was also introduced as potentially a space to talk about how these feelings kick against each other. Joe said that there was once 'thinking time' in childhood with 'Nan' but since she died there has been no one to think with. The helper said pointing to both 'thinking time' and 'Nan' on the map, 'I wonder if we could create some "Nan" time between us in honour of your relationship with her. We could sit down now for an hour and you could come back for "Nan" time over a number of sessions'. Joe pointed to the map and said, pointing to the different feelings 'I am still ragingly angry. I am still sad, and I am still hoping and expecting to get special attention'. Joe touched the words on the paper in naming each of the feelings that are still in the air. The helper tore the piece of paper off the flip chart and suggested sitting down at a table to mull over it some more and see how it all played out.

The preceding illustrative vignette is a fictionalised and dramatic account of what can sometimes happen in helping people who are working hard to survive a lot of emotional chaos and abuse in their lives. Joe's orchestral sense of self is lost in the jumping between different states. We might call them self-seeking states and, as some stability returns, a person in Joe's situation might settle into one of these states as a home for their sense of self. This is explored more in the preceding chapter on trauma and a divided sense of self. What is needed in such a first encounter with someone jumping from emotional state to state is compassion for the vulnerable search for a more secure emotional sense of self. Early and active mapping of the shifting self-states is essential.

In such circumstances any of us would find it difficult to orchestrate our conflicting feelings without being overwhelmed with anxiety. We would jump from one high-emotion state or over-controlled state to another. The helper in response can barely get a space to help because there is too much pressure to be pulled into responding to one strong pull of emotion or another. In CAT terms each separate emotion word on the map is a marker of a powerful call to reciprocate in a harmful or restrictive role. CAT practitioners have found that multiple state maps are a good way of catching the gaps, and missing links, as someone's sense of self jumps between these different emotionally charged positions in search of a containing haven. For the person in distress, it is a painful, retraumatising process. Helpers find it very hard to resist joining in the harmful jumps between emotions and states of mind. One source of help is the active, fast, side-by-side process of putting the shifting states, and emotions onto paper. In the above illustration the active, early, immediate mapping of multiple positions can offer a starting point for stability. It is a step towards lowering emotion enough to gain perspective and gain a side-by-side alliance from which, and only from which, thinking time or 'Nan' time can emerge. There is always the idea that someone who has been through abuse and trauma and denial has had a family figure who has been able to offer space and perspective in which thinking about self was allowed and more securely orchestrated.

Shared 'notes' preparation for the reformulation

The shared mapping can lead to, and be enhanced by, writing short notes in session, in a self-consciously therapeutic way as preparation for the therapy letter (pages 188-192). These are short, single paragraph, prose descriptions of patterns that are being drawn out from life-stories. There is an emotional immediacy in co-writing and then reading them aloud to get the procedural, sequential and dialogic feel of them with the client. Writing in the room proceeds at a different pace and with a different rhythm to mapping together. Making the choice of who does the writing and reading out, and who is being addressed, is therapeutic. The subsequent naming and sharing of the emotions involved is all part of the continuous process of helping the client become their own therapist. The style of such therapeutic writing and the various ways of doing 'dear therapy' letters and therapeutic sentences is described in chapter 6 on writing and voicing therapeutically. Either client or therapist may initiate such writing. It always needs dating and coding. Just as bits of mapping help prepare the ground for the therapy map, so also bits of writing can help prepare the ground for the sharing of the therapy letter.

Therapy goals, problems and patterns maintaining them

Not all issues and problems facing the client can be addressed within the limited time of a therapy. The primary task, therefore, is to identify together one or two goals on which to concentrate. Within CAT, the things that are blocking the client reaching their goals, or are at the heart of their distress, are called target problems. For example, the goal of therapy might be to socialise more, and the target problems might be 'I am critical of myself and do not think others will want to spend time with me'. These target problems are the difficulties or issues on which the therapy will focus, and by which success or failure will be jointly measured at the end of therapy.

As target problems are identified then the next task is to work out the habitual patterns of relating to self and others that are sustaining these target problems. These are called 'target problem procedures.' Teasing them out in detail can arise from mapping and sketching but it can also be helped by reference to, and discussion of, the psychotherapy file, once completed by the client.

Identifying the target problems and procedures, alongside the client's goals, are the important initial work of the therapy. Following a discussion of the psychotherapy file in the pages below, the shaping and mapping out of a target problem procedure will be described.

The psychotherapy file

The psychotherapy file is one of the tools that has played a role in the development of the cognitive analytic approach. It arose from the outcome research work of Ryle (1979), as already mentioned. It offers a selection of brief sequential descriptions of typical, high-level patterns of relating to self and others. These target problem patterns are described in clusters as traps, dilemmas and snags. A trap is a narrow view about achieving aims that then shapes behaviour and produces response from others which fits and ramps up the narrow view. Traps are like self-fulfilling prophecies or vicious circles. They highlight the cognitive side of CAT in that their focus is the thinking component of the self-defeating pattern.

Dilemmas are like two linked traps. However, the focus is on the limited choice of behaviour. They are forced polarised choices of behaviour. If I don't do this and end up here, I will do that and end up there. There is no middle ground. They are signposted on maps as 'either/or'. An example would be brilliant but anxiously exposed, or useless and unworthy but safe from challenge. One extreme seems to offer an escape from the other. If I am at one end of the polarised choice, then the other end may be partially dissociated and out of awareness. In the psychotherapy file some of the dilemmas are interpersonal, and some are internal and divided forms self-management.

Finally, a snag is a situation where what I want is okay and potentially achievable but, in the process of moving towards achievement, progress is blocked by a forbidding voice from within or from society. These snags are the deeper analytic dynamics or the socially constructed imbalances of power and opportunity. In the former case, I may be making progress in a career as woman or working-class man but then sabotage success because, in my mind, I am not allowed to succeed more than my mother or father without betraying them. In the case of a snag, what I want, think or do is okay but it triggers another position from outside or within which stops or undermines my healthy aims and/or beliefs. Any of the patterns whether traps, dilemmas or snags will be enacted in therapy as part of a transference laden interaction.

The psychotherapy file lists these common patterns in ordinary language and the client is invited to take the file home, go through it, and edit or add to some of the statements to make them fit their own experience. They may note patterns which once applied but are less so now, or which apply to important people in their lives. Listing these patterns in everyday language offered the client a ready reckoner against which to prepare to work out their own patterns with the therapist. The psychotherapy file and the idea of traps, dilemmas and snags has been somewhat replaced as a tool by mapping and sketching out patterns in the early sessions. It can still be a supplement to this mapping work. At the least the psychotherapy file helps develop psychological awareness and relational thinking. The file includes self-management and interpersonal patterns and forms of self-sabotage. It is concluded with a list of helpful and limiting or disturbing states of mind that are very useful in linking back to the kind of rapid state shifting described in the preceding pages under the title of multiple states maps. A copy of the psychotherapy file is available through the following link (http://internationalcat.org//pdf/ThePsychotherapyFile-inwords.pdf).

The target problem procedures

The phrase 'target problem procedure' is a CAT concept that is technically accurate but not so easy to convey in the ordinary language of therapy. They are the problem patterns located in the wider context of self and of personal history drawn out from the map. The felt experience of them and their 'push and pull to repetition' are best described in writing in one or two sentences. As discussed at different points in the book, their wording and their sequencing, and their part in a larger orchestration may change as the therapy progresses. Target problem patterns stand at the heart of the therapy letter and are the most identifiable sequences within and between reciprocal role positions on the therapy map (see below). The work of drawing them out and gathering a shared sense of clarity about them between client and therapist is the pivotal work of the therapy. The relationship pattern that makes up a target problem procedure within and between reciprocal roles on paper has been explored in detail in **Chapter 2** on relational mapping.

The therapy maps

The therapy map is a reformulation diagram, or in the technical and specialised language of CAT, a sequential diagrammatic reformulation

(SDR for short) or multiple self-states diagram (MSSD for short) in the CAT literature. In this book it is referred to more simply as the therapy map. The therapy map is the overall, tidy map for the client to take away and refer to as a source of reference for therapeutic work within and between sessions.

Over the first four or five sessions, the process of reformulation results in a jointly reworked and refined therapy map which draws up an understanding of the client's problematic patterns or target problem procedures. Such a map can help shape, contain and guide a therapeutic journey. It can become a focal tool and reference point for the client and therapist during therapy, and for the client, beyond the end of therapy. It may do the work of the therapy reformulation letter in a more visual way.

To some extent client and therapist are hedging their bets that one of the tools (letter or map) may bring the desired breakthroughs. The making and shared ownership of a therapy map by client and therapist is one of the central concerns of supervision during reformulation at the beginning of therapy. With a map the therapist, client and supervisor can hold in mind several parts to a conversation and make links across several stories, between past and present and inner and outer realities. A map can link the bigger picture and small details of life experience, and link symbolic thought processes with actions and behaviours. It is the vehicle for testing and tracking therapeutic change and building a greater degree of relational and orchestral awareness.

It is the result of the variety of work of the earlier reformulation sessions with sketches, the psychotherapy file, life maps and, if needed, multiple state maps.

The therapy map is for the therapist and the client. The therapist may feel able to make this overall and tidy map together with the client. Equally the therapist may feel freer and more able to gather their thoughts by saying they will go away and put the map together to present at the next session. This process mirrors the bringing together of writing in the reformulation letter. The use of one enhances the understanding of the other.

Whether worked on with the client or taken away between sessions, it is a different kind of activity to mapping as an immediate therapeutic process. It is a drawing together of the therapy. The therapist needs to feel they have done their best in thinking it through and getting it right enough for it to work for the therapy and for the client. It is the map that will ultimately guide the therapy, whereas preceding sketches and life-mapping might be valued more as stepping-stones to the therapy map and a means of building an alliance.

The therapy map is usually extracted from the early sketches and the life-map. In many cases it may greatly resemble a simplified life-map. It is best if it is tidy, clear, and simple enough for the client to take home and routinely refer to as a way of monitoring the enactment of problems patterns of interaction.

One client called it the 'fridge door map' because that is where she kept it for reference, pinned up with a magnet. Its language and structure have been refined for the business of practical therapy. It should not be too complex or crowded so that there is space for recognition of gaps and additions. It might have different coloured ink for different patterns.

As described in Chapters 1-6, the process of arriving at a therapy map can be anxiety provoking. As one client said, 'At first I thought we were going around the houses to get to the point of eventually trying to tackle my problem. Now I realise that we needed to go around the houses to see my problems in the context of my life'. Therapy maps do what CAT does best by linking the solving of problems and management of symptoms, to the bigger story of self-functioning and self-identity.

The therapy letters

The CAT therapist, having gathered a picture and found a focus, puts this down in plain language as a personal letter to the client. Writing and letters (like mapping and maps) need considering as both process and product. The process follows distinct steps; gathering the material for the letter, making a first draft and sharing this draft by reading it out, handing a copy over to the client, who then may revise and extend it, and finally agreeing a completed letter. This process is a powerful distillation of the whole reformulation journey at the beginning of therapy. Like the map, it can be an activity which brings out patterns of transference, acting as an enactment magnet for characteristic ways of relating for both client and therapist.

The therapy letter offers a record of shared understanding and puts it into a clearly organised shape for use as a therapy guide in the weeks ahead. It is best written early on at around session three or four and read out in draft form. It is important to make a distinction between reformulation as a narrative, which is the story of what the therapy is about, and the story of how the therapy is going to be achieved and is being experienced. This latter story is part of the creation of a healing narrative and is the story of how the therapy works. (For more consideration of the idea of therapy as the art of holding open four different stories that can easily be lost one within the other see page 140 and in the next chapter on page 201.)

The therapy letter has the following components.

1. A positive, welcoming opening sentence at the beginning should give hope. It is indicated as a draft to be read out and shared and revised. It is offering a plan for the therapy in an open and transparent way. It is a summary of 'our' work so far, addressed to the client but also to the therapy. It is proposing to shape the future therapy journey and the healing narrative.

2. It is usually written in the form of a letter from the therapist to the client. The therapist has indicated the preceding week that she or he will go away and write up all the bits of writing, thinking, and mapping they have done so far. There are variations on this as indicated in chapter 6 on writing and voicing. The letter could be co-written in the therapy session with the therapist as scribe. Or the letter could be written in the first person as if from the point of view of the client to themselves. More likely it will have multiple forms of addressing ranging from 'you to I' to 'me and we'.

3. The help seeking story (as a reciprocal role procedure?) may be described giving context to the place of this therapy has in the client's life and pointing to the initial goals for help that led the client to the therapist. This is a useful source of reference for client and therapist at the end of therapy to see if the original need for help has been met and the dynamics of help seeking have been understood.

4. Target problems are the agreed focus of therapy. They are the problems that the therapy will target (with an open understanding that there may be other problems that are not the target at present or not suitable for therapy to tackle). For each target problem there will be a sentence or small paragraph describing the target problem procedures, that play a part in maintaining problems.

5. The next part of the letter is the history of the problem procedures and the wider life story around the key reciprocal roles and past events. Its function is to give a narrative sense of the problem pattern, where it came from and how it once served a necessary, if limiting, function but is now an enduring and dysfunctional habit.

6. In writing the personal history to problem patterns it is vital that all the elements of this have been rehearsed in the early sessions. The words in the letter must come from and be anchored in the client's experience and not read out as an unexpected or surprise point of view of the therapist.

7. The next component is a paragraph about how the therapy relationship is developing and might progress, succeed, get stuck or be challenged. It is an opportunity to recap moments already in therapy where the client's pattern and the therapist's response has been alive in the room and has been discussed. These sentences will be laying down a marker that it is okay to talk about how we are doing to help or hinder the therapy. They need care in writing so that it is something more than a general statement of hopes and fears but more precisely naming something that has already happened and might happen again as a help or a hindrance.

8. At this point there may be a statement about possible exits from the patterns identified but not yet experienced or worked with. These become more of a focus in the middle of therapy and are discussed in the next chapter on pages 209.

9. The letter ends with an optimistic and concluding sentence about the use of the letter to review progress. Increasingly there is the option in CAT to invite the client to write a reply, if they are happy to use the medium of writing, and this can be read out the following week.

Therapists sometimes confuse writing a history of the client's life with writing a historical summary of the target problem procedures. Not only can reading an entire life history be overwhelming for the client, but the meaning and implications for the therapy can be lost.

An exception to this is when the goal of therapy is to achieve a healing narrative to help restore a sense of self in response to hurt and trauma in childhood. In this case the therapist may write a narrative account which is explicitly confirming and validating the client's story. The letter is an invitation for the client to recover side-by-side with the therapist a capacity to be a reliable and honest narrator of their lives. It is worth considering meeting this need separately from the reformulation letter. It may, for example, be powerful and helpful to write it side-by-side with the client over a therapy session or two. Or it might be an exercise in the middle of therapy writing 'a life story' letter together in session.

Getting the balance between too little history and too much is crucial. Letters which contain too much can be beyond the client's reach and readiness, can feel accusing and can make the client feel stupid, guilty or overwhelmed. Therapists gets stuck writing reformulation letters because they are investing it with too much. In this context, it is worth exploring the tension between the letter which invites further work, and the letter which has been worked on so much that there is nothing for the client to do or add.

Functions of a reformulation letter
The following highlight functions of the reformulation letter.

1. The letter functions as a record and source of reference as to where the therapy began and as a guide for the middle and end phases of therapy

2. As with other therapy tools it will function as an expression of the co-creative partnership of the therapy and be an enactment magnet for elements of the transference alliance.

3. It may be experienced as a controlling or judging process or as collusive and being 'taken-in', since the truth has been bypassed from the client's private point of view.

4. If the mapping process is an expression of shared responsibility, the writing of the letter may function as an expression of care and validation during the reading out of the letter or in the client's private re-reading of it when they get home. In all events it is a channel for the transference processes that are current in the therapy.

5. An opportunity for the client to be more the observer than the participant in their lives. (An opportunity for outsider empathy for self.)

6. It can serve as a brake on or accelerator of the therapy process, as it is an aid to looking forward into the therapy work ahead and giving it shape and coherence.
7. Helps counter therapy drifting around without direction.
8. A focus for outcome review at the end.
9. It models transparency and openly working together.

As previously discussed, the reading of the therapy letter may already have been rehearsed with earlier bits of writing that have accompanied the mapping process. This ensures the therapist can pitch the letter within the client's reach or zone of proximal development. It guards against the client feeling overwhelmed.

These reflections may make the letter sound daunting but if mapping and writing has been done collaboratively throughout the beginning of therapy, then the letter should appear as something made together and not as a stand-alone object. This reduces the pressure to provide the 'perfect' letter and allows both client and therapist to add their input. One check is to think who the letter is for; it is written for the therapy and, therefore, can be as much for the therapist to gather, structure and check out their understanding as it is for the client. As one client said to his therapist. 'This letter of yours to me doesn't really help me much but it has obviously helped you and that is going to help me indirectly.'

When writing the letter, it is important not to see it as an enduring document but something for the therapy which is good enough to work with in the lifetime of the therapy. It is not meant to be an assessment or character portrait of the client and so careful consideration should be given to whether it is stored in the notes of the client. Different systems have different rules about this. However, it is important to consider whether what is written in the letter will be read by those who might accept it as 'truth' about the person, rather than an aid to the process of therapy, leading to information from it to be used inappropriately. If so, and if the letter must be filed, it should be accompanied by an explanation and guidelines of how the information is to be used.

The reading and voicing of the therapy letter

The therapist indicates a wish to read the letter aloud to the client. It is proposed as a means for both to connect more fully with the ideas. The client knows that they will have a copy to take away and read through on their own at home. Some therapists prefer to read the letter all the way through, without interruption. They see it as a more intense and complete experience. Mostly therapists should be flexible and see what works best with which client and, of course, be consultative with the client as to what might work for them. It can take a whole session to work through a letter and ideally the therapist will pause and comment at points during the reading out, and the client will equally interrupt or want to add comments. In addition, there will be moments of resonance and emotional connection that need noting.

Giving voice in a compassionate and open way to key phrases and points in the letter is an invitation for the client and therapist to connect interpersonally and for meanings from the letter to resonate emotionally and cathartically. The client needs a clear invitation to interrupt, comment upon or to let the reading of the letter flow through to its conclusion.

The therapist needs practice to be able to read out the letter in a way that is neither too anxious nor too disconnected and is ready to accept challenge, be vulnerable and sometimes to own and advocate for their perspective if challenged by the client.

The reading out of the therapy letter is often overlooked as a key therapeutic activity. Therapists are not typically the most theatrical of people and nor should they be. However, the process of reading a letter that they have spent time and effort composing is the central dramatic moment of the developing therapy relationship. In staging and working through therapeutically focused writing there is an opportunity to be in contact with the interplay of *what* is spoken and *how* it is spoken. The voice may touch unspoken thoughts and feelings that lie beyond or beneath what is being read out. The voice may shimmer and hover over specific words. When the reformulation letter is read out, it is a different quality of talk to that associated with earlier therapeutic conversation; the voicing is more deliberate, more staged, has more of an 'addressing' quality of 'me' self-consciously saying this to 'you' now. It is an invitation with the client to feel the emotions and ideas evoked by the writing in a different, more resonant, and connected way as they are freed from their side of conversational turn taking.

Sometimes, CAT therapists 'bypass' the exposure and anxiety of giving voice to what they have written and read in a monotone, as if only the verbal aspects of the voicing matter and the vocal aspects can be ignored. The voicing of the letter is an invitation to re-vocalise, to hear familiar life experience in a different voice and to take the opportunity to reword, revisit and further 'reformulate' the reformulation. It is an act of bringing implicit knowing (Stern 1985) to a more explicit and conscious level of knowing. The reading out as a therapeutic mechanism should not be overlooked in preference for a focus on the content and structure of the writing. Therapists who give attention to the process of reading out the letter and the tone and pitch of their voice are more likely to connect with their own and the client's feelings. Supervisees can practice by reading out each other's letters.

Writing is not the only medium

Writing as the key medium will not suit every client and therapist. The first five years of writing reformulation letter predated the common use of personal computers and the letters were handwritten. They still can be handwritten and there is something more immediate more mutual and 'honest' about writing and sharing a handwritten letter. They may also be more efficient in the use of time since there is no scope for editing and revising.

The personal reformulation letter is a compassionate retelling of the client's life story. It is not a chronological story but a telling in personal terms of the client's evolving relationship with themselves and the world, including the key people over two or more generations who have shaped that relationship. Again, this can be done in different ways with different people. One client might dictate the personal reformulation from the life map with therapist typing it out on a laptop. Or client and therapist might finger walk around the life map, recapping the patterns, roles, positions, and times in the person's life story whilst capturing it by video or audio recording. This can be a very therapeutic, clarifying, and empowering activity. However, many if not most CAT therapists find something special in the gift of writing a letter, carefully composed, and drawing upon the first four sessions, building on the therapy map, and then read out to the client. It is a form of bearing witness to the client's struggles and successes in life.

As a final thought to the process of mapping and writing to co-create the experience of reformulation, it is worth considering how the map and the letter feed into and build on each other. More and more CAT therapists are finding that the early mapping activity creates a clear scaffolding for writing the letter. The first things to be clear about the letter writing from the map are the identified target problem patterns. Writing these out from the map in session is a sure way of clarifying them and connecting with them. Once they have been agreed between client and therapist, they can be the centre piece of the reformulation letter.

In sharing the draft of the letter with the client, the prose description of the patterns identified on the map may be modified. The language may deepen, or the sequence of the pattern may change. It is quite okay, and likely to be therapeutic, to go from the letter back to the map and change the map somewhat. In this way the writing builds on the map and the mapping builds on the writing. In the process a reformulation story is established, and a healing narrative comes alive.

Common problems at the beginning of therapy

Therapy is rarely a smooth ride, though often the challenges, conflicts, and difficulties we encounter and negotiate lead to therapeutic breakthroughs.

It can be helpful to think about some of the problems that can arise at the beginning of therapy, and some possible responses.

Too deep, too quickly

One of the great advantages of working transparently and openly through mapping is that the client can see the route that the therapy is taking. It encourages the therapist to check on the direction, pace, tone, drama and progress of the therapy. Passive listening without the map can risk the client imagining a depth of understanding and empathy from the therapist that is not yet there. Or, in the spirit of attention and empathy, the client goes deeper than they can cope with or personally track unless there is a mapping activity to monitor and pace progress. Emotions may be delved into and expressed without the accompanying scaffold, digging a deep emotional hole very rapidly without a therapeutic ladder to climb back out. Mapping can contribute to tracking and pacing the conversation as it deepens. Through recapping and stopping and seeing the bigger picture, there are ways to work back to safer, or more surface territory.

Wow, I am sorted!

The initial sessions may be quickly effective in helping the client see patterns around problems that are long standing but now appear easy to change. The client then makes an apparent 'flight to health', disengaging from therapy. For example, James was able to engage in the mapping process to make sense of some of the difficult patterns he experienced in relationships, and some ideas about how he might move forward were emerging. At the end of the second session he sat back, surveyed the map that he and the therapist had begun together and announced that he was incredibly grateful, he was now 'sorted'. He stated emphatically that it would be fine to stop the sessions and give someone else a chance, and that he would be recommending the therapist to others!

He was persuasive and reassuring. Without the initial sketch to hand it would have been natural to go along with his view, and perhaps also indulge the therapist's narcissism in believing something the therapist had done had elicited such miraculous results. Together they looked over the sketch they had made and wondered whether there was much more to discover. There is a difference between gaining insight and relief from therapy and learning to be your own therapist. The therapist was able to think together about how James's wanting to end therapy might relate to his patterns in relationships of giving up on himself and making room for others, often ignoring his own needs.

Ally or accomplice?

At the beginning of session three, Jenny announced that she had fallen love with someone after some time being single and unattached. By her account, she had got very involved very quickly and in therapy was now talking nineteen to the dozen about her new partner, her hopes for their future and how their lives might progress. Much of the session was taken up by the news of this new relationship and Jenny's obvious joy at meeting someone who she felt was strong and would take care of her. The new partner sounded quite firm in his views and was giving Jenny much advice about how to live her life.

The therapist was hovering and shimmering between wanting to share Jenny's delight but also to wonder about the power of this new relationship to stop any therapeutic relationship developing. Would the new person be an ally of the therapy or an accomplice to limiting any breakthrough in the therapy? It was Jenny who raised the issue of keeping the two important spaces separate. It led to a productive discussion through mapping out different kinds of appropriate intimacy and the importance of meeting needs in different ways with different people.

Delaying the reformulation

Therapists may bring with them a pressure to get things right and make a perfect reformulation map and letter. They keep postponing the day for reading out the reformulation letter or sharing a tidy therapy map. Procrastination makes them more anxious to get it right but less able to know what the evidence for getting it right would be. By sharing something that is less than perfect, the therapist is offering an 'open-story making' relationship that depends as much on the client's contribution as that of the therapist.

Brilliant or no good

There might be many reasons that the therapist or therapy becomes idealised. High regard for the therapy or the therapist is not always a problem if it can be noticed and negotiated. For example, the therapy might become idealised as 'the thing that is definitely going to help', or the reformulation lauded as brilliantly helpful, original, and transformative. Idealisation should not be confused with genuine appreciation for the therapeutic work. However, if the client is unable to offer any constructive criticism or feedback about how therapy is progressing, alarm bells should start to ring. Likewise, attempts to keep the therapy and therapist 'good', despite obvious mistakes such as being late to a session, should act as an alert that something needs exploring. There may also be times when the therapist or the therapy is dismissed, 'this is rubbish, how qualified are you anyway'? The aim is to work side-by-side in a realistic and 'good enough' way. Noticing, naming and exploring both idealisation and dismissal can illuminate times when this has also happened outside the therapy room.

We are confused

It would be odd, given the complexity of therapeutic work, if both client and therapist did not have times of being confused. In such cases, it can be extremely helpful to place the words 'confusing - confused' at the centre of a sheet of paper. The words and arrows pointing to or away from both ends of this reciprocation can help them work it out together thereby uniting therapist and client in mutual exploration. The key shift is in verbing the noun 'confusion': 'something is **confusing**, and we are feeling **confused**'. At the top of the paper above the **confusing to confused** reciprocal role could be put the magic words '**sorting to sorted**'. In asking each other what it would be like to be 'sorted' and how natural it is to have times of being 'confused', a more honest and collaborative relationship can emerge.

Forgetting to routinely map the moment

It is easy to overlook talking about the relationship in the room until there is a crisis and then it is like to be embarrassing or anxiety making. A weekly progress map as described on page 84 helps set up a routine of talking about the therapy relationship by having a five minute 'here and now' progress review assisted by mapping immediate moments of interaction in the room. Having the routine in the background can give a framework for talking about more difficult, therapy threatening, enactments when, or if, they arise.

Sessions are missed

When sessions are missed at the beginning of therapy it needs to be talked through. A simple map can help. The tone should be of curiosity about what we are doing. Missing sessions may be for external reasons but also may be symptomatic of something that needs negotiating together. CAT therapists tend to actively contact clients who don't attend and offer, by phone or in a short letter, possible links of the missed session to the focus of therapy. It is always worth considering a temporary pause to the therapy if there are important short-term factors affecting attendance such as new job, relationship or bereavement.

Supervision

For therapists working relationally supervision is not a luxury. If a more senior or experienced supervisor is not in reach or affordable then peer supervision, if given a reliable routine and good shared authority, can be just as good. The measure of value of supervision of any kind is its easy accessibility, reliability and its capacity to function as a space where we take our concerns about the relationships between ourselves, the client and the activity of therapy.

Early sketches and bits of writing can be fruitfully shared in supervision and help prepare the ground for reformulation. It is common to take a draft of a reformulation letter or therapy map to supervision. It makes even more sense to take a first draft of the target problems and procedures to supervision. These are the lynch pin of the shaping and holding of the therapy. Since the time of supervision is limited it can help to choose one paragraph form the draft letter to read out, or map what might have been a troublesome or breakthrough moment with the client.

Experienced therapists need to use supervision as much as beginners. One short exercise to bring to supervision is a simple and short 'dear therapy' letter which the therapist writes for five minutes about their view of the possibilities, challenges, and scope of the therapy as it stands at present. It is addressed to the therapy but can be useful for the therapist and the supervisor. It may give a new focus to carry back to the client.

Concluding comments

The beginning of a therapy relationship is an engaging and testing process. By the end of the beginning stage, client and therapist will have a sense of having worked hard at shaping the work to be done. They should have a small portfolio folder of sketches, a messy life map and bits of writing in the form of therapeutic notes and 'dear therapy' letters, the centre piece of which is a reformulation letter and a therapy map. Alongside such work the client and therapist hopefully will have a sense of beginning a unique kind of relationship with the shared use of tools and activities for a co-creative therapy which may hopefully build a healing narrative.

Chapter 10: What to do in the middle of therapy

'In an analytic situation, the analyst is concerned with trying to make conscious, trying to bring to awareness to something which the patient has often spent his life trying to make unconscious.' (Wilfred Bion, a Seminar held in Paris, 1978)

Introduction

These pages are about the middle phase of therapy. They explore time and tasks in the middle and the quality of the relationship with specific reference to therapist versatility. The work following reformulation and the use of progress rating sheets is considered. There is a focus on some of the mechanisms of change linked to the use of mapping therapeutically in the middle of therapy.

In the chapter on the beginning of therapy there was the story of reformulation and a compassionate understanding with the client of the trouble they are in. Now in the middle of therapy a second story takes centre stage alongside the reformulation story. The recurring name for this second story throughout this book is the 'healing narrative'. This is the story of how therapist and client go about sustaining a process of change together. In this vein, there are illustrations of working and consideration of some common problems that arise in the middle of therapy. The chapter concludes with notes on what to take to supervision.

Time in the middle of therapy

Being in the middle of a relationship is a good place from which to look back to the beginning and forward to the ending. It can so easily be a place to get lost or come to a premature conclusion or resolution. Both client and therapist can mistake the heightened awareness and engagement of the reformulation work at the beginning as the high point of insight and, given the struggle of getting this far, see it as a job now done. Another risk is to lose the focus of the reformulation and set off in a new direction. For the therapist the task in the middle of therapy is to hold onto the focus of the journey as understood in the beginning phase of therapy. Time can seem to stand still and the work feel less structured. The challenge is to keep the shape of the therapy whilst responding to the immediate experience of the relationship.

All models of therapy create time boundaries and structures; it is both containing and clarifying to have a clear sense of a beginning, middle and end from the start of therapy. A clear 'timetable' of sessions helps shape and pace the work and it models an open, honestly negotiated, limited relationship.

It is easy to procrastinate, give more time, collude or get distracted or lost in the middle of therapy. We can become over-concerned with welfare and solving immediate life problems, whilst losing sight of the therapy plan and focus on target problems.

Mixed feelings about the passage of therapy time might resonate with mixed feelings about change. At the beginning, it may feel like sixteen or twenty-four weeks is too much time. In the middle the time may feel like it is running out and may be used to avoid change, 'If only I had more time with you then change would be possible.' Patterns like this may be caught in a moment of expression, or an aside, and might be voiced by the therapist or the client. These are ideal moments for process mapping, as they may be a direct route to a deeper concern. All therapies have recurring patterns of attachment. The value of the weekly, five-minute slot to 'map the moment' (page 84) and review progress cannot be overstated.

The middle phase will vary in length but may be four, eight, twelve sessions after the reformulation and before a 'four session' phase of ending. Even a long term, open-ended therapy should have an episodic structure with times to review and end and thereby be in the middle of a focused piece of therapeutic work. There are times in the middle when the client has a sense of being their own therapist and there is movement between the three tracks of personal problem solving, developing self-understand and recovering or discovering relational awareness.

In CAT the aim is to see and experiment with exits from the targeted problem patterns and these exits can take many forms. These exits are the new resources with which the client protects and validates their sense of self and builds safety and self-esteem. The middle phase of therapy is a valuable time to access deeper feelings of hurt, anger, loss, or shame against which the target problem procedures are often an important defence. Or to visit lost dreams and see where new motivation to achieve may be rekindled. This might be a time when client and therapist yoyo between work with more surface ways of coping and going deeper beneath the problematic patterns to unmanageable feelings, unmet needs, or unformulated experiences. As described in Chapter 8 on relational healing, if these can be encountered, held and can be made meaningful through re-thinking, retelling and rewording, the client can learn to live with them in different ways and discover untried skills by letting go of high-cost ways of coping.

There can be a pressure for both therapist and client to 'make things better'. The client may pretend, and the therapist may collude in being overly positive. Deep change in relation to self and personal problems takes time and needs patience to sit with a full awareness of what is going wrong - the hidden and unresolved hurt - alongside working out alternatives which are freer or more healing. Moments of mapping an exit onto the map, or on a separate sheet, can help validate new resources that are being developed and enabled.

In the middle of four stories

In **chapter 7** the idea of holding a therapeutic space open between four distinctive stories was introduced (page 140). To recap these were the client's stories of their present life distinguished from stories of earlier life and especially childhood. Linked to these two distinctive areas of storying telling was the distinction between the story of diagnosis and formulation and the story of treatment and the emerging healing narrative.

In the middle of therapy, it may help to understand therapeutic work as a joint struggle to sustain relational awareness in the spaces between these four stories. There is space for the delicate, co-creative and uncertain process of 'narrative weaving' making links and finding gaps between and among these four stories as part of a therapeutic process of memory reconsolidation, problem solving and developing the therapeutic capacity of the client and the therapy relationship.

Reformulation becomes the basis of a healing narrative

The therapist's job in the middle is to compassionately hold to the agreed shape of the therapy. The therapy map and letter are a source of shared authority and reference as the therapy plan. The target problems and procedures are best written out on one sheet of paper separate from the letter with accompanying map, or maps, making them easy to locate, if needed, during the middle sessions of therapy.

The therapy map and reformulation letter (described in the previous chapter) play a key role in the management of the middle phase. They are a scaffolding and evidence of a collaborative agreement to work in a certain way on certain things. The therapy map is a 'root and route' map for the therapy. The collaboration over the reformulation is the prelude to building and testing a collaborative working alliance in the middle of therapy.

> *'The role of reformulation is to illustrate and challenge the negative consequences of the individual's social formation and to support the patient in the recognition and revision of what has not gone well but was previously not recognised.'*
>
> (Ryle & Kerr, 2002)

Reformulation in CAT is both a healing process and a clarifying product. The process of **how** we do the reformulation is as important as **what** we do with it. The process of doing the reformulation serves to build a collaborative alliance, create a therapeutic space and set a healing narrative in motion. The shared understanding that is agreed through the therapy map and letter serves to guide and evaluate the work. These come together in the middle of therapy, week by week and incident by incident.

CAT therapists refer affectionately (in the English language) to the three R's: **reformulation** of problems, recognition based on the **reformulation** and **revision** arising out of **recognition**. However, even at the beginning of reformulation there will be moments of recognition and opportunities for revision of patterns. The relative emphasis on reformulation, recognition and revision will vary with the stage of therapy. As the overall picture of the reformulation becomes clear, and is jointly established by therapist and client, then recognition becomes the main concern. With recognition comes the opportunity to micro-manage, opportunities for exiting from problematic patterns and developing different ways of coping. Most often in a CAT therapy there are two or three target problems and procedures. They are likely to be linked, therefore recognition and revision of one procedure may help with recognition and revision of others.

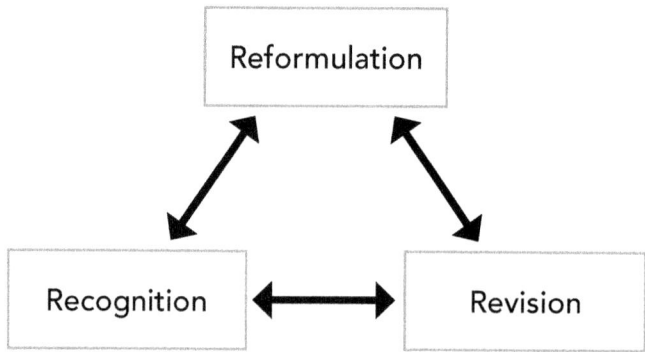

There may be many a client for whom increased ability to reformulate is the important therapeutic exit. This is the over-riding idea of relational awareness as one of the general gains in therapy and one of the exits from distressing patterns. I may still be suffering in my life, but I can understand it and steer it better. In response to relational trauma, the problem is not with a chain of faulty cognitions but a general absence of ability to think relationally and compassionately about one's self in the world. In the chapter on relational trauma this was described as gaps in self-knowledge. Developing some adult (or teenage) confidence in the capacity to think about the patterns of hide and seek with these gaps may be a major therapeutic step of recognition.

In the middle of therapy, specific educational and therapeutic activities can come to the fore under the general title of 'working at change'. This includes using the therapeutic space consciously to work through in-session enactments, agreeing, setting and reviewing homework tasks, monitoring change and reviewing breakthroughs and setbacks. The middle might be thought of as 'hovering and shimmering time' characterised by an increased tolerance of the anxiety and ambivalence that accompanies increased awareness. There is space to be versatile and to use the shared understanding built around the mapping and writing of reformulation to apply a wide range of specific interventions drawing upon other approaches to therapy.

The relationship in the middle of therapy

Client and therapist will now have a sense of working together and a shared idea about the focus and direction of therapy. The reciprocal role of 'compassionately exploring and understanding leading to accepted, valued and understood' will ideally have been noticed, named and placed on the therapy map (see figure below).

The middle of therapy is where the therapeutic relationship is balancing containment and support with experiment and exploration. Enactments that happen in the therapy space are noticed and explored against the backdrop of the therapy map and the reformulation work. Enough of an alliance or partnership has been created to maintain a transference friendly climate. Ruptures and conflict might emerge, testing both the client's and therapist's capacity to work side-by-side to make sense of what is happening.

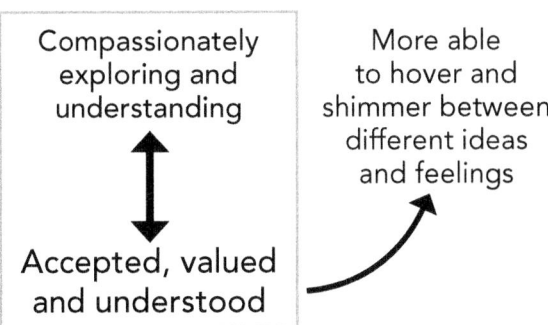

Patterns of the clients will be carried over and activated in the therapy relationship as transference into the middle of therapy. Also, the therapist's professional, and personal transference will be in play. This will be either as an element of a counter transference response to the push and pull of the client's patterns or as a response to the push and pull of the system, agency and profession around them. The therapist will have the organisation's voices in her or his head. 'See more clients, be effective, don't promise what you cannot deliver.' Against this may be their mother's voice. 'Be nice to people, especially to those who are hurt or wounded.'

The ideas and skills of hovering, shimmering, constructive dithering and processing highlighted by the chapters on therapeutic mapping have their moments in the middle stage of therapy. We are continuously learning how to be in, and near, contrasting feelings, role responses, positions or viewpoints. As a reminder here are some activities, qualities and concepts that can support the therapeutic partnership in the middle of therapy.

- Be aware of 'being' together in therapeutic conversation rather than 'doing' it. Look for and allow moments of participating sincerely, spontaneously and wholeheartedly in the retelling and reworking of the client's life stories.
- Tolerate and get alongside the moments of ambivalence as interpersonal entanglements and misunderstandings arise. Rather than seeking to tidy up, make neat or make absolute, allow contact with uncertainty.
- Acknowledge the push and pull between ideally desired and feared and forbidden positions and coping responses that are harmful or avoided.
- Allow the idea that we may be projecting, identifying with or working through patterns that originate elsewhere but are being enacted in the space of the therapy.

The goal is to be touching and encountering troublesome feelings without being overwhelmed or engulfed by them. Client and therapist are learning together, week-by-week, how to be in a therapeutic relationship. They should neither rest on their laurels, assume or expect defeat, nor take the relationship as fixed.

It is part of the therapist's training to seek to be present in a consistent manner week by week. It would be a mistake for the therapist to think that the client will do the same. One week, life events may have left the client feeling low. Another week there might be an unusual level of vulnerability and willingness to trust the therapy space with hard to manage emotions. The following week the client may feel upbeat and full of ideas. The therapist needs to be willing to meet the client anew in each session (and within sessions sometimes) whilst holding in mind the enduring patterns that have been identified in the reformulation phase.

In this vein it could be that what really brings change is not what the therapist does, or the model of working involved but the clients experience of a safe and open space week by week that, uniquely, is for them. Sometimes the wisest thing the therapist can do is follow the client on their journey of discovery. The client is the actual therapist in the room.

Ryle describes CAT with rich detail in ways that would define it as a corrective cognitive experience but in the process identities his developing model as a 'corrective emotional' experience (1997, page 16) The middle phase is also a stage on which a 'corrective relational experience' can be played out, if both therapist and client have a feeling for what is unfolding between them and are able to critically and compassionately reflect together. A corrective relational experience works with the transference dynamics and reciprocal roles of the client, the therapist and the system. The therapist, from within the safety of the CAT scaffolding and the mapping process, is saying. 'What happened in the past and happens in your life now is happening in some similar ways between us.' And, 'the exit from this pattern is being played out between us also.'

At risk of repetition, the middle stage of therapy is an important time for the routine use of the weekly 'progress review map' described on page 84. It is worth persisting with this routine task, as it is so easy to drift away from looking at the progress of the here and now relationship in therapy. If it draws a blank or does not reveal much, that is also interesting.

The versatile therapist and therapy

The middle of therapy is a place for versatility in the mix of technique and method used. It will show up in the client's changing attitudes and skills, as the client seeks to be more versatile in their lives. A wide range of therapeutic techniques can be woven into the CAT framework in the middle phase of therapy. The techniques used will vary with the range of expertise of the therapist and with the needs of the client. CAT offers a framework through its emphasis on reformulation that is flexible enough and strong enough to help work in whichever way most benefits the client during the middle of therapy. The soft structure of the scaffolding with a therapy map allows the various interventions to be pinpointed and evaluated in terms of changes to reciprocal role patterns.

Psychotherapy in the twenty first century has the potential to be a dialogue between the psychoanalytic, the behavioural, the humanistic, the existential, the constructivist, the cognitive, the neuro-scientific, the spiritual and the body-based approaches.

The variety of interventions that therapists can do within the CAT framework is unlimited. All are possible: cognitive restructuring, behavioural experiments, work with treatment protocols, trauma focused work using 'EMDR' or allied approaches, body focused work, dream work, emotionally focused work on building skills such as compassion and acceptance and meditative work aimed at increasing mindfulness by gaining control over rumination. No single approach holds the key. All are enriched by each other. A third and fourth generation of therapies often combine two or more of the above. Therapists will increasingly be versatile, which also means integrative and relational in spirit, to find their own joined up way of working.

At such moments, the value of the therapy map and the versatility of the mapping process come in to their own. The goal is always to do two things at once; solve or exit from a specific life problem and learn a general lesson. Ryle was one of the first to point out that, with the aid of the therapy map, all well conducted therapies are likely to be equally effective as they impact on different part of the whole interacting system. Therefore, changes in behaviour will lead to changes in thinking or relating and these in turn will lead to mind or body changes.

The reformulation, with its explicit therapy plan, is the guide and reference point for the use and evaluation of any specific additional intervention. The relational style of any of these activities may vary from direct education to guided exploratory work to engage with past trauma. It is not a case of either continuing with recognition and revision or working at some other therapy intervention. The two go hand in hand. In all cases, the CAT therapist continues to work on the general therapy tasks of developing the healing alliance, allowing the therapeutic relationship to be tested and used, and attending to moments of breakthrough or breakdown in the alliance as they arise in the room. The focus continues to be on supporting the client to become their own therapist, increasing versatility, and developing a wider repertoire of relational roles. Examples of CAT plus other approaches and CAT in dialogue or mapping in dialogue with other approaches can be found on www.mapandtalk.com/catplus/.

The healing power of rating sheets

The rating sheets (sample sheet below) allow therapist and client to evaluate their work in detail, identify areas for attention and develop a sense of shared ownership of the process of change. Rating sheets can be used to assess the level and quality of recognition and revision of problematic patterns. These can be linked to marking up 'exit' points on the therapy map at points where something different can be done or a new path can be taken.

Week by week, the focus is maintained on the target problems and target problem procedures by allocating time, often towards the end of the session, to explore the rating sheets together. It is a change of gear within the therapy session and offers a sort of 'reality check' to link the work of therapy in the room to the process of change outside. It offers a way of recapping the work of the session and keeping it in mind until the next session. This is also an opportunity to be realistic about difficulties with either recognising a pattern or revising it. Continuous awareness of problematic patterns which have been ignored in the past may be challenging and embarrassing. An increase in anxiety may arise and a conflict emerge between the uncertainties of changing and the predictability of staying the same. There may be distancing from family members, or situations whose contribution to harmful patterns is now more visible or more confusing.

Difficulties with revision can be exposing and shaming if not talked about compassionately and linked to the reformulation work. It may trigger self-critical procedures and be a source of an enactment of assuming the therapist will be disappointed, critical, or abandoning if efforts to change are not made. The quality and stability of recognition might vary from week to week. Discussing the detail of what helped or hindered recognition will help with developing reflective capacity and relational awareness. A guide for weekly self-monitoring, using a rating sheet, is as follows.

Rating sheet example

These are the patterns I am troubled by. I can get caught up in them with myself and others. I want to spot them taking hold of me and find ways to soften them or step out of them and do something more helpful for me and others. [The text that follows is a rough guide and mirrors the basic steps in relational mapping (chapter 2). This sheet should have appended to it a map of the one, two or three patterns described.]

> *When I am feeling 'a.....' in response to me or someone else doing 'b....' then I want or need 'c......' and tend meet that need based on thoughts and ideas about my needs, and about me in the world by a belief or assumption that I have to do 'd.....' or get others to do 'e......' for me. This results in taking me back to the role I was in (trap); or into a divided choice between two contrasting options (dilemma); or I start getting somewhere and then hit a brick wall either because I forbid getting for myself what I need or others or society forbid it (snag)*

Over this last week these are my examples of recognising the pattern...

I was kind to myself, critical, dismissive etc, to myself about their recognition...

I realised I was in the pattern straight away, or sometime after or not at all (say when)...

I was able to soften, change the pattern, heal the damage to myself or to others by talking it through or making changes...

My exits from the patterns are...

General feedback to myself is...

What to take back to therapy is...

Like any therapeutic activity, rating is a shared process. Helping the client write out a brief description of the target problem procedures can support the transition from reformulation to recognition and revision. As described in chapter 4 on process mapping, each therapeutic activity and tool is an enactment magnet for the transference from therapist or from the client. Time should be spent discussing the feelings about self-monitoring alongside discussion of the details of change for better or worse.

Sara's illustration

It was only when Sara wrote out her pattern on to a rating sheet that she connected with it. She said.

> 'This is me. I am taking it home with me. I have written it out with my own hand. I saw it on the map, but nothing clicked. I didn't want to own it. Who would behave like that? When you read out the letter. I agreed it was me you were talking about it. After all, it was what I had said, but I was all head and no heart. Now, written in my own hand, it is like it is distilled. This is my pattern pure and simple. It has got me, but I have got it'

In the following week she wrote her own short single sentence letter to the pattern.

> 'Dear my problem pattern. I love you and I hate you. You are my homespun addiction and I am going to see you out of the house.'

Sara knew what she meant, and in that moment, she was more an owner and co-author of the therapy.

Steps to relational awareness and a healing narrative

These ten steps have been derived from teaching and supervision, and the wisdom of many practitioners and clients both in the UK and internationally using the cognitive analytic approach. They are geared to working with a therapy map and the target problems and patterns written out on paper. They can be supported also by further moments of mapping and writing in session. Each step, in its turn, helps in developing relational awareness and reflective capacity. Each step adds up to a healing narrative. The steps invite the therapist to be versatile and make use of what works, whilst staying within the reformulation framework of the therapy map and letter. They show an integrated view of the social, emotional, cognitive, behavioural and relational tasks in the middle phase. They draw upon methods and techniques from many others approaches. They may have value for people working across the range of therapies and treatments. They can be used as a help list for clients and are written in the voice of addressing the client directly. They draw on parts one and two of the book.

1. Track, locate and recap it
Trace the problematic pattern in detail, locate its roots and present context. We need to go over the same dance, seeing it routinely played out, to truly connect with its character and its impact on us emotionally. Each pattern has its context within a larger arrangement or picture. If we track it, we get to know how the pattern works; the logic of the thinking, the push and pull of the action and the back and forth of feelings. Recapping and talking through one or more patterns in detail helps develop familiarity with how the pattern works and build reflective capacity.

Talking about the pattern, on and through the map, engages with it at a distance. It is both live in the room and not in the room. Tracking the detail of the pattern with the assistance of the map helps us get to know our way around and can lead to quicker and more confident recognition in the future with or without the map. Recapping always brings a different angle or stance and often additional information. We never tell the same story twice in the same way. In this way each act of recapping and recognition is a small experience of re-formulating the existing reformulation which is to say it is an act of memory reconsolidation.

2. Accept and get alongside it here and now
A pattern that can be located and tracked is also one that can be approached and encountered more safely. It is a more securely formulated experience out there in words mapped on paper. By hovering and shimmering alongside the problem pattern in the here-and-now, the gaps in self-knowledge can be more easily engaged along with the forgotten links and hidden feelings. This stance echoes that of Marsha Linehan's (1993) radical acceptance. Rather than trying to actively change something, we give it space to be met, encountered and understood. The push for change gives way to the push for awareness, trusting that in time this will lead the client closer to their goals. Literally sitting side-by-side and exploring a pattern on a map allows the associated thoughts and feelings to emerge.

3. Expose it
Make it visible (colour coding it on the map helps) and externalise it so it stands apart from you and is no longer so familiar to you, and so much a part of you that you cannot see it. Sometimes change is hard to make because the pattern is hard to see and stand back from. In psychoanalytic language (Greenson, 1967), the pattern is ego-syntonic and needs help to be made ego-alien or dystonic. A good map helps show where the troublesome points are and where things might get stuck or be avoided. Viewing the problem clearly, and as something external, allows a different relationship to emerge. Something that has been known implicitly and accepted as part of you, becomes explicit, separate, and available for exploration. Being able to

move back and forth between familiar and new or strange perspectives is an element of relational awareness.

4. Befriend it

Make a kind and compassionate relationship with the pattern. Compassion helps us sustain the demanding work of recognition and revision. Patterns that we want to change now may feel hard to change because they were once our way of surviving. Make friends with the pattern and thank it for the work it has done in helping you survive thus far. Accept it and the thoughts, behaviours and feelings that go with it, as one of my ways of being. It is a part of my world but not all my world. Speak compassionately about the work it has done in helping you adapt. Thank it and let it know it is no longer needed. Or at least, won't be needed very often. This can be done through writing a 'Dear Old Pattern letter' (as described on page 122) as if writing to an old friend. Read it out and work with the feelings that follow from hearing it voiced. The letter may serve as an ongoing tool for nurturing compassion and the compassionate emotional resources in the brain, as described by Paul Gilbert and illuminated by the compassionate mind approach (Gilbert, 2013).

5. Safely re-live it

The processes of change in therapy are likely to work within and between sessions. Old patterns, and the memories of experiences in which they played a part, are more likely to surface in the heat and light of therapy. We need to be prepared as clients to note the layers of feelings that come along with these memories. Often it is the second level of feelings, such as distaste or shame or anger, that matter most, or it is the gaps in memory and feeling. It takes time for client and therapist to spot what is being replayed. This may happen through the push and pull of transferred feelings and roles in the therapy room, or through the tracing and touching of lines and circles by hand on the map. It may be triggered by events in the present that resemble or hark back to earlier experience. Although it may feel difficult at the time, the process of walking through past troublesome experiences (which may well be the source of current distressing patterns of coping) is a key therapeutic and healing mechanism (Patricia De Young, 2015)

Safely reliving past patterns and some of the feelings tied up in them is helped by all the other points in this list and by the general stance of therapy with a map seeking to develop self-understanding and relational awareness. Many CAT therapists are using techniques from the more body (Bessel van der Kolk, 2014) or brain-based therapies (Corrigan, 2018; Shapiro, 2018), to work through unsettling or hidden trauma memories. The role of transference and the compulsion to repeat unresolved patterns remains important as a common element in the search for healing.

6. Hover over and shimmer with it

Seeing the bigger picture and all the points of view can add context. It can support the person in stepping back from their immediate thoughts and feelings. Each point on the map invites reflection from a different standpoint. Working side-by-side with a map enables rehearsing and practising hovering and shimmering in-session. Both client and therapist can keep rediscovering that there is more than one perspective and more than one feeling. Shimmering between overlapping and contrasting emotional states develops feelings skills. Both must tolerate the anxiety and ambivalence of not having a fixed position for a while and share the experience of uncertainty.

7. Left/right brain it

Mapping helps us link our brain's executive suite of skills (Donald, 2002) to multiple senses of touching, seeing and hearing with the map. We can see the shapes of the map, and touch and trace the lines of the map with our hands. We give voice to the words as we tell, rethink and retell the stories which are 'scaffolded' by the map. We rework the words to reach softer or stronger meanings, to connect cognitively, viscerally, and emotionally in the same breath. At present, it is a guess how this co-creative 'mapping' mechanism of change works in the brain. Some clues are in the way that mapping might help re-engage the different strata and sides of the brain, opening new pathways and integrating the components of the brain in a new dialogue between memories, emotional sub-systems and experience. A review of how working memory is optimally taxed in the process of EMDR (Van den Hout, 2012) seems worth linking to the multi-sensory process of emotion-focused mapping. It seems plausible to think that the mapping process helps the work of re-orchestrating the interplay between various emotional sub-systems of the brain (seeking, playing, rage, care, grief, fear and lust) in the substrata of the brain (Panksepp). Equally it makes sense to draw on the view of McGilchrist (2009) that the point of interest is in the re-orchestration of the two sides of the brain. Mapping, with its joint activity of hand, heart and head is a continuous process of recombining left and right sides of the brain in a different balance.

8. Tame it

This involves seeing how milder versions of problematic patterns have quite different results. Often therapy meets resistance because we feel, or fear, that change means giving up a life-long way of coping. The coping pattern might be quite different in its impact if it is toned down or slowed down a bit. Or if the flow of the sequence of action, reactive feeling, coping intention, belief, and consequential action is edited, redirected, or rebalanced. Less intensity or speed of response allows some of the nuance of feelings to come out. More awareness of the response may change the place of the pattern within the wider orchestration. This can be supported by learning to tame and soften feelings in session. Equally, it may help to learn to turn up the volume of some responses which are too muted. Such work may specifically come through 'giving voice to 'hoped for' alternative patterns.

9. Re-route or 're-root' it

This involves making new patterns of thought, feeling and action by mapping and trying alternative ways and paths to the pattern. It is useful in this context to invoke the '5 degrees of difference on the compass' rule. Ryle (informal communication) maintained the sailor's point of view, that a slight change in direction of the sailing boat five degrees north or south would not feel much at the point of departure but at the end would turn out to be a very different destination. In other words, we may not need to change very much in the short term to feel quite different in the long term if we sustain the change. The advantage of thinking in terms of new routes is that it promotes relational awareness and seeing our self in the light of a new procedure for coping and dealing with life. Relational awareness may thrive on the noticing and naming of small differences which are local and manageable.

It is hard to avoid the word play of re-route and re-rooting. Most of our patterns carry with them a founding story such as, 'I learnt my people pleasing pattern from my mother.' Re-rooting this as, 'I learnt my people pleasing pattern as a working-class girl', might offer a very different starting point for a healing narrative.

10. Re-orchestrate and re-integrate it

The therapy map offers a space for repeatedly going over the link between problem patterns and ways of relating to self and others in the wider world. Something is being re-orchestrated and integrated differently each time therapist and client try and exercise the compassionate understanding of a reciprocal role position. They are jointly participating in the difficulty; living in the transference feelings; being in the procedural 'dance' and stepping out of it. Such repeated attempts at re-orchestration and integration in a compassionate relationship builds a behavioural skill, like practising the scales on a piano or working at painting technique. This exercises the 'orchestral-integrative muscle' and builds a capacity for relational awareness. It solves problems and develops reflective capacity at the same time. In cognitive analytic terms, this might be described as increasing the repertoire of reciprocal roles, but it is more than this. It is extending the variety of ways of orchestrating many reciprocal role procedures into a more coherent or empowering whole, and in the process building a sense of agency in one's self. One might think of the therapist as a tutor in the cognitive, emotional and relational integration of patterns that have been fragmented, stuck and out of conscious dialogue.

Illustrations of working in the middle of therapy

The following are illustrations in quotations (fictionalised and anonymised) of the variety of work that might be done in the middle of therapy within the framework of the CAT reformulation and mapping process. Each is an example of a moment within a healing narrative and a movement towards greater relational awareness.

Going to the doctor
'For the past six years I have avoided going to the doctor about my health problems. I could see it on the map as a fear of being criticised and feeling ashamed. In the middle of therapy, we micro-mapped how I thought the doctor might respond. I knew I had to report back to the therapist, so I took the map seriously, kept it with me and was watching out for my moments of wanting to avoid saying what was concerning me to the doctor. I was battling with embarrassment. It went okay. It was like two victories. Or perhaps three victories. I got treatment which reduced my physical symptoms which helped me sleep better. That boosted my self-esteem and made me take more care of myself. But thirdly, I valued more the "thinking things over" which I had been doing with the therapist. I could look myself in the eye.'

Rewriting the reformulation letter for my husband
'We revised the reformulation letter so that I felt I could share it safely with my husband without going head-to-head. It had four benefits: I thought more about the difference between compulsively hiding and choosing to hide myself from him. Re-writing the letter with him in mind made me get alongside the choices I had in the push and pull of control and power between us. Sharing the letter made him more of an ally and less inclined to label me as crazy. The therapist and I also saw a bit more in the reformulation letter than we had at first. I felt more like it was mine. It was not just rewriting the letter. It was 'rewriting' my relationship with my husband.'

An exit from comfort eating without resorting to self-harm
'The map shows me that when I get home alone, I feel so lonely and empty in my heart that I just need some love. Food is the only thing that is available. I realise I eat without thinking until I feel stuffed. Now I see it doesn't bring comfort, which is the desired place on my map but brings me escape from despair. When we got closer to the despair in therapy, I wanted to harm myself and we got that on the map as well. In the middle of therapy, I knew the despair was the challenge I needed to face. As an exercise I wrote to the hurt child I had been when young and felt for her but also felt when she wrote back to me that she and I could join forces now and didn't need to be so afraid of the despair but leave it in the past and not load it on to the future. This deeper change within myself is eventually going to help me change the pattern of stuffing myself with so called comforting food.'

Separating out starving control from triumphant superiority

'I think I had become addicted to the feeling of superiority when in control by not eating and being thin. I looked down on other people. By separating out the reciprocal roles of "being in control or controlled" from the role of "feeling superior and looking down triumphantly" on other people, I could see that I wanted to keep some of the feelings of control but that the looking down on people served to keep everyone away and hid how lonely and vulnerable I felt. I wasn't yet prepared to give up being in control but really noticing and naming the triumphant and superior part of me took a lot of pressure off me and I am becoming more sociable and less worried about my body.'

Experimenting with 'chipping-in'

'I am so shy in groups. I am mute. I know it is not always going to work but I have an exit on my map which says prepare, in my mind without any intention, to chip in, catch one person's eye, nod to them and give it a go. My real therapy is in my evaluation of what I do when I fail to get noticed. I try to notice when I turn on myself. Instead, I step back and see what was going on. The key idea is to nod to people and keep physically involved even if I don't manage to get a word in. Once I was on nodding terms, I tried just voicing one word. Yeah or okay or something like that. I know it is going to take a while and I am more aware of how loud the voices are of those in the group who speak most. As my isolation goes down and my inward and anxious pre-occupation lessens, I am more able to think about what I want to say. I feel like I am on the pitch, and in the game, which is a massive change even if I rarely touch the ball yet.'

Celebrating my spikey blue hair

'In tracing my life history, and mapping and talking more in the middle of therapy, me and my therapist linked up how an attempted sexual assault on the street (I managed to run away) when I was twelve made me very shy and socially scared. I became a "teenage mouse". No one understood what was wrong. No one could help me. Because I never told anyone about the assault and didn't make the link to shyness myself. I thought it was a fault in my personality. Then one day, by chance my friend and I, when we were stuck and bored at home, cut our hair very short and spikey, and dyed it blue. My friend got into trouble, but I found that with spikey blue hair and a punk style I was someone with a special power of self-protection. It is hard to define how it happened and the links only became clear through mapping it out in therapy some years later, but gradually I felt more confident going out. People seemed a bit wary of my spikey blue hair and didn't hassle me. I went to pubs and could order a drink. In hindsight, I now realise that, I "piggy backed" my way to social confidence off that spikey blue hair.

It was a fake part of me but underneath the disguise, a real part of me was freer to heal and recover. Once we had figured this out in therapy, it was easier to look back at the trauma and link more widely to my awareness of who I could relate to and who felt unsafe in early years, in all my interactions. I also used the "blue hair story" as a kind of model or metaphor for trying out new behaviours. We called them "blue hair" experiments because they had the same pattern and relationships as the spikey blue hair.'

A happy map instead of a 'crappy' map

'The therapy map was true but did not have any good things on it. It was miserable. As part of accepting the limited world in which I evolved as a human being, I wanted to make a happy map with all the good things which I wanted to bring into my life. We didn't dream a dream or cheat but made the happy map as a sequence of exits from the crappy map. Looking at the two maps side-by-side with my therapist gave me hope and allowed me to look full on at the past hurt. The bad stuff was my bad stuff and I survived. It was not all of me. The happy map was like a hopeful alternative and it allowed me to see other possibilities for myself and imagine a more resourceful and supported life. There was something fresh and liberating about making the happy map. It was as if I was saying: I don't want to be weighed down by the past. It helped me connect with some of the happier things in the past as well.'

Noticing, naming and negotiating angry moments

'I don't get angry all the time and seem to get angrier with people with whom I am close. My job in the middle of therapy is to notice when I get upset but don't feel angry, when I feel angry and negotiate with it and when I behave in an angry way that is hurtful to someone else. If I notice it more, then I hope, I can negotiate with myself or others. I don't like being an angry person. My aim is to practice having a choice whether to show or hide my angry feelings. There is nothing automatically wrong in feeling angry but there is something wrong in not having a choice. Having a choice may allow me to sit with the feelings longer and understand them better.'

Common problems in the middle of therapy

There are many challenges that might face the client and therapist as they navigate the middle stages of therapy. Here are some common issues that supervisees describe:

The reformulation letter is ignored or never referred to again. Perhaps the therapist is unsure of it, or the feelings the client has about the letter have not been discussed enough. The purpose of the letter is to shape and hold the therapy journey, therefore, if it is being ignored, it might need returning to. At the very least its lack of use should be discussed.

The map and the letter don't tie up. If the letter is written before the map is finalised, it may be superseded by the map as the key therapy tool. Or if the letter has not evolved in a collaborative step-by-step way with the client then there might be a lack of co-ownership and shared investment. Sometimes difficulties integrating the map and letter point to challenges the client has with acting and thinking in an integrated way. It is important to explore this with the client. Are the goals, target problem and target problem procedures clear? Are they clearly articulated in the letter and depicted on the therapy map? If not, then the therapy should re-visit the tools to ensure they are supporting the therapy as intended. The therapist should always share responsibility for the letter or map not helping. Care should be taken not to leave the client or therapist taking on the blame.

What is in the room is not on the therapy map. New and deeper understanding may emerge in the middle of therapy and the therapy map may be out of date. This is not a problem, as it indicates the therapy is alive and progressing. However, it is helpful to review whether the new developments are in line with the goals of the therapy. If so, either update the map or acknowledge the need for a new map or sketch of what is happening just now. The routine uses of checking in on progress maps as detailed in Chapter four on process mapping (map the moment, page 84) can help work with such moments.

Recognition triggers resistance, helplessness or hostility. Moving from reformulation with the very active helping hand of the therapist, to monitoring recognition of patterns on one's own between sessions, is a big step requiring motivation and attention. It may feel lonely and may trigger old patterns in relation to it as an activity. Our contemporary lives don't exactly offer spare time to reflect. It is worth encouraging clients to try mindful mapping (and indeed, there will be more chance of the client doing this if the therapist is also engaged in this way with themselves) as described on page 103.

Unexpected life changes take centre stage. Bereavement, illness, adverse life events, childcare difficulties, or moving jobs and location can happen at any time in therapy. A personal crisis is likely to have its own timeline and the different routines of the therapy can be returned to when ready. It may make sense to stop the therapy clock and have one or more sessions geared to getting through an immediate life crisis. Marking this out as a different focus of therapy may protect the therapy work, and prevent it from being taken over by supportive, or crisis interventions. It may be unhelpful to stop meeting all together. The changing circumstances may act as a catalyst to the therapeutic work. Client and therapist should seek to work out the meaning of what has happened together, using the reformulation work at the beginning of therapy as a source of reference. If possible, the therapist needs to catch difficulties along these lines early on and rehearse options and agree choices. All, or any, of these events can be a source of important therapeutic understanding, but not in the moment until the crisis has passed.

Unplanned therapist absences. If the therapist is unexpectedly ill or unavailable, it might be useful for a colleague to have, what might be called, a 'broker session' to consider collaboratively with the client what the best options might be. The client might well be able to explain from the maps and reformulation letter how far they have got and the best way of maximising the benefit of the therapy at this stage. Care should be taken by the temporary therapist to value the client's account of, and ownership of the therapy and, if possible, to maintain the work.

Everything in the list above comes back to one over-riding theme; notice, name and negotiate. Therapy with a map and the skills and tools of cognitive analytic therapy stress the work of developing relational awareness as a general good but also as a resource when difficulties do arise. If the ground for sincere and thoughtful negotiation over difficult feelings has been prepared, then there is more chance of working things through at a time of crisis.

What to take to supervision?

Therapist who work collaboratively and relationally need routine supervision. In choosing what to bring to supervision the following list may be helpful.

- Micro-supervision of a moment with a client. What was the process? Where was it going? How did it fit into the bigger picture? Prepare by doing some self-supervision (map the moment for yourself).
- Thoughts about where the therapy is in relation to the target problem patterns. The most common supervision question during the middle of a CAT therapy concerns the relationship of the therapy to the target problem or problems. Has it wandered off track or does the target problem need refining?
- Talk about planned interventions around recognition and revision (as already discussed in relation to the therapist versatility). These can be like a minor therapy within the larger therapy. How will the specific therapeutic technique or approach be structured within the CAT framework? Does the therapist, the supervisor or the co-supervisees have enough expertise in respect of the minor intervention?
- Bring to supervision troublesome thoughts and responses that were left at the end of the therapy session. These don't need to be clearly formulated and may be a half-formed feeling. Supervision is a place for finding the words for tendencies, responses and transference dynamics that are in play but out of awareness or unformulated.

Some common reciprocal roles and procedures the therapist and supervisor might enact in respect of supervision in the middle of therapy are:

- Looking after and sorting out the client: it is tempting to take over in the middle on the back of the confidence and clarity of the reformulation letter
- Waiting and seeing what happens which may lead to a passivity that misses key turning points in the therapy.
- Turning attention to the drama of beginning or ending of another case and neglecting the client who is in the middle of therapy.

All of these, and any reciprocations like them that seem to be generated in the here and now relationship of the therapy, can be talked through in supervision.

Conclusion

The middle is where the therapy is sustained, and a healing narrative begins, or it falters in some way. The strength of the open and transparent CAT approach to reformulation (with its emphasis on the co-creative relationship and tools such as mapping) is that difficulties can be more easily spotted and negotiated. As described on page 92, the therapist needs to watch out in the middle phase after the reformulation that the therapy does not become a process of doing therapy for or doing therapy to the client. The progress of working and recognition and revision of patterns and various exercises to bring about change need to be in the reach and in the hands of the client. As detailed in the preceding chapter (page 180), client and therapist may need to approach the middle phase by 'pushing where it moves'.

Chapter 11: Ending therapy

> *'There is a beginning to a song, and there should be an end of a song, and of course there's a middle. And I like to take the middle any place it wants to go. But whenever I take it to the end, I like to bring it somewhere familiar, someplace that people feel it's resolved, it's settled; it comes back home at the end, whatever home means.'*
> **Carole King, p144 in Songwriters on song-writing (2000)** by Paul Zollo

Introduction

This chapter explores the therapeutic use of the end of therapy. It begins with our experience of endings and the mixed feelings that arise of relief or abandonment, challenge, or opportunity. Managing a planned ending is a shared, self-conscious, activity which can be aided by using the tools of mapping, writing, and voicing already described in this book.

As part of preparing for the ending there are guidelines on mapping the ending phase of the therapy relationships with a 'goodbye' map. The focus of the 'goodbye' map may come from the weekly progress maps that have been checked briefly, session by session, on how the therapy is going. There is a list of prompt statements that might help shape a dialogue about how things end. The use of goodbye letters is described as a key part of CAT practice. Preparing, writing, and reading out these letters helps make the most of the final sessions therapeutically. It is the vehicle for describing and reviewing the healing narrative that has been the story of how the therapy has helped.

The chapter itemises some challenges of appropriately managing the endings for the client, for the therapist and for the system around them. After reviewing the part of supervision in working with the ending, the chapter concludes with attention to the 'self-help' phase of the therapy, when the client seeks self-consciously to be their own therapist. This is reviewed at the follow-up session and its role is discussed.

Our experience of endings

The ending of the therapy relationship may evoke feelings related to past endings and the replay of lifelong patterns of coping with separation and loss.

The unique qualities of a therapeutic partnership with its intensity of self-focus, curiosity and compassion, may result in the ending being felt more keenly. It may feel to the client as if this new way of relating is being ended prematurely and will be hard to replicate out there in the everyday world.

Michael was surprised by the attention the therapist was giving to a proper ending. Usually people just say, 'push off.' Maria saw endings as a completely unfamiliar territory. Her parents had found it hard to let her grow up and go. Deep down she assumed we should all cling on to whatever intimacy came our way. For both Michael and Maria, the therapeutic attention to the ending was an encounter with some of their deepest patterns of showing our need for others. Many of us have experienced endings that are difficulty to face, unexpected or unmarked and hurriedly skipped over, or just denied. Learning to manage the ending is indicative of self-consciously managing our choices about relationships more generally.

Feelings of working well together may only be fully experienced towards the end of therapy. Indeed, the impending loss of this working partnership may bring it sharply into focus. Michael said, 'Only when I was losing it, did I realise how much it had come to mean to me'.

Past experiences of loss and separation may well have been characterised by denial from powerful others. The client might cope with the impending ending by pulling away from the therapy, dismissing the work or rejecting the therapist, to reduce its impact. Relational patterns that arose at the beginning of therapy, but then became less marked, may resurface towards the end. For example, the therapist who has tried hard and been supportive throughout the therapy, doubles their efforts at the end. Or the client who placed huge demands on the therapy at the beginning might return to this position at the end.

Managing the ending therapeutically

The end stage is a chance to take stock. Can success be celebrated and owned? What disappointments can be acknowledged? Can failure be discussed and can these difficulties in appraising the successes and limits of the therapy be shared without a hidden agenda of blame or self-criticism? It would be odd if our lives were sorted out by a short course of therapy. Inevitably, some fixed habits and deep problems persist. Missed opportunities, setbacks and disappointments in the therapy should be openly and sincerely acknowledged.

The ending of the therapy meetings, and of the direct relationship with the therapist, is simultaneously an important beginning. It is the beginning of a therapeutic self-help phase. The struggles, breakthroughs and enactments that might accompany it should be anticipated as part of the ending process. Such attention fits the educational and empowering theme of coaching the client to be their own therapist.

Managing the ending therapeutically involves being more explicit than we might usually be with endings. If the ending is not managed consciously and explicitly, it will be managed unconsciously and through enactments. By the tenth or eleventh session of therapy, hopefully there is a predominant sense of the therapy being actively managed and worked on by two people working in partnership. The spirit of co-creativity has taken centre stage. As the ending approaches, the experience of managing and being managed is brought into view. How have we worked together? How has the space been managed, and by whom? Here follows a list of aspects of managing the ending that might apply. This is the point where the four 'stories' of therapy mentioned in chapter 7 and 10 may stand out apart from and in relation to each other. How have we managed the links and gaps between stories from the past and stories in the present? How has the reformulation story at beginning stage of therapy and the insights that flow from it helped develop a healing story of changes in behaviour, feeling and thinking through the middle and now the end of therapy?

Don't wind down
Once the date of the final session has been set and the last few sessions remain, it is important not to let 'ending time' become 'winding down time', but to keep up the momentum. There might be many reasons why it is tempting to slow down. Both client and therapist might look at the ending as a source of relief and a chance to escape the scrutiny and demands of the therapeutic space. Mapping and writing about the ending process can help maintain therapeutic momentum to the end of the final session.

The unexpected ending
Always be ready to manage the ending; it may come out of the blue. One client left a note.

> 'I cannot come today. I am finding the sessions hard work. Sorry, I want to give the session to someone else whom you can help. If you think I should see you, please phone me. Otherwise thanks very much for your time.'

The therapist felt confused by the unexpectedness of this and aware that he was being put in a dilemma. He noted, 'I had either to encourage him to come back and rescue him or ignore him and thereby reject him. I needed to find a compassionate way of naming the dilemma and of managing the confusion hanging in the air between us. I rang him and thanked him for his note and said that I appreciated the sessions had been hard, and his concern for my other clients. 'However.' He said. 'I suggest we meet to think through the issues raised by this note and explore the choices to make together about continuing or ending the therapy'. The client did re-attend and the subsequent mapping and discussion of the note and the therapist's response, took them to the heart of the therapeutic relationship and re-activated it.

People unexpectedly drop out of therapy for a myriad of reasons. One good reason for building up a routine progress map (page 84) is to be prepared for the more difficult and powerful enactments that threaten the therapy or put the client at risk. Enactments around ending therapy are always important to name and negotiate for the benefit of both client and therapist, even if they are unexpected.

Consider whether to touch hidden feelings or respectfully bypass

There might be times when feelings are hinted at but are being warded off. For example, the client has warned that they don't like endings. They will talk intensively about earlier losses and the grief involved. Suggestions by the therapist of parallels with the current situation are dismissed. One way of negotiating this is to map the feelings and memories of past losses and not stress or push the link with the present time. By experiencing respect and thought for past losses, the client may then be able to negotiate the one in the room. One therapist, when faced with a client's reluctance to talk about the relationship, at the end wrote down in the middle of a piece of paper between them, 'It is okay not to go there'. The phrase on paper helped to substantiate an agreement between them to not discuss something. Avoidance is always a choice as-long-as, in some small way, it is acknowledged and owned as a choice.

Balancing equity of provision with the needs of an individual

There is a tension between equity of provision and meeting a pressing individual need. By ensuring therapy is available in the public sector for those who need it, there is not always room or flexibility for additional sessions even if there is a pressing and justifiable need. A longer run of sessions may be needed in relation to working through severe trauma, working with complexity or high levels of risk. If it does feel to the therapist or the client that not enough time has been given but the ending must take place, then sincere honesty is called for about what has not been achieved through lack of time. The therapist needs to say that he or she is sorry for the untimely ending and to do what they can to find other sources of help for the client.

Old endings impact on or distract from negotiating this ending

The approach of the ending of this therapy is likely to bring up memories of and connections with old patterns of ending, or not ending, relationships. It can be of great value to work through the parallel process between the story of ending then and the story of ending now. The challenge is to stay in contact with both endings and not to become exclusively focused on the ending many years ago. The therapeutic work is found in the repetition of old roles and feelings and beliefs in the present, and the possibility of a different, more knowing response now. This is a situation where a goodbye map can be helpful along with the exchange of goodbye letters. The healing narrative in and through the goodbye letter should point to the hoped for, different experience of this ending and the fears of it repeating past endings.

The course is completed but the journey continues
If the high-level task of therapy is to help the client learn to be their own therapist, then it could be argued that the therapy should end when the client has made some progress in this respect. However, for some this could be a long time, or a lifetime's work. In any case, the process of learning, growing, integrating, and re-orchestrating the 'orchestra' of me and myself in the world will continue past the end of therapy. This can be named with the client to highlight that the therapeutic work does not cease at the point where meetings end. This is discussed more in the section on self-help and follow-up.

Holding the boundaries
To sustain a therapeutic space and maintain a therapeutic relationship involves an awareness, sensitivity to, and capacity to hold the boundaries. There is a view within the CAT communities that it is never advisable to extend a therapy beyond agreed time limits. This is linked to the view that extending sessions may be part of a process of rescuing and a need, in the therapist or from the client, for a relationship of perfect care as depicted in the trauma diagram on page 160. A shared collusion with ideal care risks spoiling or devaluing the 'good enough' work that has been done. Both client and therapist need to discover, take ownership over, and adjust to the experience of good enough care. These are words that are easy to put down on paper but hard to work through in practice. If therapy is extended by a run of follow-up sessions, or through a second course of therapy, the end of this piece of shared therapeutic work, at this time, should still be marked by a proper goodbye and a gap before starting again.

Disappointment and failure
Feelings that the therapy is not working or helping need exploring early on. There can be many reasons for difficulty or disappointment, and another approach or another therapist might be a reasonable choice to consider. If a co-creative alliance is not developing by session two or three and is not being sustained, then naming the difficulties without blame or shame is the most helpful thing to do. It invites a variation on the progress maps described on page 84. The therapist's stance is to explore along the following lines: 'I wonder where we are and what we are doing? Or what I am doing that is not helpful at this time'. It is very important not to convey that therapy does not work, or therapy is not right for the client, or they are not ready for therapy. Therapist should always have thoughts about, and signposts for, other kinds of helpful or neighbouring therapies and therapists who might be worth contacting. In the process of exploring disappointment and failure it may emerge in quite a helpful way that the client did not want, or did not feel ready for therapy, but that should not be assumed or jumped to as a first line of explanation. Saying goodbye and managing the early ending of a therapy that is not felt to be working can be a helpful and protective process.

Raising awareness: a checklist of prompt questions

Drawing upon the preceding discussion, the following list of questions are an aid to talking about the ending of the therapy relationship. The list is a brief prompt for client and therapist for discussion and a small aid to overcoming hesitation or embarrassment about talking about ending a relationship. There are no statements that are right or wrong. Talking about endings can be hard and it might be helpful to notice, name and negotiate how this ending now is shaped by prior assumptions and patterns of response from other endings in life, or by assumptions about each other's needs or expectations. We are all capable of being party to any one of these responses.

For both client and therapist

1. Awkward: talking about us ending feels awkward so we don't discuss it.
2. Interruption: ending now feels like interrupting something that is unfinished.
3. Mixed feelings: some success and failure, some reasons to stop and some to continue.
4. Thanks: we thank each other and appreciate our efforts.

For the client

5. New beginning: ending this is also a new beginning with new possibilities.
6. Return to my way: I will cope by going back to doing things my way. It is what I know.
7. It feels like a loss: I am going to miss this, and I feel sad about it.
8. Ready now to begin - let's make the most of the last few sessions. There is so much to do.

For the therapist

9. Don't go it alone: let's talk about how you find other allies in your continuing therapeutic journey.
10. The turning points: the ending brings in mind the key moments where change occurred, difficulties were faced in ways that add up to a healing narrative.
11. Learning from you: I will remember you as a client and feel I learnt with you.
12. I believe in you: I have trust and confidence in you coping alone and carrying on.

Mapping the experience of the ending

It can be useful to spend some time mapping hopes and fears about the ending, as a way of it being reflected upon and managed. If the routine of mapping the therapy relationship week-by-week has been established and maintained, then the map of the feelings about ending is a continuation of this work. If not, it is worth setting time aside a few sessions before the final meeting, and mapping how the therapy has progressed and how it might face the ending. Here is an example of how mapping helped deepen the discussion about ending.

Therapist: 'I need to remind us about the end of therapy. We have four sessions remaining. I wonder how we are both feeling about this. Or what we can do about it?'

Client: 'So, I suppose it is time to wind up then?'

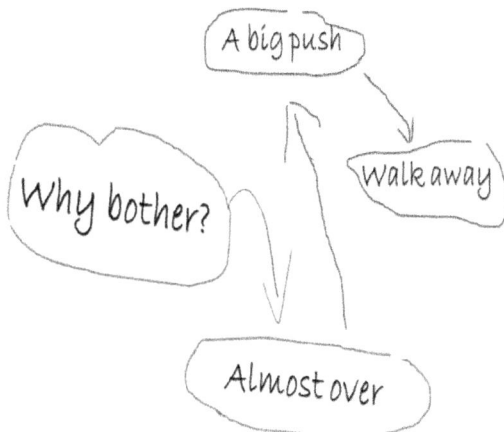

Therapist: 'We can do more. In fact, we are only three quarters of the way through.'

Client shrugs: 'Yes but, a bit, I am feeling why bother now? It is almost over.'

Therapist: 'Oh, that feels a bit sad or disappointed. What is almost over?' (she writes on a blank sheet of paper 'almost over' and then across the page 'why bother'. The client leans into the writing activity. As an afterthought the therapist asks: 'What can we do about it?'

Client: 'It feels difficult to have a big push at the end of things. It's better to walk away as everyone does, or I do, or did...' (therapist writes 'walk away' and 'big push').

Therapist: 'I am touched by this (pointing to the words "why bother" and "almost over"). You don't want to walk away like other times, and yet we might need to make a big push and bother. One thing that might help is for us to write a draft good-bye letter for ourselves and each other, to reflect on what we have done and experienced together'.

Client: 'You won't let me slip, away will you?' (the atmosphere between them is more hopeful and active).

'Goodbye maps' awareness training exercise

General awareness of working with the ending can be developed by therapists and helpers by practising mapping the ending process. This can be done in pairs. One person in the pair thinks of a recent ending in therapy which went well, was rewarding, or challenging and difficult. The other person is the mapper. They are mapping the story of the therapy relationship, the places it has been and its highs and lows. They have an eye to the conversational process of telling the story and the patterns of relating in the story. Mapper and talker work side-by-side and use the map to help draw out the story of the therapy. They are mapping out the elements of a healing narrative. They recap and hover and shimmer etc as described in part one of this book.

After ten minutes the person who has been telling the story leads a shared 'walk around the emerging map'. The two partners to the mapping process recap with the map together. The person telling the story takes some time to sit back and reflect upon what they have learnt through the process of telling the story of the ending with the help of map. He or she will wonder about what it might have been like or might still be like to do such a mapping activity with the client involved. As with other forms of supervision, or speed supervision mapping in this style (see page 110), it can add another layer of reflection for each party to write a short 'five-minute' spontaneous letter using the map as a reference. This can help develop the skills and feelings for writing the goodbye letters. The person telling the story might write to the client or to themselves. The mapper would write to the person telling the story, or to the map of the ending relationship. They would both read their letters out with the map between them.

Writing, exchanging and voicing goodbye letters

The goodbye letters look back on the work done and look forward to the 'self-help' phase of therapy ahead. Looking back involves asking the questions, 'how it helped or not?' 'what has been missed?' 'where did things get stuck or go well?' The actual writing of the goodbye letters is a reflective occasion and an aid to private reflection. It brings other aspects of ending the therapy into sharp relief. The reading out is a potential experience of heightened interpersonal and emotional connection. It is addressing the question of the story of the therapy; how the co-creative process of therapy has become an experience of the therapy story as a healing narrative.

The introduction of the letters and negotiation over how and whether to write them is a rich therapeutic process. It is important that throughout the therapy both client and therapist know of this task at the end. It leaves something to work on and revisit as a memorable focus of the therapy. The goodbye letter is a chance to undertake a compassionate and sincere review of how the therapy has addressed, or not, the target problems. As with the other activities of mapping and writing, it is part of a process of memory reconsolidation.

The goodbye letter brings the here and now relationship into focus and challenges both therapist and client. It builds a bridge to the self-help and follow-up session. It maintains the co-creative approach and offers a transitional object from the shared experience of the therapy. It serves as a reflective tool for both therapist and client. The goodbye letter is both a personal exchange which, at its simplest, is a thankyou letter but at the same it is a review letter and letter of anticipation of the road ahead.

The prevailing address of the letter should between us (what we have done), I (how I now see things) and you (what this faces you with or what you – the client – have achieved). It is important not to write just with one pronoun and one direction of address.

Writing a good-bye letter is helped by using the therapy map as a source of reference. Also, the goodbye map as described earlier may offer multiple entry points into the writing of the goodbye letter. A new angle on things or a new response may arise through the sharing of the letter.

For some clients it may be right to co-write one goodbye letter together in session, or to write side-by-side in silence a letter each to be read out there and then. This can be a good way of managing an ending that, out of necessity, has come up prematurely.

There may be anxiety about the exposure of writing, fears about spelling and language. The importance of spontaneity and not feeling judged on writing should be stressed. If there are real concerns about writing as a medium, it is possible to consider an audio or video version of the goodbye letter using the same structure but voicing what otherwise would have been written with the same amount of deliberation. Or in some cases it works well for the therapist to be the scribe for the client.

The ideal aim is two perspectives being separately committed to paper, written alone between sessions, and then read out in session. The client might opt to leave the letter with the therapist and, as with the reformulation 'therapy' letter, there may be fears or hopes about who else will read it, intentionally or otherwise. Whilst keeping in mind the above concerns, the therapist needs to watch out for the protective kind of rescue around the tasks of writing that stops the client reaching a new level of ownership over their therapy journey through composing and reading their own letter.

Sharing goodbye letters takes a full session and there is wisdom in using the penultimate session, rather than the final session, to do the exchange of letters. A rushed exchange of letters in the final session, with no time to process them is not therapeutic. Nor is it advisable to send an unshared letter as an indirect communication or after thought. Some therapists give the client a choice as to whether to read the letter out loud or let them read it out on their own after taking it away. It is likely to miss the therapeutic point of working co-creatively with mapping and writing if the letter is not read out.

Guidelines for introducing and preparing the letter

In setting up and sharing the good-bye letters, it is not enough to announce to the client. "Please write a letter to me to read out next week about how the therapy has been." This activity needs preparation and the preparation needs to be used in a therapeutic way. The client might be given an information sheet, like the one in the box below. On top of this, it helps to rehearse how the letters might be written and how 'we' plan to share them. This rehearsal may itself be therapeutic and an enactment magnet.

As the ending approaches, we are hoping that feelings of gratitude, loss and adventure are within reach of the client and therapist. If the shared and courageous nature of the work (its moments of difficulty and breakthrough) can be realistically acknowledged and not idealised or diminished, then the ending is more likely to be managed in a shared way. This will become clear in the exchange of the goodbye letters. Therapy might be thought of as successful if the there is some sense of shared ownership of the therapy and that a new place on the map has been found that is curious and compassionate through the process of writing and exchanging letters.

Guidelines for the client

If we both write a goodbye letter to each other about the therapy, it will help us reflect on the work we have done, the feelings we have had, and the ideas involved. We could speak of where there have been some successes or setbacks and what remains to be done or carried on after the therapy.

- Write as you speak in your own words and keep in mind you are writing to me the therapist but also to yourself.
- Don't worry about spelling or punctuation. The feelings and ideas matter most.
- Say something about us and how we have got on with the activities of therapy.
- Then focus on what you feel has gone well for you, what you might need to do more of and what has been frustrating or disappointing.
- Refer to how much the target problems and the patterns behind them have been tackled and how much your relationship with yourself has changed.

- If there is a moment or two that stand out, mention it/them.
- Say what you plan to keep working on in the months ahead.
- Feel free to ignore these points and write the letter spontaneously for yourself.

Like any piece of reflective writing, it is worth having the goodbye letter in mind throughout the therapy. When something happens that is memorable or troublesome or a breakthrough during the therapy, note and bank it for the goodbye letter. CAT involves building a small portfolio of maps and writing and notes, and the 'secretarial' skills of the therapist can draw on all this material for the goodbye letter. Here is an example of a short goodbye letter from a client.

> **Dear Therapist,**
>
> *I will miss you and our conversations together. I am grateful for the effort you have put in. You have been a real help and your maps have shown me what is going on. I have had the chance to think differently about my life I think I can be a kind of therapist to myself. We have had some tricky moments and it was hard to keep going with the therapy when crises got in the way. I don't know if I will miss these sessions, but I will remember them. One thing I value is that you took me seriously and, in a warm but challenging way, challenged me out to take some responsibility for my part in my problems.*
>
> *Thank you*

Guidelines for the therapist

The guidelines for the therapist are like those for the client, though more thought is needed about remaining in the reach of the client and enabling and responding to the client's letter.

The emphasis is on a limited, tentative and accurate shared description in ordinary language. The therapist is addressing the client directly, describing the work together both as a formulation of problems and the creation of a healing narrative. The letter is linking back to the reformulation work at the beginning of therapy and specifically to the target problems and procedures. The letter will follow two threads. One reflects on how much there has been recognition and revision of problem procedures during the therapy. This is honouring the reformulation story. The other thread looks at how much self-understanding, relational awareness and compassion has developed in the process of change. This is honouring the healing story of personal growth and recovery. The letter refers to these in ways that implies the work is not done or dusted, a success or a failure but work in progress. The two threads of revising problem patterns and developing understanding may have their best moments in the final sessions.

Dear client

I hope this goodbye letter is a way of telling the story of our therapy together. I am proud of you for battling through these sessions together with me. You have put yourself on the line and shared the best and worst of times in your life. You have helped us work out the patterns which you have carried with you from childhood and how they play a part in your present difficulties. In mapping these out we could see where change might be tried out and we set out your version of a weekly rating sheet to see if change is possible. You have made more progress than you expected and are hopeful that more change can come. More importantly you have felt more knowingly in control of your life. Our story is one of finding out together what lies behind your ways of interacting and coping. You have been a good ally to yourself on your journey of therapy.

I have valued working together with you and I hope you feel enough of what we have done is now a part of you. You have found some allies in your family and friends who are going to show interest and solidarity with the changes you want to make. I look forward to hearing the ups and down of progress when we meet at our follow up session in 3 months' time. I wish you the best. yours sincerely

Things to look for in the letter from the client

There are various signs to look for in the client's letter. Be clear in advance that you would like the client to write a letter and bring it to the session but, if it is not done for whatever reason, you don't want the client to not attend out of embarrassment or fear of disappointing the therapist. As already mentioned, one fallback position to offer is to do the letter free style during the final sessions, either by writing it out together or through joint dictation on your phones.

We are interested in how the client evaluates their own role in making the therapy progress. Can they hover and shimmer in between desired and feared outcomes and have some sense of increased ownership and agency over the difficult parts of their lives? Does their letter point to new patterns of relating and interacting with others or self? Are feelings and emotions acknowledged? Can they stand apart from the past and present stories of their lives and distinguish the formulation story of the therapy from the healing narrative with which they have been involved.

Be curious about how the letter might be written, or in retrospect how it was written. Do this without judgement or wanting to put the client on the spot. However, it would be an interesting aspect of understanding the goodbye letter if, for example, the client had written it in the waiting room just before seeing you. In this vein, be open and reflective about how you and they went about writing the letter.

In listening to the client's reading out of their letter, pay attention to reciprocal role procedures and invitations to join an old or new dance. What might be being unsaid or avoided? Who else if anyone had a hand in the letter? Did a partner help write it or was a keyworker involved in discussing it? Don't discount praise and gratitude as the therapist; it is likely to be genuinely felt and is important to accept and work with. Gratitude and admiration should be directed to the therapy relationship and to the work we have done together. One value of having tools in the therapy room like letters and maps is that you can redirect praise for the therapist on to the map. It is not down to me. It is down to our letters, or the maps and mapping processes.

If not arising from the exchange of letters, look for and discuss both swings to idealising and overvaluing or dismissing and undervaluing the therapy. One argument in favour of the letters being exchanged in the penultimate rather than the final session is that the letters may be received and explored in one state but then re-read some days later in another state. For example, I may be in my grateful and pleasing mood in the session as a client but in my anxious and self-critical mood when re-reading on my own a week later. The contrast between the two states may filter how I work with the therapeutic potential of the letter.

Like all therapeutic writing, it is tempting to strive to write a perfect letter. As ever, it is better to write something that can be built upon in dialogue, in the therapy room than have it all done and dusted. Writing that is too polished and too complete tends to be silencing and leave the client and perhaps the therapist with nothing left to say or do. Like the big reformulation letter, it can be consumed but not digested.

Challenges and opportunities

These are some of the challenges arising from ending therapy and in each case, they can be opportunities for further therapeutic understanding, or at least to avoid harming or spoiling the preceding work. They may be moments when mapping the conversation or the interpersonal process of help bring out the issues involved.

- The client or therapist do not share responsibility for the ending and find it difficult to remember the focus of therapy and evaluate it. Stopping and mapping this loss of direction is essential. If the focus of the therapy is not routinely worked on and discussed week by week, then the anxious position at the end will be 'I don't know how or why to end because I don't know what we have done'.

- Progress towards working collaboratively established at the beginning of therapy and sustained through the middle may be lost as the client feels the ending is something being done to him or her. The challenge is to talk about the feelings involved and a simple map may help the necessary conversation begin.

- The client and the therapist have been too engrossed in the therapy to notice the ending. It is the role of the therapist to orientate the client to time within the therapy, most often by noticing and naming the session number thoughtfully within the overall context of the therapy duration. It is easy to become swept away in the work, or to avoid endings if they are likely to provoke strong and difficult emotions. The challenge is to step back and see the whole therapy journey at regular intervals with the client so as to ensure the ending is kept in mind at the beginning and middle of the therapy journey.

- The client or the therapist may be reluctant to face the ending and look to life events or external constraints to relieve them of responsibility. The therapist may be ending their job; the client may be moving away. External reasons for ending therapy are real but care needs to be taken to see how externally imposed ending is being used to avoid feelings about the therapeutic relationship.

- Another person is recruited as an accomplice to manage the ending or non-ending. For example, the GP might be drawn in to insist on more sessions.

- There is an abundance of gratitude and admiration between client and therapist. This might draw the unsuspecting therapist into feeling magnificent and assuming the ending is both timely and correct. It might lead the client into thinking they are more resolved and resourced than is possible within the limits of therapy.

- In the urgency of the imminent ending, the pressure to address traumatic or shaming memories before it is too late may lead to a disclosure that creates a need for further therapy. Though this cannot always be avoided, it is worthwhile asking frequently during the therapy, 'is there anything we are not touching or exploring because it is difficult?' If this does arise, it is still possible to do an ending of this round of therapy at this specific time, with further work scheduled subsequently where appropriate.

- Negotiating gifts at the end of therapy can be challenging, even with statutory and professional structures in place to guide the therapist. The choice of gift might indicate a far greater attention to the therapist's needs than has been realised or expressed, or a sense of repayment of an emotional debt. The giving of a gift can be the expression of a real gratitude and the therapist should acknowledge this. Such gift giving can be an expression of something healthy and culturally appropriate, but the meaning and relational quality should be explored. The first requirement is to negotiate its meaning as a communication and to give worth to the intent and the enactment of the gift giving. Other than token gifts, however, gifts of financial value must be compassionately refused or be directed to a worthy cause.

- One client brought her teddy bear to the final session as the object that had comforted her during lonely times in childhood. She said that as the therapy had worked, and she no longer needed it, she wanted the therapist to have it as a token or as gift for someone else who might need it. The therapist was moved by the intensity of the gift and the story behind it. The client had brought the teddy bear to several sessions. He didn't want to refuse it but didn't want to accept it either. Together they worked out a clever and emotionally satisfying solution. The client took a photograph for the therapist of the therapist holding the teddy bear to symbolise the thought behind the gift and promised to keep the teddy bear and look out herself for someone for whom it would meet a need. The symbolism of the gift was separated from the substance of the bear.

- There is a sudden onset of courage and insight in both client and therapist. The ending triggers a late rush of willingness and capacity to work therapeutically. One client said. 'When you reminded me of the ending coming up, it felt like you really cared, and I suddenly realised that I mattered to you. I am ready to trust you now and you seem to expect more of me.' It takes courage for the client to handle the emotions and connections raised by the ending and the therapist needs to be open to expression of this courage. They need courage as well.

Small things can happen in the final few sessions that shift a therapeutic relationship into areas that were hitherto stuck. It can, therefore, be tempting to extend the work. However, this negates the fact that it was the ending that galvanised the client and therapist and was necessary for this work to take place. Feelings of regret at time not fully utilised, or frustration should be given space but any suggestion of extending therapy should be thoroughly explored and discussed in supervision. However, the energy and increased motivation at the end should be valued and one or more extra sessions for genuinely break through work may have great value. The point is they are only happening because the ending was declared. Hopefully, these points convey some sense of the active, dynamic, and therapeutic use of time at the end of therapy and not the rigid use of time.

Explore the outcomes of therapy

At the end of therapy, it is natural to turn our attention to the goals, target problems and procedures that were identified as the focus of the work at the outset. It is what the therapy is about and a key indicator when reviewing how therapy progressed.

Has the client remembered his or her goals for therapy, the target problems that block them and the procedures which maintain the push and pull between goals and target problems?

Have the tools and activity of therapy helped develop relational awareness not just in the therapy sessions but more generally in everyday life? A measure of relational awareness and of the value of relational mapping is available at www.mapandtalk.com/research/

Is there a lighter and more optimistic sense of self, even if not everything has changed for the better? It is a good sign if rating sheets and diaries are a living part of the therapy that might outrun the end of therapy sessions. This sense of the client being prepared to work on their own and take some charge of creating their own therapeutic activity and spaces, is encouraging.

We are interested in the end of therapy measures and what changes these highlights. Clients can find the process of completing these measures helpful, but they can also bring home the fact that the therapeutic work is coming to an end. For this reason, there might be a temptation to avoid them. Completing them together in session can support a helpful conversation around change. Other positive outcomes of therapy might also include a reduction of risk, improved problem-solving ability and improved self-esteem. Whatever measures, domains and indicators are used, the end of therapy should involve a frank, open exploration about what has changed and the impact of these changes. Sometimes the outcomes might be surprising, or a departure from the original goals.

Self-help and follow up

Brief therapies establish the conditions, the frame and understanding for change, but the therapeutic process continues after the ending. Revision of patterns may have only partly begun by the end of therapy. The underlying structure of the therapy is geared to what might best be called a 'self-help' phase, when the client tests out their ability to use the skills and understandings, the tools and work done, and the exit strategies identified. In learning to be our own therapist, the learning materials are our own life-problems, struggles and stories. The self-help phase is a period of two to three months, finished with a follow-up session. Normally the date for the follow-up session will be set in the final session of therapy, and a reminder sent a week or two before it is due. The client may well have help and support in the form of a key worker or support group, but the idea of continuing to work at recognition and revision is central. A new, more negotiable relationship with self takes time to practice and develop.

The follow-up session will check how things are now and how they have been. The therapist, as ever, will have an eye on the quality of the alliance in this follow-up session, and the push and pull of feelings and expectations between them and the client. As the client reports in on progress and setbacks, the therapist will be looking to make connections with the patterns and themes that were the focus of therapy.

In this spirit the follow-up session reviews two things; how much the target problems and patterns have been addressed and how much a general therapeutic and reflective capacity has been sustained. There should be scope for open-ended questions (how do you think that you have coped? How have you managed to reflect on that? How does that link to the procedure here?). It can be worth enquiring about the use of tools for self-monitoring, rating and recognition of repetitions of patterns, enactments with people, and exits and alternative patterns. Without getting too much into revisiting the maps and letters at the beginning and end of therapy, it is worth having them out and wondering about any specific memories of places on the maps or points in the letters.

The follow-up session is more structured in reviewing progress and setbacks. Care must be taken not to enter in another open therapeutic relationship. However, it is possible that something unresolved from the therapy might be returned to in the follow up session, and both therapist and client might have in mind to deal with unfinished business. Something too hot to handle at the time of the final few sessions may have settled or taken a different shape by follow-up and can then be talked through.

It is tempting for the therapist to steer clear of troublesome questions for fear of being drawn back into an ongoing therapy relationship but it is important to know about the worst moments and the best moments and of risky times, and how these were coped with. This may naturally lead to discussions about allies or helpers; those who have been a positive influence on maintaining the work of therapy. Equally it is worth knowing of old, renewed, or new accomplices who are inviting a return to harmful patterns of interaction. The follow-up session should conclude with reflection on challenges in the weeks and months ahead. There may also be time for renewal of thanks and gratitude for the work done, and appreciation of the efforts involved and, if appropriate, regret that more cannot be done.

Options after follow-up

Depending on the context, the psychotherapy contract may have ended but not the contract of help or the duty of care. The specific problems addressed in therapy may point to joining a group, couple or family therapy programme or treatment for a specific need that emerged in the therapy in specific ways, such as a phobia, unresolved trauma memories, confidence building or emotional expression and regulation. There are assorted options after a follow-up session that will vary with setting and context. There may be decisions about the need for further follow-up, more CAT, or other treatments but these should not detract from the ending of this therapy at this time. For people working privately or in voluntary roles it might be quite productive following a time-limited course of therapy to offer, or assume the value of, a six monthly or annual follow-up session.

The managerial role of supervision

There is a tendency for supervision of endings to be after the event, or when trouble has arisen from a difficult ending. If it has gone well, the helpful elements of the ending might be overlooked and the opportunity to reflect on what made a difference is lost. A lack of curiosity about finished business is understandable, where new challenges and demands are making their claims on time. However, for all the reasons explored generally in this chapter about the ending phase of therapy, it makes sense to talk in supervision before, during and after the process of ending. It helps bring to the front of attention what it is like for the therapist to create time-limited, therapeutic relationships and for the client to be an active participant.

Conclusion

Everything discussed in this chapter comes back to one overriding theme. If we can talk about this ending, we can build on it and talk about other endings. A compassionate conversation about endings reveals much about relationships with life in general. From such reflections relational awareness grows.

The ending is one of the richest and most troublesome parts of the therapy process. A well-managed therapeutic ending is one that acknowledges the mixture of gratitude, hope, regret and sadness in what is happening. It is given space and attention by the client and therapist. The hope is that the sincerity and style of the relationship will be taken to heart and called upon in the future, as part of a healthy dialogue with self and others.

The focus at the end has been the bringing together of four stories or modes of storytelling mentioned earlier. The first two modes of storytelling are of the past and the present. They may now hopefully be richly linked. The third mode of storytelling is of what the therapy has been about. It is the story of formulations of problems and distress, and the models of self-understanding that have been mapped out and explored. Implicit in this work has been a fourth story or mode of storytelling of how the therapy relationship has developed and how it has helped or hindered. As the ending of therapy approaches, this fourth story needs its own distinctive space. This is the story of how we have struggled together. There is a relational history of co-creativity, of rupture and repair, of breakthroughs and setbacks which needs remembering, remarking upon, and honouring in the process of saying goodbye. It is always a unique story. Reflecting upon it and voicing it at the end of the therapy sessions will be jointly owned and, in the best sense, is something messy, flawed and less than perfect. It is the story of a healing narrative and hopefully this is the story which is carried by this book.

References

Introduction

Barkham, M., Guthrie, E., Hardy, G. and Margison, F. (2016) *Psychodynamic-Interpersonal Therapy: A Conversational Model*. London: SAGE Publications.

Bromberg, P. (1998) *Standing in the Spaces*. Brighton: Psychology Press.

Brummer, L. and Coid, P. (2018) *Cognitive Analytic Therapy -distinctive features*. London: Routledge.

Bruner, J. (1990) *Acts of Meaning*. Cambridge, MA: Harvard University Press.

Calvert, R. and Kellett, S. (2014) Cognitive analytic therapy: A review of the outcome evidence base for treatment. *Psychology and Psychotherapy: Theory, Research and Practice*, **87**, 253-277.

Compton-Dickinson, S. and Hakvoort, L. (2017) *The Clinician's Guide to Forensic Music Therapy*. London: Jessica Kingsley.

Daniels (2005) *An Introduction to Vygotsky*. London: Routledge.

Eliot, G. (1876, 2002) *Daniel Deronda*. London: Penguin Random House.

Eliot, T.S. (1940) *East Coker Four Quartet's*. London: New English Quarterly.

Gilbert, P. (2009, 2013) *The Compassionate Mind (Compassion Focused Therapy)*. London: Constable.

Hayes, S., Strosahl, K.D. and Wilson, G. (2012) *Acceptance and Commitment Therapy: The process and practice of mindful change (2nd Edition)*. London: Guilford Press.

Hepple, J. and Sutton. L, (2004) *Cognitive Analytic Therapy and Later Life*. Hove: Routledge.

Hobson, R.F. (1985) *Forms of Feeling*. London and New York: Tavistock.

Howells, E. (2003) *The Dissociated Mind*. New Jersey: The Analytic Press.

Hubble, A., Duncan. L. and Miller Scott D. (1999) *The Heart and Soul of Change: what works in therapy*. Washington: APA.

Josselson, R. (1995) *The Space Between Us*. London: SAGE Publications.

Kabat-Zinn, J. (1990, 2013) *Full Catastrophe Living*. London: Little Brown Book Group.

Knox, J. (2011) *Self-Agency in Psychotherapy*. London: Norton.

Lane, R. (2018) From reconstruction to construction: the power of corrective emotional experiences in memory reconsolidation and enduring change. *Journal of the American Psychoanalytic Association* **66**(3) 507-516.

Le Doux, J. (1996) *The Emotional Brain*. New York: Simon and Schuster.

Leiman, M. (1992) The concept of the sign in the work of Vygotsky, Winnicott and Bakhtin: Further integration of object relations theory and activity theory. *British Journal of Medical Psychology*, 65, 209-221

Leiman, M. (1997) Procedures as dialogical sequences; a revised version of the fundamental concept in cognitive analytic therapy. *British Journal of Medical Psychology*, **70**, 193-2007

Leiman, M. (2004) Dialogical sequence analysis. In H.J.M Hermans & G. Dimaggio (Eds) The dialogical self in psychotherapy, London, UK: Brunner-Routledge

Linehan, M. (1993) *Cognitive Behavioural Treatment of Borderline Personality Disorder (Diagnosis & Treatment of Mental Disorders)*. New York: Guilford Press.

Lloyd, J. and Clayton, P. (2014) *Cognitive Analytic Therapy for people with intellectual disabilities and their carers*. London: Jessica Kingsley.

Lloyd, J. & Pollard, R. (eds) (2018) Cognitive analytic therapy and the politics of mental health. Abingdon, UK Routledge.

Margison, F. Guthrie, E. Hardy, G. and Barkham, M. (2016) *Psychodynamic-Interpersonal Therapy: A Conversational Model*. London : Sage

McCormick, E. (2017) *Change for the Better* (5th Edition). London: SAGE Publications.

Meares, R. (2016) *The Poets Voice in the Making of Mind*. London: Routledge.

Mitchell, S. (2000) *Relationality: From attachment to intersubjectivity*. Brighton: Psychology Press.

Pickvance, D. (2017) *Cognitive Analytic Supervision – A Relational Approach*. London: Routledge.

Pollard, R. (2008) *Dialogue and desire: Mikhail Bakhtin and the linguistic turn in psychotherapy*, London, UK: Karnac.

Pollock, P., Stowell Smith, M. and Gopfert, M. (2006) *Cognitive Analytic Therapy for Offenders: A new approach to forensic psychotherapy*. London: Routledge.

Ryle, A. (1969) *Student Casualties*. London: The Penguin Press.

Ryle, A. (1975) Self-to-self, self-to-other: the world's shortest account of object relations theory. *New Psychiatry* 12-13.

Ryle, A. (1978) A common language for the psychotherapies. *British Journal of Psychiatry* **132** 585-94.

Ryle, A. (1994) Persuasion or education? The role of reformulation in cognitive analytic therapy. *International Journal of Short-Term Psychotherapy* **9** 111 - 118.

Ryle, A. (1998) The whirligig of time. *Psychiatric Bulletin* **22**(4) 263-267.

Ryle, A. and Kerr, I.B. (2002, 2020) *Introducing Cognitive Analytic Therapy*. Chichester: Wiley-Blackwell.

Ryle, A. (2006) Transferences and counter transferences: the cognitive analytic perspective. *British Journal of Psychotherapy*, https://doi.org/10.1111/j.1752-0118.1998.tb00384.x

Safran, J. (2000) *Negotiating the Therapeutic Alliance*. New York: Guilford Press.

Shapiro, F. (2018) *Eye Movement Desensitization and Reprocessing (EMDR) Therapy: Basic principles, protocols, and procedures* (3rd Edition). New York: Guilford.

Solms, M. (2015) *The Feeling Brain Selected Papers on Neuro-psychoanalysis*. London: Routledge.

Stern, D. (2004) *The Present Moment*. New York: Norton

Trevarthen, C. (2017) The affectionate intersubjective intelligence of the infant and its innate motivation for mental health. *International Journal of Cognitive Analytic Therapy and Relational Mental Health* **1** 11-53.

Wallace, R. (1989). Cognitive mapping and the origin of language and mind. *Current Anthropology* **30** (4), 518-526.

White, M. and Epston, D. (1990) *Narrative Means to Therapeutic Ends*. London: Norton.

Winnicott, D.M. (1953) Transitional objects and transitional phenomena – a study of possession. *International Journal of Psychoanalysis publisher* **34** 89–97.

Chapter 1: Conversational mapping

Bakhtin, M. (1981) *The Dialogic Imagination*. Texas: University of Texas Press.

Bromberg, P. (1998) *Standing in the Spaces*. Brighton: Psychology Press.

Daniels, H. (2005) *An Introduction to Vygotsky*. London: Routledge.

Heaney, S. (2010) *Human Chain*. London: Faber and Faber.

Hobson, R.F. (1985) *Forms of Feeling*. London and New York: Tavistock.

Horney, K. (1945/1992) *Our Inner Conflicts*. New York: Norton.

Horowitz, M. (1998) *Cognitive Psychodynamics: From conflict to character*. Chichester: Wiley.

Knox, J. (2011) *Self-Agency in Psychotherapy*. London: Norton.

Panksepp, J. and Biven, L. (2012) *The Archaeology of Mind*. New York: Norton.

Pickvance, D. (2017) *Cognitive Analytic Supervision: A relational approach*. London: Routledge.

Segal, H. (1992) The achievement of ambivalence. *Common Knowledge* **1** (1) 92-104

Smith, E. (2020) *This is Shakespeare*. London: Pelican.

Stern, Daniel. (2010) *Forms of Vitality*. London: OUP.

Stern, D. (2004) *The Present Moment*. New York: Norton.

Trevarthen, C. (2017) The affectionate intersubjective intelligence of the infant and its innate motivation for mental health. *International Journal of Cognitive Analytic Therapy and Relational Mental Health* **1** 11-53.

Wittgenstein, L. (2011) *Wittgenstein Day-by-Day*. Available at: http://www.wittgensteinchronology.com/3.html (accessed April 2020).

Chapter 2: Relationship mapping

Greenson, R. (1967) *The Technique and Practice of Psychoanalysis*. London: Karnac

Howells, E. (2003) *The Dissociated Mind*. New Jersey: The Analytic Press.

Kahneman, D. (2011) *Thinking fast and slow*. London: Penguin.

Kemp, N., Bickerdike, A. and Bingham, C. 2017 *'Map and Talk' – A Cognitive Analytic Therapy Informed Approach to Reflective Practice in a Forensic Setting*, International Journal of Cognitive Analytic Therapy and Relational Mental Health. www.internationalcat.org/journal-contents-volume-1/

Mitchell, S. (1988) *Relational Concepts in Psychoanalysis*. Cambridge, MA: Harvard University Press.

Ryle, A. (1975) Self-to-self, self-to-other: the world's shortest account of object relations theory. *New Psychiatry* 12-13.

Ryle, A. (1975) *Frames and Cages: Repertory Grid Approach to Human Understanding*. Brighton: Sussex University Press (AbeBooks.co.uk)

Ryle, A. (1997) *Cognitive Analytic Therapy and Borderline Personality Disorder*. Chichester: Wiley.

Ryle, A. (2003) *Reflections on the Development of CAT Diagrams* ACAT website: www.acat.me.org (20th Oct 2003)

Ryle, A. and Kerr, I.B. (2002, 2020) *Introducing Cognitive Analytic Therapy*. Chichester: Wiley.

Sullivan, H.S. (1955) *The Interpersonal Theory of Psychiatry*. London: Tavistock Press.

Van der Hart, O., Nijenhuis, E. and Steele, K. (2006) *The Haunted Self, Structural Dissociation and the Treatment of Chronic Traumatization*. New York: Norton.

Chapter 3: Narrative mapping

Beckett, S. (1953). *Waiting for Godot*. New York: Grove/Atlantic, Inc.

Bird, J. 2000 *The Heart's Narrative*. Auckland: Edge Press.

Booth, W. (1983) *Rhetoric of Fiction*. Chicago: University of Chicago Press.

Bromberg, P. (1998) *After the Tsunami*. Brighton: Psychology Press.

Bromberg, P. (1998) *Standing in the Spaces*. New York: Psychology Press.

Bruner, J. (1990) *Acts of Meaning*. Cambridge, MA: Harvard University Press.

Donald, M. (2001) *A Mind So Rare*. New York: Norton.

Dostoyevsky, F. (1848, 2016) *White Nights*. London: Penguin.

Hobson, R.F. (1985) *Forms of Feeling*. New York: Tavistock.

Holquist, M. (1990) *Dialogism*. London: Routledge.

Horowitz, M. (1998) *Cognitive Psychodynamics; From Conflict to Character*. Chichester: Wiley.

Lane, R. (2018) From reconstruction to construction: the power of corrective emotional experiences in memory reconsolidation and enduring change. *Journal of the American Psychoanalytic Association* **66**(3) 507-516.

Le Doux, J. (1996) *The Emotional Brain*. New York: Simon and Schuster.

Malloch, S. and Trevarthen, C. (2010) *Communicative Musicality*. Oxford: Oxford University Press.

Mann, J. (1973) *Time-limited Psychotherapy*. Cambridge, MA: Harvard University Press.

McGoldrick, H. (1985) Genograms in family assessment. *Assessment and Intervention* 9-38.

Panksepp, J. and Biven, L. (2013) *The Archaeology of Mind*. New York: Norton.

Potter, S. (2010) *Words with arrows: The benefits of mapping while talking. Reformulation* **Summer** 37-45.

Potter, S. (2014) 'The helper's dance list'. In J. Lloyd and P. Clayton (eds) *Cognitive Analytic Therapy for People with Intellectual Disabilities and their Carers*. London: Jessica Kingsley.

Reese, E., Haden, C., Baker-Ward, L., Bauer, P., Fivush, R. and Ornstein, P. (2011) Coherence of personal narratives across the lifespan: a multidimensional model and coding method. *Journal of Cognitive Development* **12** 424–462.

Ryle, A. (1997) *Cognitive Analytic Therapy and Borderline Personality Disorder*. Chichester: Wiley.

Ryle, A. and Kerr, I.B. (2020, 2002) *Introducing Cognitive Analytic Therapy*. Chichester: Wiley.

Safran, J. (2000) *Negotiating the Therapeutic Alliance*. New York: Guilford Press.

Sennett, R. (2002) *The Fall of Public Man*. London: Penguin Books.

Sennett, R. (2012) *Together: The rituals pleasures and politics of co-operation*. London: Yale University Press.

Trevarthen, C. (2017) The affectionate intersubjective intelligence of the infant and its innate motivation for mental health. *International Journal of Cognitive Analytic Therapy and Relational Mental Health* **1** 11-53.

White, M. (2000) *Reflections on Narrative Practice*. Adelaide: Dulwich Centre Publications.

White, M. and Epston, D. (1990) *Narrative Means to Therapeutic Ends*. London: Norton.

Chapter 4: Process mapping

Bromberg, P.M. (2011) *The Shadow of the Tsunami and the Growth of the Relational Mind* Oxford: Taylor and Francis.

Horney, K. (1945/1992) *Our Inner Conflicts*. New York: Norton

Knox, J. (2011) *Self-Agency in Psychotherapy*. London: Norton

Ryle, A. (2006) Transferences and counter transferences: the cognitive analytic perspective. *British Journal of Psychotherapy* https://doi.org/10.1111/j.1752-0118.1998.tb00384.x

Ryle, A. and Kerr, I.B. (2002) *Introducing Cognitive Analytic Therapy*. Chichester: Wiley.

Chapter 5: Learning to Map

Bion, W.R (1961) *Experiences in Groups and other Papers*. New York: Basic Books.

Potter, S. (2014) *Speed Supervision*. Available at: www.mapandtalk.com/speedsupervision (accessed April 2020).

Potter, S. (2014) 'The helper's dance list'. In J. Lloyd and P. Clayton (eds) *Cognitive Analytic Therapy for People with Intellectual Disabilities and their Carers*. London: Jessica Kingsley. Copy also available at www.mapandtalk.com/helpersdancelist/

Ryle, A. (1990) *The psychotherapy file*. Available at: www.Internationalcat.com/tools/file www.acat.me.uk (accessed April 2020).

Ryle, A. (1994) Persuasion or education? The role of reformulation in cognitive analytic therapy. *International Journal of Short-Term Psychotherapy* **9** 111 - 118.

Chapter 6: Writing for the therapeutic voice

Bolton, G., Howlett, S., Lago, L. and Wright, J.K. (2004) *Writing Cures*. London: Routledge.

Booth, W. (1991). *The Rhetoric of Fiction* (2nd ed). Harmondsworth: Penguin Books.

Forrester, J. (2016) *Thinking in Cases*. London: Polity Press.

Heaney, S. (1995) *The Redress of Poetry*. London: Faber and Faber.

Jenaway, A. (2011) *Whose Reformulation is it Anyway? Reformulation* **Winter** 26-29. Available at: https://www.acat.me.uk/reformulation.php?issue_id=22&article_id=219 (accessed April 2020).

Linehan, M. (1993) *Cognitive Behavioural Treatment of Borderline Personality Disorder (Diagnosis & Treatment of Mental Disorders)*. New York: Guilford Press.

Leiman, M. (2019) How assisting client self-observation has changed in CAT. *International Journal of Cognitive Analytic Therapy and Relational Mental Health* **3**. Available at: http://internationalcat.org/wp-content/uploads//Journal-3-LEIMAN.pdf (accessed April 2020).

McCulloch, G. (2019) *Because Internet: Understanding how language is changing* New York: Penguin

Pennebaker, J.W. and Smyth, J.M. (2016) *Opening Up by Writing it Down: How Expressive Writing Improves Health and Eases Emotional Pain* (3rd edition). New York: Guilford Press.

Potter, S., Bernardy, M., Amleh, I., Cutler, L. Crothers, L. and Dewshi, R. (2020) Innovations in writing. *Reformulation* www.acat.me.uk.

Seferis, G. (1974) *A Poet's Journal, Days of 1945-51*. Cambridge, MA: Harvard University Press

Smith, A. (2012) *Artful*. London: Penguin Books.

Stern, D. (2010) *Forms of Vitality*. London: OUP.

White, M. (2000) *Reflections on Narrative Practice*. Adelaide: Dulwich Centre Publications.

Wordsworth, W. (1807) *Poems in Two Volumes*. London: Longman.

Wordsworth, W. (1802) *Preface to the Lyrical Ballads*. Available at: https://sites.udel.edu/britlitwiki/preface-to-lyrical-ballads-full-work/ (accessed April 2020).

Chapter 7: Relational awareness

Ainsworth, M. and Bowlby, J. (1965) *Child Care and the Growth of Love*. London: Penguin.

Bonfield, S. and Potter, S. (2020) *Developing a measure of Relational Awareness* www.mapandtalk.com/research/

Bromberg, P. (1998) *Standing in the Spaces*. Brighton: Psychology Press.

Donald, M. (2001) *A Mind So Rare*, New York: Norton.

Flax, J. (1990) *Thinking Fragments: Psychoanalysis, feminism and postmodernism in the contemporary west*. Los Angeles: University of California Press.

Forster, E. M. (1910, 2012) *Howard's End*. London: Penguin Books.

Fotopoulou, A. and Tsakiris, M. (2017) Mentalising homeostasis: The social origins of interoceptive inference. *Neuro-psychoanalysis* **19**(1) 3-28.

Fromm, E. (1978) *Fear of Freedom*. London: Jonathan Cape.

Gallese, V. and Umilta, M. (2002) From self-modelling to the self-model: Agency and the representation of the self. *Neuropsychoanalysis* **4** (2) 35-40.

Knox, J. (2011) *Self-Agency in Psychotherapy*. London: Norton.

Holquist, M. (1990) *Dialogism*. London: Routledge.

Horney, K. (1945/1992) *Our Inner Conflicts*. New York: Norton.

Howell, E. (2003) *The Dissociated Mind*. New Jersey: The Analytic Press

Hubble, A., Duncan, L. and Miller, S.D. (1999) *The Heart and Soul of Change: What works in therapy*. Washington: APA.

Josselson, R. (1995) *The Space Between Us*. London: SAGE Publications.

Panksepp, J. and Biven, L. (2012) *The Archaeology of Mind*. London: Norton.

Rogers, C. (1954, 2015) *On Becoming a person* Mariner Books

Selasi, T. (2015) www.ted.com/talks/dont_ask_where_i_m_from_

Smith, E. (2020) *This is Shakespeare*. London: Pelican

Stern, D. (1985) *The Interpersonal World of the Infant*. New York: Ingram

Sullivan, H.S. (1955) *The Interpersonal Theory of Psychiatry*. London: Tavistock Press

Tokarczuk, O. (2019) https://www.nobelprize.org/prizes/literature/2018/tokarczuk/lecture/

Trevarthen, C. (2017) The affectionate intersubjective intelligence of the infant and its innate motivation for mental health. *International Journal of Cognitive Analytic Therapy and Relational Mental Health* **1** 11-53.

Van der Kolk, B. (2014) *The Body Keeps the Score*. London: Penguin.

Chapter 8: Relational healing

Corrigan, F. and Hull, A. (2018) The emerging psychological trauma paradigm. *International Journal of Cognitive Analytic Therapy and Relational Mental Health* **2**.

De Young, P. (2015) *Understanding and Treating Chronic Shame*. Hove: Routledge.

Fotopoulou, A. and Tsakiris, M. (2017) Mentalising homeostasis: The social origins of interoceptive inference. *Neuro-psychoanalysis* **19**(1) 3-28.

Foucault, M. (1975,1991) *Discipline and Punish: The birth of the prison*. London: Penguin Social Sciences.

Gilbert, P. (2009, 2013) *The Compassionate Mind (Compassion Focused Therapy)*. London: Constable.

Herman, J. (1992) *Trauma and Recovery*. New York: Basic Books.

Howell, E. (2003) *The Dissociated Mind*. New Jersey: The Analytic Press.

Josselson, R. (1996) *The Space Between Us*. London: SAGE Publications.

Luborsky, L. and Crits-Christoph, P. (1990) *Understanding Transference: The CCRT method*. New York: Basic Books

Mann, J. (1973). *Time-limited Psychotherapy*. Cambridge, MA: Harvard University Press.

Panksepp, J., Biven, L. (2012) *The Archaeology of Mind*. London: Norton.

Ryle, A. (1997) *Cognitive Analytic Therapy and Borderline Personality Disorder: The Model and the Method*. Chichester: Wiley-Blackwell.

Savege Scharff, J. and Scharff, D. (2005) *The Legacy of Fairbairn and Sutherland*. London: Routledge.

Sennett, R. (2012) *Together, The Rituals, Pleasures and Politics of Cooperation*. London: Allen Lane.

Shapiro, F. (2018) *Eye Movement Desensitization and Reprocessing (EMDR) Therapy: Basic Principles, Protocols, and Procedures* (3rd edition). New York: Guilford Press.

Siegel, A. (2016) *Heinz Kohut and the Psychology of the Self*. London: Routledge.

Smith, E. (2020) *This is Shakespeare*. London: Pelican.

Solms, M. (2015) *The Feeling Brain Selected Papers on Neuro-psychoanalysis*. London: Routledge.

Stern, D (2003) *Unformulated Experience -From Dissociation to Imagination in Psychoanalysis* Hillsdale, NJ: Analytic Press.

Sullivan, H.S. (1955) *The Interpersonal Theory of Psychiatry*. London: Tavistock Press.

Van der Kolk, B. (2014) *The Body Keeps the Score*. London: Penguin Books.

Caldwell, L. and Taylor Robinson, H. (2016) *The Collected Works of Winnicott: Volume 9, 1969 – 1971*. Oxford: Oxford University Press.

Chapter 9: Beginning therapy

Booth, W. (1991). *The Rhetoric of Fiction* (2nd edition). Harmondsworth: Penguin Books.

Bordin, E.S. (1979) The generalizability of the psychoanalytic concept of the working alliance. *Psychotherapy: Theory, Research & Practice* **16**(3), 252-260.

Luborsky, L. and Crits-Christoph, P. (1990) *Understanding Transference: The CCRT method.* New York: Basic Books.

Ryle, A. (1979). The focus in brief interpretive psychotherapy: dilemmas, traps and snags as target problems. *British Journal of Psychiatry,* **134**, 46-54.

Ryle, A. (1982). *Psychotherapy: A cognitive integration of of theory and practice.* London UK: Academic Press

Ryle, A. and Kerr, I.B. (2002, 2020 Revised) *Introducing Cognitive Analytic Therapy.* Chichester: Wiley-Blackwell.

Stern, D. (1985) *The Interpersonal World of the Infant.* New York: Ingram.

Talmon, M. (1990) *Single Session Therapy.* San Francisco: Jossey Bass.

Chapter 10: In the middle of therapy

Bion, W. (1978) *A Seminar Held in Paris.* Available at: http://www.psychoanalysis.org.uk/bion78.htm (accessed April 2020).

Donald, M. (2001) *A Mind So Rare.* New York: Norton.

Greenson, R. (1967) *The Technique and Practice of Psychoanalysis.* Madison, CT: International Universities Press.

Gilbert, P. (2009, 2013) *The Compassionate Mind (Compassion Focused Therapy).* London: Constable.

Linehan, M. (1993) *Cognitive-Behavioral Treatment for Borderline Personality Disorder.* New York: Guilford Press.

McGilchrist, I. (2009) *The Master and His Emissary: The divided brain and the making of the western world.* London: Yale University Press.

De Young, P. (2015) *Understanding and Treating Chronic Shame.* London: Routledge

Van der Kolk, B. (2014) *The Body Keeps the Score.* London: Penguin Books.

Ryle. A, and Kerr. I.B, (2002, 2020) *Introducing to Cognitive Analytic Therapy,* Chichester: Wiley.

Van den Hout, M.A. Engelhard, I.M. (2012) How does EMDR work? *Journal of Experimental Psychology* **3** (5) 724-738

Chapter 11: Ending therapy

Zollo, P. (2000) *Songwriters on Song-writing.* London: Plume Penguin.